Silver Burdett Ginn Science
DISCOVERYWORKS

HOUGHTON MIFFLIN

Boston • Atlanta • Dallas • Denver • Geneva, Illinois • Palo Alto • Princeton

Authors

William Badders
Science Resource Teacher
Cleveland Public Schools
Cleveland, OH

Lowell J. Bethel
Professor of Science Education
The University of Texas at Austin
Austin, TX

Victoria Fu
Professor of Child Development
Virginia Polytechnic Institute and
State University
Blacksburg, VA

Donald Peck
Director, Center for Elementary Science
Fairleigh Dickinson University
Madison, NJ

Carolyn Sumners
Director of Astronomy and Physics
Houston Museum of Natural Science
Houston, TX

Catherine Valentino
Senior Vice President for
Curriculum Development
Voyager Expanded Learning
West Kingston, RI

Consulting Author

R. Mike Mullane
Astronaut, retired
Albuquerque, NM

Acknowledgements appear on page H40, which consti-
tutes an extension of this copyright page.

CONTENTS

UNIT B

Sun, Moon, and Earth

THEME: SCALE

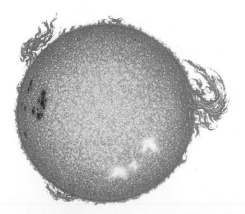

Motions of Earth and the Moon B32

UNIT C
Forms of Energy

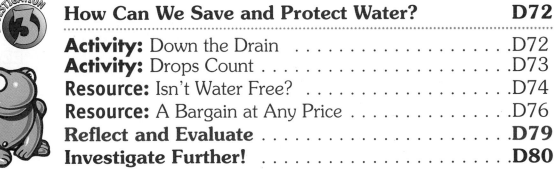

UNIT
F

What's for Lunch?

THEME: SYSTEMS
GET READY TO INVESTIGATE!

The Foods We Eat

SCIENCE Handbook

UNIT A

LIFE CYCLES

Theme: Models

GET READY TO

OBSERVE & QUESTION

How do adult animals care for their young?

Animals are all around you. Close observation will help you learn about them. How do the animals you observe care for their young?

EXPERIMENT & HYPOTHESIZE

How do plants change during their life cycles?

Measuring the trunk of a tree can help you find out the age of the tree. What else can you discover about how plants grow?

INVESTIGATE!

RESEARCH & ANALYZE

As you investigate, find out more from these books.

- ***INSECT METAMORPHOSIS From Egg to Adult*** by Ron and Nancy Goor (Atheneum, 1990). Do you know how to recognize a moth at any stage in its life cycle? This book will tell you how.

- ***Tree in a Forest*** by Jan Thornhill (Simon and Schuster Books for Young Readers, 1991). If a maple tree could talk, it would probably tell the story in this book. Read the book to find out about that story.

WORK TOGETHER & SHARE IDEAS

How can you give your pets and plants the best care possible?

Working together, you'll have a chance to apply what you have learned about plants and animals. Share the information your group finds out. Look for the opportunities in Unit Project Links to include your ideas in an Animal Sitter's Guide and a Plant Sitter's Guide.

1
LIFE CYCLES OF ANIMALS

Think about some animals that you know. What were they like when they were young? How did they change as they grew older? Do you think all members of the animal kingdom grow and change throughout their lives?

Flying With a Bear

Would you like to be alone in a small plane with a large bear? Jay Hammond, a bush pilot and biologist, was flying high above the Alaskan wilderness. Suddenly his passenger, a 275-kg (600-lb) bear, started to awaken. The bear had been drugged to keep it calm during the flight.

As the pilot dropped out of the clouds and searched for a place to land, the bear grew restless. Minutes later, Hammond unloaded the bear on the shore of a lonely lake. Now wide awake, the animal ran off to find a new home. Here the bear will mate, raise cubs, and spend the rest of its life. Like all animals, it will grow and change.

How are animals alike in the ways they change? How are they different? To find out, read this chapter!

Coming Up

Bush pilot Jay Hammond flew a bear to its new home.

WHAT IS A LIFE CYCLE?

Arrange these words in order—*teenager, child, adult, baby*. How did you do it? Each word names a stage in the life cycle of a human. All living things go through stages, or life cycles. In this investigation, you'll find out about the life cycles of some plants and animals.

Activity

The Changes Chart

How have you changed since you were a baby? How do other living things change during their life cycles? Find out.

MATERIALS

- strip of white paper
- pictures of plants and animals
- books about plants and animals
- *Science Notebook*

Procedure

1. With your group, brainstorm a list of living things that you've observed near your home or school. **Record** your list in your *Science Notebook*.

2. Make a Changes Chart. Fold a strip of paper lengthwise into four sections. First, fold the strip in half. Then fold the folded strip in half.

3. Choose a living thing from the list you made in step 1. In the first section, at the left of the chart, **draw** a picture or **write** a description of how you think the plant or animal looked when it was very young. For help, look at pictures in books. **Predict** how the plant or animal will change as it gets older.

4. In each of the other three sections of the chart, **draw** or **write** your ideas about how the animal will change. Do not name the animal.

5. Exchange Changes Charts with another group. Study the other group's chart. Name the plant or animal that this chart is about. Ask the other group if you guessed correctly.

Analyze and Conclude

1. **Make a plan** to test your predictions from steps 3 and 4.

2. Show your teacher your plan. Then carry it out. How do the predictions you recorded on your Changes Chart **compare** with what you found out?

INVESTIGATE FURTHER!

EXPERIMENT

Fold a paper strip into eight sections. In the sections write these ages: 1, 3, 5, 7, 9, 15, 25, 55. Write how you have changed in the sections. For the ages you have not reached, predict how you will change. Explain your predictions.

Step 3

A7

City Life

A city is full of life. People, spiders, ants, birds, dandelions, squirrels, roses, and earthworms are only a few of the things that live in a city. You might have to look closely to see some forms of city life. But if you observe the living things in a city over time, you'll notice that they change.

Think of the Changes Chart you made in the activity on pages A6 and A7. All living things—whether they live in a city, a town, an ocean, a forest, a desert, or your home—go through certain changes. These changes include growth, development, reproduction, and death. Growth refers to changes in size—that is, plants and animals becoming larger. Development refers to changes in plants and animals as they mature, or become adults. Reproduction is the process by which plants and animals produce offspring, or young, of their kind. Death marks the end of each plant's or animal's lifetime.

Animals go through ordered life stages, as you can see in the pictures of the dogs below. After several

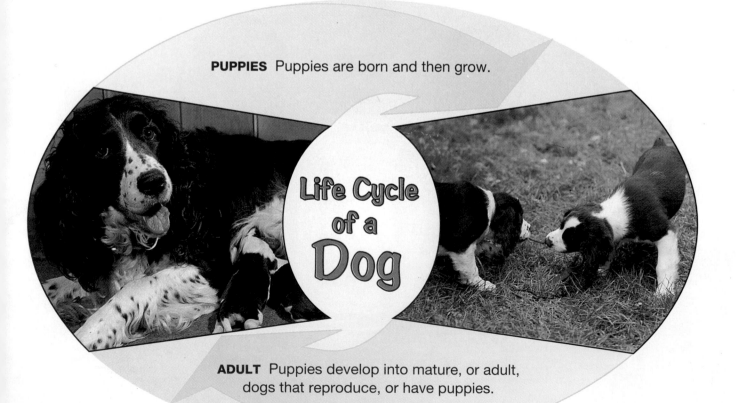

PUPPIES Puppies are born and then grow.

Life Cycle of a Dog

ADULT Puppies develop into mature, or adult, dogs that reproduce, or have puppies.

▲ **Living things in the spring**

years, an adult dog dies. But because it has reproduced, that kind of dog continues.

Plants go through life stages, too. A milkweed plant grows, blooms, and produces seeds. Some seeds fall to the ground. From these seeds new plants grow. The mature plant dies. But because it has reproduced, that kind of plant continues.

Look at the two pictures above and below. What living things can you find? Compare the pictures. What changes have taken place in the living things over time?

The ordered stages that occur in a plant's or animal's lifetime are called a **life cycle**. A life cycle is like a circle. It has no end. One life cycle leads to another. ■

Living things in the summer ▼

What's Wrong
With This Picture?

If you heard that a duck had hatched out of a chicken egg, you probably wouldn't believe it. It's a fact that animals produce young just like themselves. Chickens mate and produce chicks. Ducks mate and produce ducklings.

Chicks belong to one species (spē'shēz) and ducks belong to another species. A **species** is a group of living things that can pro-duce living things of the same kind. Now do you know what's wrong with this picture?

Passed On or Learned?

Animals of the same species pass on certain traits. A trait is a charac-teristic. It describes something. You and your classmates belong to the human species. You all have many of the same traits.

Some things are not passed from parents to offspring. These things are learned. For example, having feet is a human trait that is passed from parents to children. But using your feet to kick a soccer ball is a skill you learn. Chicks hatch knowing how to peck for food. But suppose a chick pecks at a caterpillar that tastes bitter. Then the chick learns to avoid that kind of food.

How Long Do Animals Live?

By producing young, each species can continue beyond the life span of each parent. An animal's life span is the time between its birth or hatching and its death.

Species	Life Span
Spider	1-20 years
Gray Squirrel	8-15 years
Cat	12-15 years
Eagle	20-30 years
Elephant	65 years

As you can see in the table above, each species' life span is different from another's. A spider's life span is only one to twenty years. Yet box turtles have been known to live as long as 123 years. ■

INVESTIGATION 1

1. Think about how a life cycle and a circle are alike. What must happen so that the life cycle of a species does not end?

2. Choose an animal and draw a picture of two different stages in its life. Order the stages by labeling them 1 and 2.

WHAT IS THE FIRST STAGE IN AN ANIMAL'S LIFE CYCLE?

A newborn kitten and a newborn puppy look *so* tiny. But each developed from something much tinier. What is that something? Find out and become an "eggs-pert" as you explore the first stage in an animal's life cycle.

Activity

Be "Eggs-act"!

To a scientist, observing something means much more than just looking. In this activity you must be "eggs-act" as you explore the first stage in a chicken's life cycle.

MATERIALS
- goggles
- plastic gloves
- uncooked egg
- small dish
- hand lens
- paper towel
- *Science Notebook*

SAFETY

Wear goggles and gloves during this activity. Clean up any spills immediately.

Procedure

1. Think of an uncooked egg cracked into a dish. **Make a drawing** in your *Science Notebook* to show the inside parts of the egg that you remember. If you can, label each part. Mark the drawing *A*.

2. Get an uncooked egg from your teacher. With your group, use a hand lens to **observe** the outside of the egg. **Draw** what you see.

3. Crack the egg into a dish. Use the hand lens to **observe** the egg and the inside of the shell. **Draw** all the parts that you see. Mark this drawing *B*.

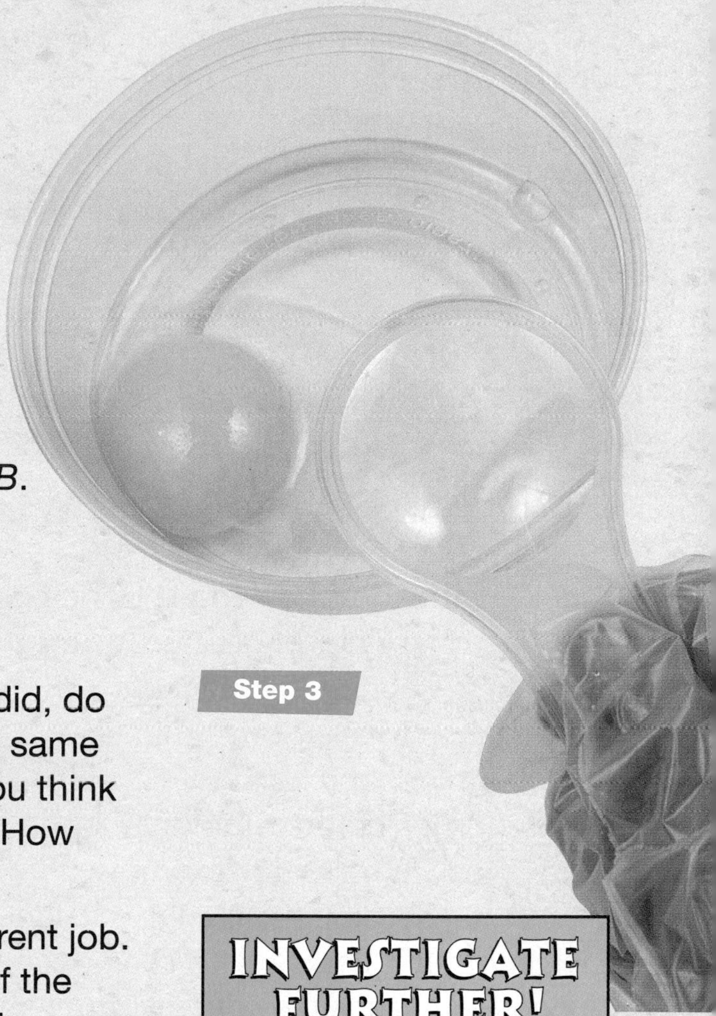

4. **Compare** drawing *A* with drawing *B*. What new parts did you discover?

Analyze and Conclude

1. Based on the drawings your class did, do you think that all chicken eggs have the same parts? A chicken is a kind of bird. Do you think that all bird eggs have the same parts? How could you find out?

2. Each part you observed has a different job. Find the white spot on the yellow part of the egg. This spot could have developed into a new chick. **Infer** how the eggshell helps the developing chick.

Step 3

INVESTIGATE FURTHER!

EXPERIMENT

Observe the eggs of another animal—for example, a fish. How are these eggs different from chicken eggs? How are they the same?

Step 3

"Eggs-traordinary" Eggs!

Do you think eggs "eggs-ist" only to boil, poach, scramble, or fry? Actually, the job of an egg is to help produce offspring, or young. An **egg** is the first stage in the life cycle of almost all animals. Some animals— for example, baby horses—develop from eggs inside their mothers' bodies. Other animals—for example, chickens—develop from eggs outside their mothers' bodies.

Eggs are "eggs-traordinary" in many ways. Even the tiniest egg contains everything needed for developing a new animal. Study the parts of the egg shown. Add labels to drawing B, which you made in the activity on pages A12 and A13.

"Eggs-actly" How Would You Describe an Egg?

Eggs come in many shapes, colors, textures, and sizes. Chicken eggs are round on one end and pointed on the other. Owl eggs are round. Plover eggs are pear-shaped. Tortoise eggs are shaped like globes and sand grouse eggs like tubes.

These photos show the actual sizes of some of the many kinds of bird eggs. ▼

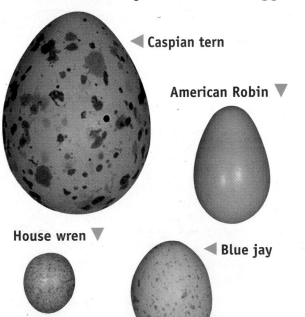

◄ Caspian tern

American Robin ▼

House wren ▼

◄ Blue jay

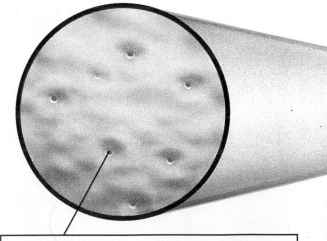

PORES A close-up look at tiny openings, called pores, in the shell of a chicken egg. Pores let water and oxygen enter the egg and carbon dioxide leave.

Eggs can be brightly colored, dull, plain, or very fancy. From green and blue to black and red, eggs can be freckled, speckled, spotted, or dotted.

There are many kinds of egg coverings, too. Bird eggs have hard, chalky shells. Fish and frog eggs have a soft outer covering. They don't dry out, because they're laid in water. Slug and snail eggs have shiny, round shells that you can almost see through.

Inside a Bird Egg

TWISTED STRANDS Twisted strands of the shell lining keep the embryo upright as the mother turns her egg. Turning the eggs warms them evenly.

SHELL The egg is covered by a shell. The shell protects everything inside the egg. A material called calcium makes the shell hard and helps to form the embryo's bones.

EMBRYO The white spot is where the embryo begins to grow as soon as the egg is laid. The **embryo** is the developing chick. By the twenty-first day, the chick will start to hatch.

EGG WHITE The egg white cushions the embryo and provides it with water.

YOLK The yolk is the stored food for the embryo.

SHELL LININGS Just inside the shell are the shell linings. At the rounded end of the egg is an air space, which allows the embryo to get oxygen.

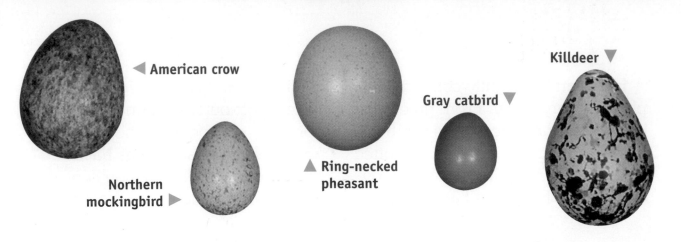

◄ American crow

Northern mockingbird ►

▲ Ring-necked pheasant

Gray catbird ▼

Killdeer ▼

Ostrich eggs are the largest in the world. Each ostrich egg is 16 cm (6 in.) long and has a mass of about $1\frac{1}{2}$ kg (3 lb). Compare this with the hummingbird egg in the picture below.

"Eggs-actly" How Many?

The number of eggs that an animal lays varies with the species.

The hornbill lays only 1 egg a year, but an oyster lays 500 million eggs a year. Chickens lay almost 1 egg a day, or up to 350 eggs a year. Each time an ocean sunfish produces eggs, it makes about 300 million.

Not every egg produces young. The eggs you eat do not contain embryos. For a chick or other animal to begin growing inside an egg, the mother must first mate with the father. Then—just think—the egg can grow into all the parts of an animal's body. An egg really is "eggs-traordinary"! ■

INVESTIGATE FURTHER!

EXPERIMENT

You can't easily see pores in a shell, but you can prove they are there. Place an egg in a clear container. A brown egg is best to use. Cover the egg with water. Observe the egg after 20 minutes. You may need to use a hand lens. Everywhere you see a bubble on the shell, there's a pore. Each bubble is formed by carbon dioxide gas that's passing through a pore from inside the shell.

A tiny hummingbird egg compared with an ostrich egg ►

Hatching Chicks

An incubator (in'kyōō-bāt ər) is a device that provides enough warmth, water, and fresh air to help keep something alive. An incubator in a hospital may help a tiny baby grow stronger. Other incubators are found on large chicken farms. These incubators are used to hatch eggs. Incubators for eggs, like the one shown here, come in two parts—the setter and the hatcher. Read the captions to find out the difference. ■

The trays in the setter move to turn the eggs many times each day. Eggs are warmed to a temperature of 37°C (99°F).

Large fans keep the air moving around the eggs.

1 **SETTER** Chicken eggs are placed on trays and loaded into a setter. Some setters are as large as rooms and can hold thousands of eggs at one time. The eggs stay in the setter for 18 days.

2 **HATCHER** On the nineteenth day, the eggs are put into metal or plastic baskets and moved to the hatcher. After 2 or 3 days in the hatcher, baby chicks hatch out of the eggs.

The Baby Book

Almost all animals come from eggs. Some animal babies develop from eggs inside their mothers' bodies. Those babies are born live. Other offspring develop from eggs outside their mothers' bodies. Those babies hatch. Whether born live or hatched, each baby develops from a single egg.

Here are some baby animals from around the world. Look at the pictures and read about them. Which were born live? Which hatched?

WALLABY

▲ Wallabies, from Australia, are members of the kangaroo family. A baby wallaby is called a joey. It is born live. Then it wriggles into its mother's pouch, where it drinks its mother's milk. The joey stays there until it is about eight months old.

Baby African elephants grow inside their mothers' bodies for nearly two years. When a baby elephant, called a calf, is finally born, it weighs as much as a fully grown man. ▼

ELEPHANT

This mother crocodile from Egypt carries her hatched babies into the water to protect them from enemies. She will crack the eggs that are slow to hatch inside her mouth and let the babies wiggle into the water. ▼

CROCODILE

BEAR

OWL

PENGUIN

◀ This bear cub had a mass of less than $\frac{1}{2}$ kg (1 lb) when it was born. The rings of fur around its eyes make it look as if it's wearing spectacles, or eyeglasses. The spectacled bear is the only kind of bear that lives in South America.

These baby snowy owls hatched in a nest on the ground. Their home in the far north is a cold place called the tundra (tun′drə). Both parents care for their chicks. All the chicks are born with white fluff, which later turns gray. The gray color blends in with the ground and helps to hide the young owls from enemies. ▶

◀ Gentoo penguins live in the Antarctic. They make their nests out of rocks. The penguin parents take turns sitting on the nest. Both parents feed and care for the chicks that hatch. When the young penguins are about eight to ten weeks old, they swim out to sea and live on their own.

INVESTIGATION 2

THINK IT WRITE IT

1. On page A15 you read about the parts of an egg. Think about each part and what it does. For each part, explain what would happen to the egg if that part didn't work.

2. The first life-cycle stage is the same for animals that hatch and animals that are born live. Describe that stage.

HOW DO SOME ANIMALS GROW AND CHANGE?

Have you ever worn a costume and found that no one knew you? As some animals go through their life cycles, they change so much that you may not know what animals they are. Find out about two ways animals grow and change.

Activity

Look at What You've Become

Imagine how you will change as you grow up. Do all animals change in the same ways you do? The animals in this activity are masters at some amazing changes. Find out what they are.

Procedure

1. Look at the list of materials with your group. **Predict** what a mealworm needs in order to survive. Explain which material meets which need. **Infer** which material might provide a mealworm with water.

2. Use the materials to make a home for the mealworms. In your *Science Notebook*, **describe** the home you made. Place the mealworms in the home.

Step 1

3. Every two days, clean the home and give the mealworms fresh food.

4. **Observe** the mealworms with a hand lens each day for three weeks. Use a ruler to **measure** changes in size. **Record** any changes you observe.

Analyze and Conclude

1. How did the mealworms change?

2. The adult stage of this insect is called a beetle. How many different stages did you observe in the life cycle of the mealworm beetle? **Draw** each stage.

INVESTIGATE FURTHER!

EXPERIMENT

Pet store owners keep mealworms in a refrigerator. Find out how a cold temperature affects a mealworm's life cycle. Use two mealworms. Keep one cold and the other at room temperature. What did you observe? What conclusions can you draw about the effects of cold temperatures on a mealworm's life cycle?

A21

Activity

That's Something to Chirp About!

Crickets are insects that are found in dark, damp places, such as under logs and rocks, in bushes, in deep grass, and in other shaded areas. Make a home for crickets and observe them as they grow and change.

Procedure

1. You're going to make a home for crickets from some of the materials provided. Look at the list of materials. With your group, **predict** what a cricket needs in order to survive. Explain which material meets which need. **Hypothesize** which material might provide water.

2. Make a home for the crickets. Be sure to put a small plastic dish, to serve as an egg chamber, in the home. When you have finished, place the crickets in their home.

3. Every two days, clean the home and give the crickets fresh food.

4. Every day, **observe** the egg chamber carefully for eggs. In your *Science Notebook*, **record** the day you first find eggs.

Step 2

A22

5. Use another box and other materials to make another cricket home. Move the egg chamber into the new home. Provide food near the eggs.

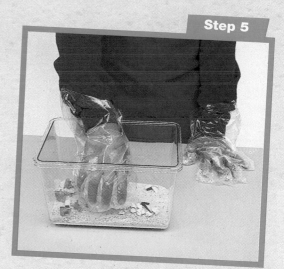

6. Watch for the eggs to hatch. Some kinds of crickets take much longer to hatch than others. **Record** the day the eggs hatch. The young crickets are called **nymphs** (nimfs). When the nymphs can hop, place them with the adult crickets.

7. Use a hand lens to **observe** the crickets. **Compare** the adult crickets and the nymphs. **Record** what you observe.

Step 7

Analyze and Conclude

1. How are the nymphs like the adults? How are they different?

2. What different stages did you **observe** in the cricket life cycle?

3. How does a cricket's life cycle differ from a mealworm's?

INVESTIGATE FURTHER!

EXPERIMENT
Observe the nymphs as they grow. What happens to them? Record what you find out.

Going Around in Cycles

▲ From one birthday to the next, people grow and change. How has this person changed?

Your life cycle is very simple. You are first a baby, then a child, then a teenager, and then an adult. Suppose you saw a baby picture of an adult friend. You'd probably be able to say who the baby in the picture grew up to be. But if you saw an insect such as a butterfly in an early stage, you might not know what the animal was.

A Four-Stage Cycle

There are four stages in the life cycles of most species of insects. The stages in order are (1) egg, (2) larva, (3) pupa, and (4) adult.

Life Cycle of a Butterfly

LARVA A larva, called a caterpillar, hatches from the egg. It sheds its outer covering several times as it eats and grows.

PUPA The caterpillar makes a covering called a chrysalis (kris′ə lis). This is the pupa stage.

ADULT After developing fully, an adult butterfly comes out of the chrysalis.

EGG The female adult mates, lays eggs, and the cycle starts over again.

A four-stage life cycle is called **complete metamorphosis** (met ə-môr′fə sis). The first stage is the egg. The second stage, called the **larva** (lär′və), is a wormlike stage that doesn't look at all like the adult. The larval stage of certain insects has a special name. Look at the pictures on this page. What is the butterfly larva called?

The larva eats and grows and then makes a covering for itself. At that time, the insect is in the third stage, called the **pupa** (pyoo′pə). Inside the pupa, the adult insect develops. When it is fully developed, the adult insect comes out. The **adult** is the last stage of a life cycle. The adult female insect then mates and lays eggs, starting the cycle again.

The beetle also goes through complete metamorphosis in its life cycle. In the activity on pages A20 and A21, you observed mealworms, the larvas of beetles. The larva of the mealworm beetle is called a grub.

Now you can see that an insect in some stages doesn't look at all like the adult. A caterpillar certainly doesn't look like a butterfly. And a mealworm doesn't look like a beetle.

A Three-Stage Cycle

There are three stages in the life cycles of some insects. The names of the stages in order are (1) egg, (2) nymph, and (3) adult. A three-stage life cycle is called **incomplete metamorphosis**.

As with all animals, the first stage in the life cycle is the egg. The animal in the second stage, called a **nymph**, looks almost like a small adult. As the nymph eats and grows larger, it sheds its outer covering several times and then develops into an adult.

Then the female adult lays eggs that can go through the same cycle. Look at the pictures of the life cycle of a grasshopper. In what ways is the nymph like the adult grasshopper? How is it different?

A cricket goes through incomplete metamorphosis. On pages A22 and A23, you did an activity with crickets. How are cricket nymphs and grasshopper nymphs alike?

SCIENCE IN LITERATURE

INSECT METAMORPHOSIS
FROM EGG TO ADULT
by Ron and Nancy Goor
Atheneum, 1990

Did you know that after a caterpillar sheds its skin, it has to puff up the new skin with air, like a balloon? That's one of the strange but true facts about the life cycles of insects told in *Insect Metamorphosis: From Egg to Adult*.

As you read this book and examine the close-up photographs, think about what amazes you the most. Make a list of strange but true metamorphosis facts. Share your list with your family and friends. Were they also amazed?

Life Cycle of a Grasshopper

NYMPH A nymph hatches from an egg. The nymph looks almost like the adult, but it is smaller and has no wings. As the nymph eats and grows, it sheds its outer covering several times.

EGG The female adult lays eggs in a hole that she digs in the ground.

ADULT Finally, after 40 to 60 days, the nymph has developed into an adult. Most adult grasshoppers have wings. The adult female mates and lays eggs, and the cycle continues.

INVESTIGATION 3

THINK IT WRITE IT

1. When a frog hatches from an egg, it has a tail that it later loses. Then it looks like an adult. Tell whether the frog's life cycle is complete or incomplete metamorphosis and explain why.

2. Compare the life cycles of two animals—one that goes through complete metamorphosis and one that goes through incomplete metamorphosis.

HOW DO ADULT ANIMALS CARE FOR THEIR YOUNG?

Have you ever had a sitter? Hiring a sitter is one way adult humans might care for their children. In this investigation you'll learn how animals differ in the ways they care for their young.

Activity

The Animal-Sitter's Guide

What's a sitter's job? Suppose an animal such as a baby whale or a young giraffe had a human sitter. What do you think that sitter would need to know to care for the young animals? In this activity you'll find out.

MATERIALS

- animal-sitting assignment cards in a box
- construction paper
- colored markers
- discarded magazines
- reference books
- *Science Notebook*

Procedure

1. Take a card from your group's animal-sitting assignment box. Look at the name of the animal on the card and **record** the name in your *Science Notebook*. Find out about the baby animal's needs and how the parents care for the baby. **Record** what you find out. **Infer** the care the baby animal should receive.

panther

hawk

turtle

Step 1

2. On a sheet of construction paper, write a list of instructions for an Animal-Sitter's Guide for the class. Give information that would answer questions such as these: What kind of food does the baby animal need? When does it sleep? Does it make unusual noises? What might threaten or harm the baby animal?

3. Include a drawing or picture of your animal.

4. Put your instructions in the class Animal-Sitter's Guide, where others can refer to them.

Analyze and Conclude

1. What would be the hardest part of taking care of the animal you wrote about? Explain your answer.

2. **Compare** the care needed by your animal with the care needed by other baby animals in the Guide. Which animal would be the hardest to sit for? Which would be the easiest? Explain your answers.

Step 2

UNIT PROJECT LINK

Pet owners are like full-time animal sitters. Predict which pets are hardest to care for. With your group, interview owners of different kinds of pets. Find out about the pets' care. Record the information in a special pet section of your Animal-Sitter's Guide.

Out of Sight, Out of Mind

It's easy to forget about something that you can't see. "Out of sight, out of mind" is a short way to say this. You might use this saying to describe how some animals behave toward their eggs. For example, a cowbird lays her eggs, one at a time, in the nests of other, smaller birds. Then she flies away. The "foster parent" birds hatch, feed, and care for the young cowbirds. You can see that for the mother cowbird, her eggs are "out of sight, out of mind."

Many Eggs—Few Survive

Frogs and most fish lay many eggs but don't protect them. A frog lays thousands of jelly-covered eggs. Many frog eggs become food for other animals, such as the cat-eyed snake of North and South America. The frog eggs that survive develop into tadpoles. Some of the tadpoles also become food for snakes. But others survive.

Some animals hide their eggs before leaving them. A female sea

1 A female sea turtle swims to shore.

2 The female lays her eggs.

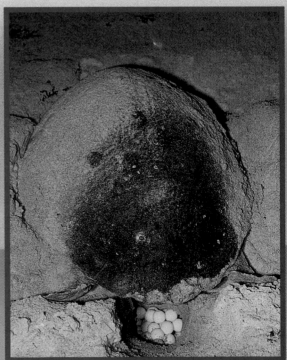

turtle crawls out of the sea at night. Using her flippers as shovels, she digs a nest, in which she lays at least a hundred eggs. Then she covers the eggs with damp sand. When daylight comes, she crawls back into the sea and never sees her young.

Although she has laid many eggs, probably only one baby turtle out of a hundred will survive. Other animals, such as raccoons, steal eggs from turtle nests. When the eggs that survive do hatch, the baby turtles crawl toward the sea. But sea birds swoop down upon them for food. And many of those that reach the water become food for sea animals.

Survival Kit

How do animals that hatch from out-of-sight, out-of-mind eggs sur-

▲ **A Colorado potato beetle and its eggs on a potato plant**

vive? One thing that helps cowbirds survive is that the adult females lay their eggs in nests of smaller birds. Because the young cowbirds are larger than the other young birds in the nests, they get more food.

Other animals lay their eggs at food sources. A Colorado potato beetle lays its eggs on a potato plant. The larva hatches just when the potato leaves are ready to eat. ■

3 The baby turtles hatch.

4 The baby turtles crawl to the sea.

A Whale of a Baby

Did you know that the world's biggest baby is about 8 m (26 ft) long and has a mass of about 1,800 kg (2 T)? It's longer than a station wagon and weighs as much as a small truck. This baby is a blue whale calf. The blue whale calf's mother is much bigger than her baby. She's about 30 m (100 ft) long and has a mass of over 90,000 kg (100 T). That's as long as two big tractor-trailers and heavier than the largest dinosaur. A land animal's legs couldn't support that mass. But ocean water can.

A Whale of a Birth

A whale develops inside a mother whale and then is born live. Whales are born underwater in early winter, almost a year after the mother and father mate. A mother whale is called a cow. The baby is a calf. Normally, the calf slithers out of the cow's body tail first.

The mother watches the newborn calf float to the surface. There the calf takes its first deep breath and sends up a fountain of mist from the blowhole on top of its head.

A mother humpback whale with her calf ▼

From the time it is born, the calf can swim. For several weeks the calf swims close to its mother. She gently strokes the calf with her flipper. A mother whale never leaves her baby unattended. She watches as it takes in fresh air before diving and as it blows out its warm breath when surfacing.

To feed, the calf dives underwater, where its mother squirts rich, warm milk into its mouth. A blue whale calf drinks about 500 L (132 gal) of milk every day and gains about 90 kg (200 lb) a day.

A Whale of a Journey

One kind of whale is called a humpback. During the winter, the mother whales never eat. They live off their stored fat. But in the spring, thousands of whales head for the colder waters of the Arctic, where there is food. The whales swim in small groups called pods. On this long journey north, the mother whale watches out for dangers. Killer whales can hurt and even kill a baby whale. A whale can get caught in nets dragged by fishing boats. Then it can't swim to the surface to breathe. A mother whale will protect her baby even if it means putting herself in danger.

▲ A closeup look at baleen

A Whale of a Summer

By summer humpback whales arrive at the Arctic. The waters there are their feeding grounds. Since the mother whale hasn't eaten for six months, she's hungry. She will eat a year's worth of food—probably a ton a day—in the next six months.

Humpback whales don't have teeth. Instead, they have baleen, or flat bony plates that hang down from the roof of the mouth like the teeth of a comb.

Humpback whales feeding
(*top and right*)

The mother whale gulps big mouthfuls of sea water. She closes her mouth part way and then squirts the water out. She swallows the food that is trapped by the baleen. A whale's mouth can hold a ton of food.

All summer, as the mother whale eats and her calf drinks milk, they build up layers of fat. They play together. They slap the water with their tails. They roll over. Sometimes the little whale breaches—it hurls itself out of the water, twists high in the air, and lands with a splash!

A Whale of a Whale

In the fall the whales travel south toward warmer waters. There the calf's mother may mate again.

The young humpback whale has grown strong. It can find its own food. Now only a year old, it has doubled its birth size. It is truly a whale of a whale. ■

INVESTIGATION 4

THINK IT WRITE IT

1. Think of a particular kind of very young animal. Suppose you found such an animal, and it was separated from its parents. Write how you might help care for the baby animal.

2. Choose an animal you have learned about in this investigation. Describe the care that the animal gets as it grows and develops.

REFLECT & EVALUATE

WORD POWER

adult
egg
embryo
larva

life cycle
nymph
pupa
species

complete metamorphosis
incomplete metamorphosis

On Your Own
Review the terms in the list. Then use as many terms as you can in a paragraph about life cycles.

With a Partner
Make a list of all the terms that apply to people. Have your partner list all the terms that apply to a butterfly. Compare your lists.

BUILD YOUR PORTFOLIO

Find out about an animal's life cycle. Glue pictures or make drawings on a large sheet of paper to show the animal's life cycle. Draw arrows to order the stages. Write the name of the animal below the life-cycle pictures.

Analyze Information

Study the photograph. Then use the photograph to name and describe all the stages in this insect's life cycle. Does the insect go through complete metamorphosis or incomplete metamorphosis? Explain.

Assess Performance

Make up a new kind of animal. Draw the egg of the animal, what the animal looks like when it is young, how the animal changes as it grows, and what its parents look like. Name your animal and label each picture.

Problem Solving

1. A mother sea turtle may have a hundred babies at one time. But a mother elephant gives birth to only one baby at a time. How do you think a mother elephant and a mother turtle might differ in the ways they care for their babies?

2. How might your life be different today if you had skipped the development that occurs between the ages of two and four in your life cycle? Tell why all the stages of growth in a person's life are important.

CHAPTER 2

LIFE CYCLES OF PLANTS

Many members of the plant kingdom grow from seeds. Have you ever planted a seed and watched it grow into a plant? What happened to the plant as time passed?

A Child, a Plant, a Poem

Gwendolyn Brooks, an African American poet, tells in this poem about a child who plants a seed.

Tommy

I put a seed into the ground
And said, "I'll watch it grow."
I watered it and cared for it
As well as I could know.
One day I walked in my back yard
And oh, what did I see!
My seed had popped itself right out
Without consulting me.

—Gwendolyn Brooks

In this chapter you'll learn how plants grow and change. And you'll discover other things plants do "without consulting you."

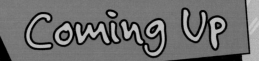
◀ **Planting flowers**

A37

What Is the First Stage in the Life Cycle of a Flowering Plant?

What a survival story! In Egypt, seeds buried for over 1,000 years were able to start a new life cycle. You'll dig up more about seeds in Investigation 1.

Activity

The Inside Story

Seeds come in many sizes. But even the smallest seed can begin a new plant life cycle. Find out what's inside a seed.

Procedure

1. Use a toothpick to pry open the halves of one lima bean seed. With your group, **observe** the parts of the seed. Place the two halves so that their inside surfaces are facing up. **Draw** the two halves in your *Science Notebook*. **Draw** arrows that point to each part. Number the arrows.

MATERIALS
- goggles
- soaked lima bean seeds
- toothpicks
- water
- paper towels
- 2 sealable plastic bags
- stapler
- metric ruler
- tape
- hand lens
- *Science Notebook*

SAFETY
Wear goggles during this activity. Clean up any spills immediately.

Step 1.

2. Place a piece of wet paper towel in a plastic bag. Staple the bag about 2 cm from the bottom. Pry open a second bean seed and separate the two halves. Place all four seed halves in the bag.

3. Prepare a second plastic bag like the first one. Add four whole bean seeds to the bag. Seal both bags and tape them to a wall or bulletin board. **Record** the date.

4. Use a hand lens to **observe** the whole seeds and seed halves each day. **Record** any changes. After three days, remove one of the whole seeds from its bag. Separate the halves. **Record** what you see. Every three days remove another whole seed and separate its halves. **Record** all observations.

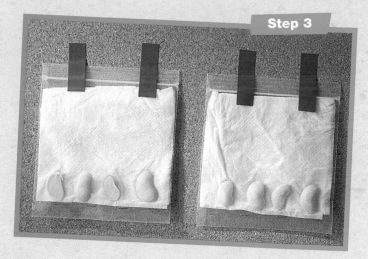
Step 3

Analyze and Conclude

1. What changes occurred in the whole seeds? What changes occurred in the seed halves? **Hypothesize** about what might account for the differences.

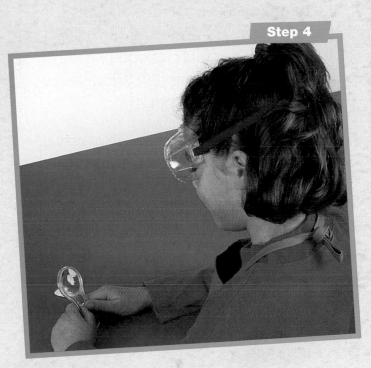
Step 4

2. How many different seed parts did you find? **Describe** each part. Beside each description, write the number that matches the number of the same part on your drawing.

3. Based on your observations, **infer** which seed part provides food for the young plant that grows from the seed. Explain your inference.

A39

Corn
Simply "A-maize-ing"

Corn is one of the most important foods in the world. People and many kinds of farm animals eat corn. Corn, also called maize, can be used to make food products, such as cooking oil and bread. The time line shows how important corn has been.

Because the action in World War I has destroyed much of the farmland in Europe, the United States sends ships loaded with food to Europe. Corn and wheat from America save thousands of people from starving.

1920

2000

1995
Farmers grow almost as much corn as they grow wheat.

Farmers grow different kinds of maize and invent better ways to store crops for winter.

800

1620
The Pilgrims land at what is now Plymouth, Massachusetts. Native Americans show the Pilgrims how to plant, grow, and use corn. The Pilgrims have a day of thanks which we celebrate today as Thanksgiving.

Maize is planted and harvested in Mexico. This corn is a type of wild plant.

2700 B.C.

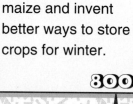

A.D. 200
Maize, along with beans and squash, becomes a main part of people's diets in the Americas. Ways are found to increase the food production.

Plant Tricks

Seeds can do stupendous tricks! Have you ever blown on the fluffy round head of a dandelion? Each little parachute that floats away is a seed that can produce a plant.

The Many Kinds of Seeds

The first stage in the life cycle of a flowering plant is a seed. Seeds are as different as the plants that grow from them. Seeds come in many sizes. A carrot seed is tiny. A coconut is a large seed. Seeds come in many shapes—round, pointed, oval, flat, and thin. They come in many patterns and colors—solid, speckled, white, brown, black, yellow, and red.

Whatever its size, shape, or color, a seed has three parts—a seed coat, stored food, and an embryo (em'-brē ō). Find out about these parts as you study the drawings below.

How Seeds Survive

Seeds are survivors. Plants have grown from lotus seeds that are centuries old. And seeds perform all kinds of tricks. Seeds can burst open, pop out, explode, fly, float, hitchhike, and parachute. These tricks help a seed get away from its parent plant. Then the new plant that develops from the seed will have space to grow.

PARTS OF A SEED

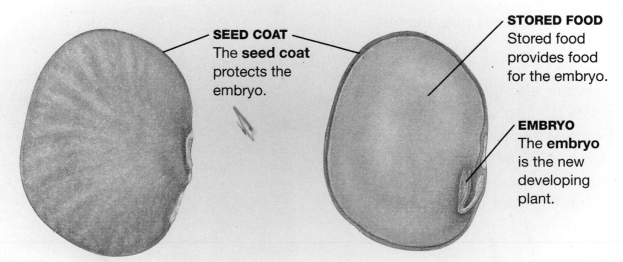

SEED COAT
The **seed coat** protects the embryo.

STORED FOOD
Stored food provides food for the embryo.

EMBRYO
The **embryo** is the new developing plant.

Wind scatters some seeds. As the tumbleweed plant is blown along the ground, its seeds scatter. Wind also blows seeds away from the parent plant. Some seeds have a shape that helps them travel in the wind. Because of its shape, the milkweed seed travels easily in the wind.

Animals also scatter seeds. As animals roam, their fur can pick up and carry seeds. Animals such as mice carry seeds away and bury them. Birds carry seeds on their feathers and in their beaks. People sometimes carry seeds on their clothing.

▲ **Seed in a bird's beak**

What Seeds Need

A seed needs warmth, air, and moisture to **germinate** (jʉr´mə-nāt), or sprout. In the activity you did with seeds, on pages A38 and A39, a wet paper towel in the bags provided moisture for the seeds. When a seed is in the ground, a tiny hole in the seed coat allows moisture to enter the seed. In addition to warmth and water, a seed needs oxygen from the air before it can germinate.

▲ **Milkweed seeds popping out**

Water also scatters seeds. Lotus seeds fall into water and float away. Some settle in the muddy bottoms of rivers and lakes and grow into new plants. Some seeds, such as coconuts, even float across oceans.

▼ **Sticktight seeds in a squirrel's fur**

With the proper conditions, a seedling develops. A **seedling** is a new plant that develops from an embryo. The growing plant has parts that help it get what it needs to grow. Some plants have long tap-roots that can reach far underground for water. Other plants have fuzzy stems and leaves that capture and hold in moisture.

Seed Plants Not From Seeds

All seed plants produce and can grow from seeds. However, some can grow from trailing plant stems called runners or from underground plant parts called tubers (too′bərz). A potato is an example of a tuber. Plants such as tulips can grow from bulbs. Some plants can even grow from a piece of stem or leaf. But all seed plants produce seeds.

Runners, tubers, bulbs, and cuttings don't produce seedlings—only seeds produce seedlings. Seedlings develop into plants that produce food, which is used by the plants and by animals that eat the plants. ■

▲ **A bean seedling**

INVESTIGATION 1

1. In Chapter 1 you found out about the stages in the life cycles of animals. How is the seed stage in the life cycle of flowering plants like the egg stage in an animal's life cycle?

2. Explain how the parts of a seed help a flowering plant produce a new plant.

HOW DO FLOWERING PLANTS MAKE SEEDS?

Have you ever picked or chosen a flower for a friend? What helped you decide which one to take? Was it the scent, the color, or the interesting shapes of its parts? In this investigation you'll find out how each of these is important for flowers to make seeds.

Activity

It's a Flower! It's a Factory!

Have you ever heard about a factory that blooms? A flowering plant is a factory. What does this factory make? In this activity you'll find out about one of its products.

Procedure

1. **Examine** a flower carefully. **Make a drawing** of it in your *Science Notebook*. **Draw** an arrow to each part of the flower. Label any part that you know.

2. Carefully pull the petals apart so that you can see the center of the flower. **Make a drawing** of what you see. Write questions about what you **observe**.

Step 2

MATERIALS
- flower
- sheet of plain white paper
- hand lens
- cotton swab
- *Science Notebook*

SAFETY
Do not smell the flowers. You may inhale pollen grains, which cause allergic reactions in many people. Wash your hands after handling the flowers.

3. With your group, **compare** the parts of your flower with the photo shown. Label the parts on both of your drawings.

4. Gently shake your flower over a sheet of plain white paper. The small powdery objects that fall from the flower are grains of **pollen** (päl'ən). Use a hand lens to **observe** the grains. Feel the grains. **Describe** how they look and feel. **Record** your observations.

Analyze and Conclude

1. The **pistil** (pis'til) is the part of the flower where seeds form. Why do you think its location in the center is important?

2. The **stamen** (stā'mən) is the part of the flower that contains pollen. For seeds to form in most plants, pollen must travel from a stamen of one plant to the pistil of another. Use a cotton swab to move pollen from a stamen to the pistil. **Hypothesize** how insects and birds might move pollen. **Talk with your group**. Explain your ideas and **record** your hypothesis.

3. A flower's petals attract insects, which feed on a sweet liquid in the plant. What is it about petals that might attract insects?

Step 3

pistil

stamen

petals

Step 4

A45

The Fantastic Flower

Many seed plants produce flowers. Flowers grow in many colors and sizes. Many people enjoy the beauty and smell of flowers so much that they give flowers as gifts on special occasions.

Plant Parenthood

Flowers might be called the parents of plants. A flower is part of an adult flowering plant. Seeds are formed in flowers. It is through the seed that the life cycle of the parent plant can continue.

Each flower has three parts that help a flower carry out its parent role. Their names are pistil, stamen, and petals. Look at the picture as you read about each part.

PARTS OF A FLOWER

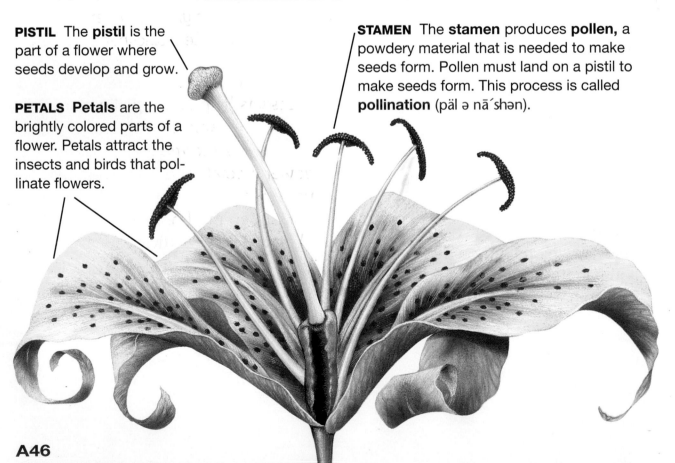

PISTIL The **pistil** is the part of a flower where seeds develop and grow.

PETALS Petals are the brightly colored parts of a flower. Petals attract the insects and birds that pollinate flowers.

STAMEN The **stamen** produces **pollen,** a powdery material that is needed to make seeds form. Pollen must land on a pistil to make seeds form. This process is called **pollination** (päl ə nā´shən).

Seed Protection

Do you like to eat fruit? Did you know fruits come from flowers? A **fruit** is the part of a flower that forms around a seed. Pea pods, tomatoes, and apples are all fruits that we eat. A fruit protects the seed or seeds inside of it.

A fruit also provides a way for the seeds to be scattered. For example, birds like to eat cherries. Inside each cherry is a single seed, which is protected by a hard shell. When a bird swallows a cherry, it digests the soft part of the fruit. But the seed passes unchanged through and out of the bird's body. If the seed falls on the ground, it can grow into a new cherry tree.

Birds also like to eat blackberries, but they do not like blackberry seeds.

▲ **Fruits protect seeds.**

The birds push the seeds aside and wipe them off their beaks. The tiny seeds fall to the ground, where they can grow into new blackberry bushes.

Plant Helpers

Insects help in the pollination of flowering plants. For example, bees are attracted to the bright colors of a flower's petals and to a sweet-tasting nectar (nek'tər) inside the flower.

Each grain of pollen, which you observed in the activity on pages A44 and A45, has a sticky coating. When an insect comes to feed on the nectar in a flower, pollen grains cling to the insect's feet and body. They then carry the pollen to the pistil of the same flower or to the pistil of another flower.

▼ **A tomato is a fruit.**

Not all flowers are pollinated by insects. Sometimes pollen is carried by wind and water. Birds and other animals, attracted by a flower's color and scent, can also carry pollen from one flower to another.

The hummingbird hovers over a flower and pushes its long beak deep into the flower to get the nectar. Pollen from the flower sticks to the bird, which then carries the pollen to the next flower.

Bats help pollinate flowering trees. Bats drink the nectar and eat the pollen. They transfer the pollen stuck on their tongues and noses from flower to flower.

Fantastic Flower Facts

Pollination can occur in some unusual ways. When an insect lands on a redbud flower, its petals spring open. This action allows the insect to reach the pollen and carry it away. Flowers of the American mountain ash, or rowan tree, grow in clusters. Near each cluster, there is a sort of platform where insects can land and then pollinate the flowers. The flowers of the catalpa tree have deep trumpet-shaped tubes. As an insect crawls inside a tube to reach the nectar, the insect picks up pollen.

Plant Cycles

The life cycles of flowering plants vary greatly in length. The life cycles of some trees, for example, may be hundreds or even thousands of years long! Many of the flowering plants you know have yearly life cycles. Such plants are called annuals. Study the life cycle of an annual shown on the next page.

▼ **Flower of a redbud tree**

▼ **Flower of a catalpa tree**

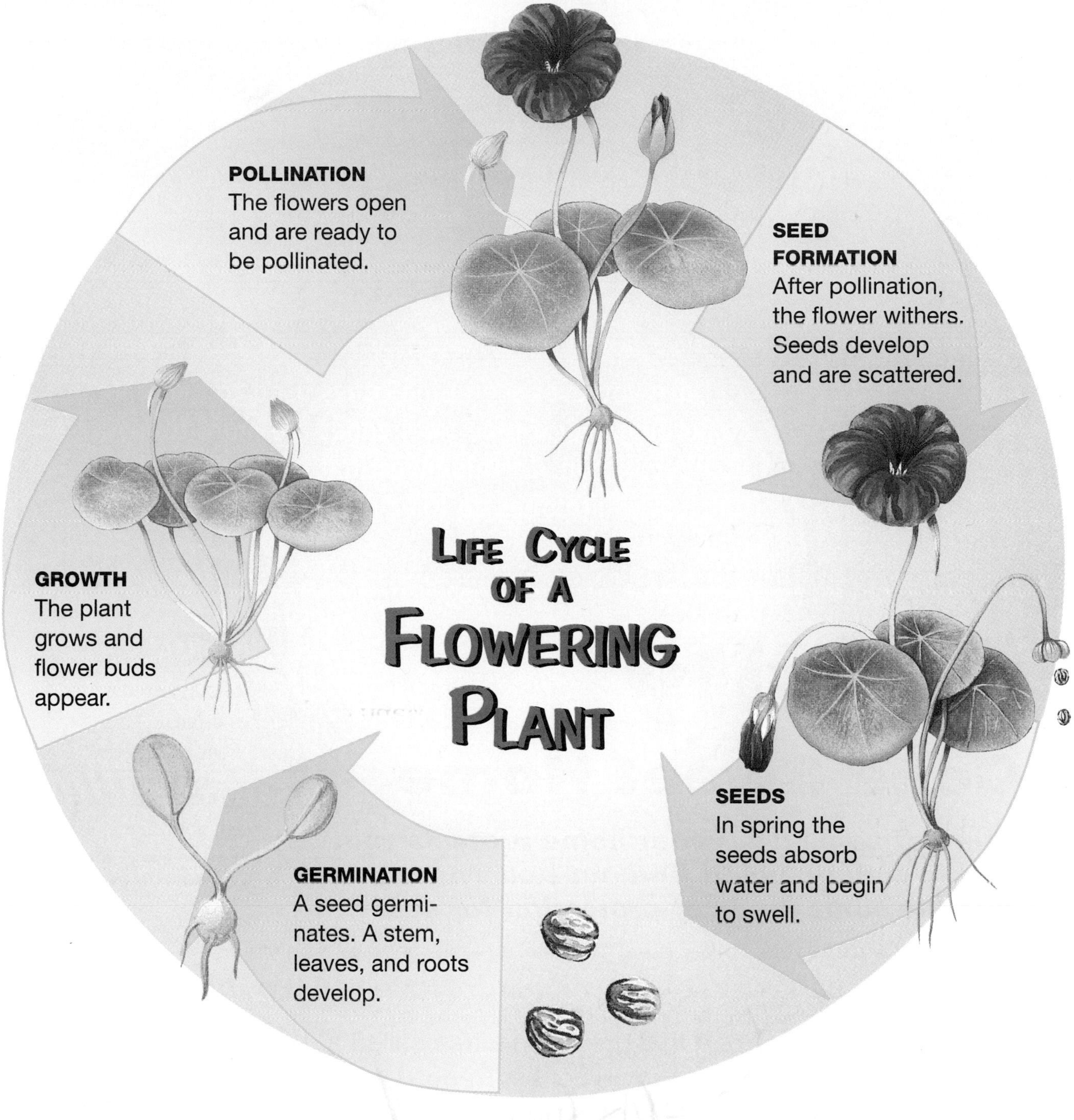

LIFE CYCLE OF A FLOWERING PLANT

POLLINATION
The flowers open and are ready to be pollinated.

SEED FORMATION
After pollination, the flower withers. Seeds develop and are scattered.

GROWTH
The plant grows and flower buds appear.

GERMINATION
A seed germinates. A stem, leaves, and roots develop.

SEEDS
In spring the seeds absorb water and begin to swell.

INVESTIGATION 2

THINK IT WRITE IT

1. Suppose you ordered a bowl of fruit at a restaurant. Your waiter delivers a bowl of sliced cucumbers. Was there a mistake? Explain your response.

2. Describe the three main parts of a flower and tell how each part helps seeds form.

INVESTIGATION 3

HOW DO PLANTS WITH CONES MAKE AND PROTECT SEEDS?

Have you ever seen pine cones used to decorate something? For a pine tree, cones are more than just decoration. In this investigation you'll find out just what cones do for a plant.

Activity

Cone Sweet Home

Think of some ways your home protects you. In this activity you'll find out how cones provide the same kinds of protection for seeds.

MATERIALS
- many assorted cones
- hand lens
- *Science Notebook*

SAFETY //////
Wash your hands after handling the cones.

Procedure

1. A cone is a plant part that grows on a tree called a conifer (kän'ə fər). **Examine** some cones. **Record** your observations in your *Science Notebook*.

2. With your partner, **classify** the cones. Each group of cones should share at least one characteristic. Use characteristics such as size, color, and shape.

3. Look at the pictures of conifers on the next page. What kinds of conifers did your cones come from?

Pine cone ▲

Cedar cone ▶    **Spruce cone** ▶

A50

4. A cone is made of woody parts called **scales**. Carefully pull off several scales from each cone. A conifer seed grows on the scale where the scale joins the cone. With a hand lens, **observe** the scales to find a seed. **Make a drawing** of what you observe on the scales.

Step 4

5. Look at the picture of the cone scale at the right. **Compare** the picture with your drawing.

Analyze and Conclude

1. Some cones can open and close. They open and release their seeds in dry weather. Cones close in damp weather to protect the seeds from moisture. **Talk with your group** and **infer** what one job of a cone is.

2. How are the cone of a conifer and the fruit of a flowering plant alike?

Pine tree

Spruce tree

Cedar tree

Evergreens

Many trees shed their leaves in the fall as part of their life cycles. But other trees have leaves (or needles) all year long. Such trees are called evergreens because they're always green. Actually, evergreens do shed their leaves, but they grow new ones at the same time. That's why they're always green.

Pine, spruce, fir, hemlock, and cedar trees are all evergreens. These trees have something else in common—they all bear cones. A **cone** is the part of an evergreen tree that produces pollen or seeds. Not all evergreens produce cones. But those that do are called conifers. The word *conifer* means "cone-bearing."

There are two kinds of conifer cones. Pollen cones make and release pollen, much as the stamen of a flower does. Seed cones receive

DIFFERENT KINDS OF EVERGREENS

Eastern hemlock ▶

Douglas fir ▶

fish scales   roof shingles   cone scales

the pollen and use it to make seeds. Each cone is a woody stalk covered with stiff **scales**, which protect the seeds under them. As you saw in the activity on pages A50 and A51, the scales overlap, like the scales on a fish or the shingles on a roof.

The Life Cycle of a Conifer

What happens to the seeds of cone-bearing evergreens? Some are eaten or carried away by animals. Others simply fall to the ground. Those seeds that are lucky enough to land on good, rich soil and receive enough warmth, moisture, and sunlight can grow into trees.

One good place for a seed to fall is on a rotting log. The log is rich in things that plants need to grow. So the log nurses the tiny seed as it sprouts and develops into a seedling. A log that feeds a seedling is called a nurse log.

As a seedling's roots grow down and its branches grow out, it develops into a young conifer. The young conifer grows taller and taller and produces cones. At the proper time, the seed cones open and let their seeds go. And the life cycle of the conifer continues.

◀ **White pine**

◀ **Blue spruce**

LIFE CYCLE OF A CONIFER

CONES In spring, dark-green buds appear on the branches. The buds develop into cones.

POLLINATION Some cones produce pollen, which drifts under the scales of cones that produce seeds.

SEEDS When new buds are forming, the cones open. The seeds fall and germinate.

SEEDLING A seedling develops and grows into a mature conifer.

Conifers, Water, and Fire

If you're like most people, you probably think that fire is always harmful to a tree's life cycle. You might also think that moisture is always helpful. Read on—you might be surprised at what you find out.

Everyone knows that plants need water. But sometimes, a conifer can get too much of a good thing. When the air is dry, the scales in the cones open, allowing air to enter. When there is a lot of moisture in the air, the scales close up tightly, because seeds need to be kept dry. Moisture can cause the seeds in a tightly closed cone to rot. So moisture is not always helpful.

Are forest fires always harmful? It's true that when fire hits the leafy top of a tree, the tree almost always dies. Shrubs and bushes also die. But the forest itself is not necessarily dead. In fact, some cones, such as those of the lodgepole and jack pines, actually *need* heat as hot as a

A forest fire ▲   **Soon after the fire** ▲

fire just to open. These cones remain closed until they reach a temperature as high as about 50°C (122°F). The high temperature melts the sticky pitch inside the cone, and the cone opens. Then the seeds can be scattered. Soon some of the seeds germinate, and seedlings appear. Fire may sometimes be harmful to plants but not to cones that contain the seeds for new conifers. ■

Within a year, regrowth begins. ▶

──────────── **INVESTIGATION 3** ────────────

THINK IT WRITE IT

1. Think back to what you learned about flowering plants. What part of a conifer do you think is most like the fruit of a flowering plant? Explain your answer.

2. Describe how cones help make and protect seeds. Explain the role a cone can play in the regrowth that takes place following a forest fire.

HOW DO PLANTS CHANGE DURING THEIR LIFE CYCLES?

You already know some changes that plants make during their life cycles. In this investigation you'll find out how some plants change as they grow and how they respond to changes around them.

Activity

Sizing Up Tree Growth

As you grow, the bones in your legs and arms get longer. What parts of a tree get longer when it grows? Find out.

- - - - - - - - - - - - - -

Procedure

1. Look at the tree in the pictures. How did the tree change?

2. **Compare** the two trunks. **Record** your observations in your *Science Notebook*.

3. **Compare** the height of the lowest branch in each picture. **Compare** the length of the branches in each picture. **Record** your observations.

▲ **Young tree**

▲ **Same tree at mature stage**

4. The trunk of most trees grows about $2\frac{1}{2}$ cm bigger around each year. **Measure** the distance around the trunk of a tree at a height of about 120 cm off the ground. **Record** your measurement. **Estimate** the age of the tree.

5. Find out how branches grow. The place on a branch where growth is occurring usually has a different color from the rest of the branch. **Observe** some branches on two different kinds of trees. Look for color differences. Where do they occur? Remember to look at the branches, not the leaves. **Record** what you observe.

Step 4

Analyze and Conclude

1. Based on your observations, **infer** where growth occurs on a branch. What happens to the branches of a tree as the tree ages?

2. How do the trunks of most trees change as the trees age?

INVESTIGATE FURTHER!

RESEARCH

How can you tell when a tree is sick or dying? Call a tree service and find out, or research diseases of trees in an encyclopedia or book about plants. What changes caused by disease would you look for? What might cause the death of a tree? Share your findings with your class.

Activity

A Change of Plants

Do you squint when you walk into bright light? Find out how plants respond to changes in their environment.

Procedure

1. Put one seedling into a shoebox. Put the lid on the box. Be sure the seedling is away from the hole in the lid.

Step 1

2. Use a pencil to make a small hole in a sheet of plastic wrap. The stem of a seedling should just fit through the hole. Gently pull the seedling in the second cup through the hole. Tape the plastic wrap tightly to the cup, as shown.

Step 2

3. Gently turn the cup upside down. Tape the cup to the bottom of a shelf or a desk-top so that the seedling hangs upside down, as shown.

4. Place the third seedling on a flat sur-face where it can receive light.

5. **Talk with your group** and **predict** how each seedling will look in three days. **Record** your predictions in your *Science Notebook*.

6. After three days **observe** the seed-lings. **Record** any changes you observe.

Step 3

Analyze and Conclude

1. **Compare** your observations with your predictions. What do you think caused any changes you observed?

2. If a plant could not adjust to changes, **infer** what might happen to it.

UNIT PROJECT LINK

Sometime you might be asked to plant-sit for a friend's plants. Ask people you know if they have had any problems in caring for their plants. Find out how the problems were solved. Record the problems and solutions in a Plant-Sitter's Guide.

Where Are You Growing?

As you get older, you get bigger. As a plant goes through its life cycle, it gets bigger, too. The stem gets taller. The roots get longer. The roots and shoots grow more branches. All plants, from a tiny violet to a giant redwood tree, grow in these ways.

Plants, like the trees you observed in the activity on pages A56 and A57, also grow in another way. Their stems get bigger around. Imagine hugging a tree. You can reach around the trunk of a young tree. But you may not be able to do this after the tree has been growing for many years.

Responding to Light

If a bright light is shined in your eyes, you'll squint. Plants respond to light, too. Have you ever seen a photograph of a field of sunflowers? You may have noticed that all the flowers are turned the same way.

Plants respond to light by growing toward it. Recall how the seedlings grew in the activity on page A58. If a plant is placed where it gets light on only one side, the stem of the plant will bend in the direction the light is coming from.

Responding to Water

In many places enough rain falls to supply plants with the water they need. But in the desert, water is very scarce.

The cactus, a desert plant, has long roots near the surface of the soil. They collect water from a wide area. The cactus also has a thick stem that stores water and keeps it from evaporating.

Amaryllis growing toward light ▶

A60

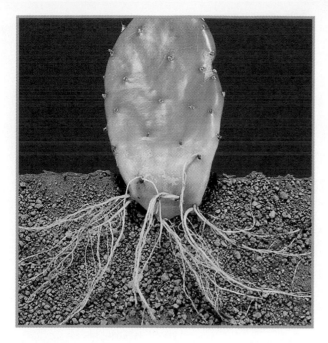

▲ Cactus roots growing toward water

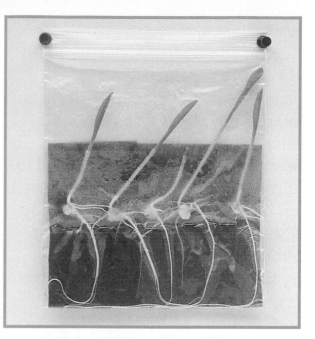

▲ Roots grow down and stems grow up.

Responding to a Pull

Roots and stems respond to the force called gravity, which pulls you toward Earth. Roots grow in the direction of the pull of gravity. So they grow down. Stems grow in the direction opposite to the pull of gravity. So they grow up.

SCIENCE IN LITERATURE

A TREE IN A FOREST
by Jan Thornhill
Simon and Schuster, 1991

Jan Thornhill tells the amazing story of the life of a maple tree in words and colorful paintings. Find out how a tree grew and changed over its 212-year lifetime.

After reading the book, retell the story in a life cycle diagram. Look back at the one on page A54 in this book to see an example. In your diagram, show what the tree looked like at important stages of its life. Use the years written at the bottom of some pages in *A Tree in a Forest* to help you label your diagram.

Plant Protection

Besides responding to light, water, and gravity, plants also respond to living things in their environment. To finish their life cycles, plants need to be protected from living things that can harm them. Adaptations (ad əp-tā′shənz) help protect them. Adaptations are behaviors or parts of living things that help the living things survive in their environment.

▲ **Sharp thorns of musk thistle**

▲ **Poison ivy leaves grow in threes.**

Quills and thorns are adaptations. Just as porcupines protect themselves with quills, some plants protect themselves with thorns. Thorns seem to say, "Stay away!"

Some plants, such as poison ivy, produce chemicals that protect them. Poison ivy can cause an itchy rash on someone who handles the plant. Mature milkweed plants are harmful for cattle and sheep to eat.

Protecting the life cycle of a plant protects the species. Species that can't protect themselves may die out. ∎

INVESTIGATION 4

1. Scientists have put experiments on the space shuttle to see how plants grow in a weightless environment. How would roots and stems be affected? Predict some problems in growing seeds in space.

2. Explain one change in a plant's environment that can cause a growth change in the plant.

REFLECT & EVALUATE

WORD POWER

cone   pollen
embryo   pollination
fruit   scale
germinate   seed coat
petal   seedling
pistil   stamen

 On Your Own
Review the terms in the list. Then use as many terms as you can in a paragraph abut the life cycle of the plant.

With a Partner
Make up a quiz, using all the terms in the list. Challenge your partner to complete the quiz.

BUILD YOUR PORTFOLIO

Design your own seed catalog. List as many different kinds of seeds as you can. On each page of your catalog, draw and label a kind of seed. Include a picture of what the adult plant might look like.

Analyze Information

On a separate sheet of paper, make a larger copy of this drawing of a flower. Use crayons or colored pencils to shade in these flower parts with the colors indicated: pistil—orange, stamen—blue, and petals—red. Label the parts.

Assess Performance

Use what you know about seeds to learn about peanuts. Study a peanut in its shell. Start by examining the outside of the peanut shell. Then carefully pull the shell apart to examine the seeds inside. Make a labeled diagram to show the seed coat and stored food.

Problem Solving

1. If the conifers in a forest did not produce cones one year, how would their life cycle be affected?

2. Fall has arrived, so you decide to clear out the dead pansy plants in your garden. The next spring you notice pansies growing in the garden. How did they get there?

3. In the park you notice squirrels collecting nuts, children picking flowers, bees buzzing around, and a bird building its nest. Explain which activities might help plant pollination.

Throughout this unit you've investigated questions related to life cycles, growth, and change. How will you use what you've learned and share that information with others? Here are some ideas.

Hold a Big Event
to Share Your Unit Project

With your classmates, plan a classroom book fair to share the Plant-Sitter's and Animal-Sitter's Guides that you have made. With your teacher's permission, you might invite other classes or adult friends and parents to the fair. If possible, offer copies of the guides to interested visitors.

Experiment

Plan a long-term project based on an activity in this unit. You might plant a flower or vegetable seed and observe as it changes from seed to seedling to a grown plant. You could measure the changes in its size, record them on a line graph, and then draw pictures to show other changes. You could also catch a caterpillar and watch as it changes into a pupa. You would have to make sure to provide it with the same food it eats in the wild. Or you might have another idea. Show your plan to your teacher before you begin.

Research

Find out how you've grown and changed since you were born. How have your height, weight, hair, and teeth changed? How have your writing and artwork changed? What toys did you like as a baby? What toys do you play with now? Report your findings in a booklet or poster about yourself. Make drawings or include photographs of yourself at different ages.

UNIT B

SUN, MOON, AND EARTH

Theme: Scale

GET READY TO

OBSERVE & QUESTION

What are eclipses?

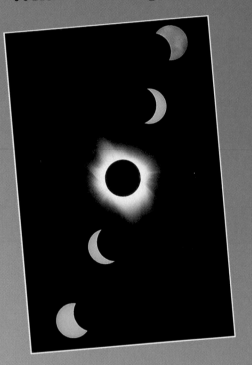

Have you ever seen an eclipse of the Sun or the Moon? Why do these awesome events happen? Can they be predicted?

EXPERIMENT & HYPOTHESIZE

What is the Sun like?

The Sun is so bright that you can't look at it directly. But you *can* make a model of a storm on the Sun. Then learn how such a storm could affect you here on Earth.

INVESTIGATE!

RESEARCH & ANALYZE

As you investigate, find out more from these books.

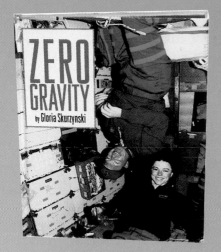

- **Zero Gravity** by Gloria Skurzynski (Bradbury Press, 1994). This book will tell you why the Moon stays near Earth and how astronauts live in space.

- **Dear Benjamin Banneker** by Andrea Davis Pinkney (Gulliver Books, Harcourt Brace & Co., 1994). Find out how a famous African American scientist learned to predict the movements of Earth and the Moon.

WORK TOGETHER & SHARE IDEAS

How would you live on the Moon?

Working together, you'll have a chance to build a model of a future base on the Moon. You'll think about the buildings your base would need and explore what a day on the Moon might be like. Look for the Unit Project Links for ideas on how to design your base.

CHAPTER 1

COMPARING SUN, MOON, AND EARTH

Some scientists pick up rocks and study them. Other scientists collect and study plants and animals. But how do scientists learn about faraway objects, like the Moon and the Sun?

Exploring Space

When Adriana Ocampo was a young girl, she dreamed of building cities on other worlds. She made spacecraft out of kitchen appliances. She pretended that her dolls were astronauts on their way to distant planets.

Today, Ocampo is a planetary geologist (plan'i ter ē jē äl'ə jist). This means that she studies the soil, rocks, and features of objects in space. Planetary geologists are interested in knowing what kinds of rocks are on the Moon. Ocampo also wants to know what the surface of the planet Mars looks like. And she is interested in rocks from space, called meteors (mēt'ē ərz), that sometimes strike Earth.

Be a scientist! What questions do you have about the Sun, the Moon, and our own planet Earth? Read Chapter 1 and look for answers.

GALILEO – MISSION TO JUPITE

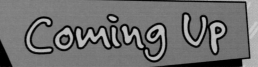

Coming Up

◄ Adriana Ocampo, planetary geologist

WHAT IS THE MOON LIKE?

What do you see when you look at the Moon? Do you imagine pictures of people or animals on its surface? In this investigation you'll learn what the Moon is *really* like.

Activity

Big Earth, Small Moon

How big is the Moon compared to Earth? This activity will help you find out.

MATERIALS

- globe
- round objects of different sizes
- string
- scissors
- metric tape measure
- paper models of Earth and the Moon
- *Science Notebook*

Procedure

1. Place a globe and other round objects on a table. Suppose Earth were the size of the globe. **Predict** which object would be the right size to represent the Moon. **Record** your prediction in your *Science Notebook*.

2. Wrap a piece of string around the middle of the globe. Have a group member cut the string so that it's the right length to wrap around the globe exactly once.

Step 2

3. **Make a chart** like the one shown. Then **measure** and **record** the length of the string.

Round Object	Distance Around the Object

4. Repeat step 2 for each object. **Measure** and **record** the length of each string.

5. Cut out a paper model of Earth and several paper models of the Moon. Place your Moon models side by side across the middle of the Earth model. **Record** how many Moons it takes to go across Earth.

Analyze and Conclude

1. Using the models you cut out as a guide, **estimate** how much bigger across Earth is than the Moon.

2. Look at your chart of string lengths for the different objects. **Identify** the object whose string is the right length for the Moon. How did you decide which object to choose? Is it the one you predicted?

Earth

Moon

INVESTIGATE FURTHER!

EXPERIMENT

How far is the Moon from Earth? Place the globe on the floor. Take the object that's the right size to represent the Moon. Place it as far away from the globe as you think it should be. To check your estimate, use the string that marks the distance around the globe. Measure nine and a half times that distance from the globe. Place the Moon object at that point.

Activity

Making Moon Craters

The Moon's surface is covered with round pits called craters. In this activity you'll discover how craters are made.

MATERIALS

- goggles
- newspaper
- sand
- baking pan
- small marble
- meterstick
- large marble
- *Science Notebook*

SAFETY ///////

Wear goggles during this activity.

Procedure

1. Cover your work area with newspaper.

2. Place a 2-cm-thick layer of sand in a baking pan.

3. **Make a chart** in your *Science Notebook* like the one shown.

Height of Drop	Width of Crater

4. Drop a small marble straight down onto the sand from a height of 25 cm. **Observe** what happens.

5. **Measure** the width of the crater you produced. **Record** the height of the drop and the width of the crater in your chart. Then carefully remove the marble.

Step 4

6. Repeat steps 4 and 5, but drop the marble from each of the following heights: 50 cm, 75 cm, and 1 m. **Record** all results. **Compare** your results with those of other groups.

7. Imagine dropping a large marble from the same height as a small marble. **Predict** how the craters will compare. Then use a large marble and a small marble to **test** your prediction. **Record** the results.

Step 5

Analyze and Conclude

1. **Compare** the width of the craters when marbles of the same size were dropped from the same height. Were the craters always about the same size?

2. What can you **infer** about the relationship between the height from which a marble is dropped and the width of the crater it produces?

3. Which marble moves faster—the one dropped from a short distance or the one dropped from a greater distance? What can you **infer** about how the speed of a marble affects the crater size?

4. Look at the pictures of the Moon on pages B10 and B11. What can you **infer** about the size and speed of the objects that have struck the Moon in the past?

UNIT PROJECT LINK

Using a map of the Moon, pick a place for your class's Moon base. Make a model of the area around your base. Include craters, mountains, and other features. As you learn more about the Moon, add buildings to your model Moon base. Think about every kind of building you would need and what each building should look like.

A Place Without Air

▲ **The Moon is about 3,476 km (2,160 mi) across. Compare that with the distance across the mainland United States, which measures about 4,517 km (2,807 mi).**

At some time in the past, someone observed the light and dark areas on the Moon and concluded that the Moon looked like a ball of green cheese. Because of all those round shapes that look like holes in the Moon, it could even have been Swiss cheese! You know better than to think the Moon is *really* made of cheese. But just what *is* the Moon made of?

A Mighty Big Rock

The Moon is a ball of gray rock covered with powdery gray soil. At about 3,476 km (2,160 mi) across, the Moon is a mighty big rock. But the Moon is much smaller than its closest neighbor, Earth. Remember the activity on pages B6 and B7? You used a globe and different round objects to compare the sizes of the Moon and Earth. You found that

Earth is about four times larger than the Moon. If the Moon were the size of a tennis ball, Earth would be the size of a basketball.

Mountains, Valleys, and Plains

Like the surface of Earth, the surface of the Moon rises and falls in mountains and valleys. The Moon's surface also has flat plains. In photos of the Moon, you can tell the mountains from the plains by differences in their brightness. Find the brightest regions in the photo on page B10. These are the hills and mountains. Find the dark areas. These are the low, flat plains.

When scientists looked through the first telescopes (tel'ə skōps) hundreds of years ago, they observed the Moon's dark regions and thought they saw seas. We now know that these areas are plains, not seas. They were formed not by water but by hot, melted rock that turned cold and solid long ago. Yet our ancestors' names for the dark areas remain in use today. The first people who walked on the Moon landed on a plain called the Sea of Tranquillity (tran kwil'ə tē).

How Craters Form

Remember when you made craters by dropping marbles into sand in the activity on pages B8 and B9? A **crater** is a pit shaped like a bowl. There are craters on

▲ **Craters on the Moon**

Earth, but not nearly as many as there are on the Moon.

The Moon's craters were formed in much the same way that you made yours. Chunks of rock or metal fell from space and crashed on the Moon's surface. Once such pieces of space material land, they are called **meteorites** (mēt'ē ər īts).

This meteorite that fell to Earth is on display in Africa. ▼

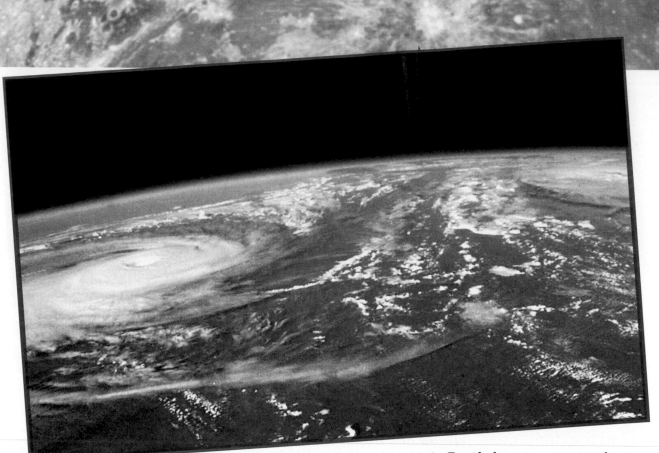

▲ **Earth has an atmosphere.**

These objects from space come in many shapes and sizes. One grain of sand is larger than the smallest meteorite. A really big meteorite can be larger than a house, but meteorites this size are very rare.

Like the meteorites that made them, some craters on the Moon can only be seen with a microscope. Others are more than 1,000 km (620 mi) across. A car traveling at highway speed would take about 11 hours to cross one of these huge pits.

It Gets Cold Without a Blanket!

Earth is surrounded by a blanket of air called the **atmosphere** (at′məs fir). This layer of gases protects living things on Earth from the Sun's most harmful rays. It also traps heat from the Sun and keeps Earth from getting too cold at night.

Earth's atmosphere gives us clouds and weather. It allows us to hear sound. It makes Earth's sky look blue. It even protects us from falling meteorites, since most of them burn up in Earth's atmosphere before they reach the ground.

Earth

▲ **The Moon has no atmosphere.**

The Moon has no atmosphere. Scientists have found evidence of ice on the Moon. But no liquid water is thought to exist. So living things would have no air to breathe and no water to drink.

Since the Moon has no atmosphere to protect it, the daytime temperature on the Moon's surface can rise to 104°C (220°F). Then, when the Sun goes down, the temperature drops far below freezing, as low as −173°C (−279°F). Because there's no air, the sky always looks dark from the surface of the Moon, even in the daytime. On the Moon you can always see the stars shining, day and night! ■

Moon

▲ The Moon is about 384,000 km (239,000 mi) away from Earth. That means you'd have to line up about 30 Earths to reach the Moon.

Learning About Space

STS
SCIENCE
TECHNOLOGY
& SOCIETY

Suppose you want to learn about the South Pole. One good way would be for you to visit. You'd need to bring along all your food for the trip, plus special clothing and shelter for the harsh climate. You'd need to arrange transportation and bring equipment to communicate with the outside world. You might want a camera and a journal to record what you learned.

Whew! If all this work is needed to study a faraway place on Earth, how do people ever learn about the Moon and the Sun?

Astronomers and Their Tools

An **astronomer** (ə strän'ə mər) is a scientist who studies objects in space. One good thing about an astronomer's work is that it can be done without leaving Earth. To learn about objects in space, astronomers use tools

such as telescopes, cameras, and space probes. They also study information gathered by human missions into space.

Look at the photograph of the Moon on page B10. That picture was taken through a **telescope**, a device that makes faraway objects look larger. You know that you can see the Moon without a telescope. But even a pair of binoculars (bi näk'yə lərz), a

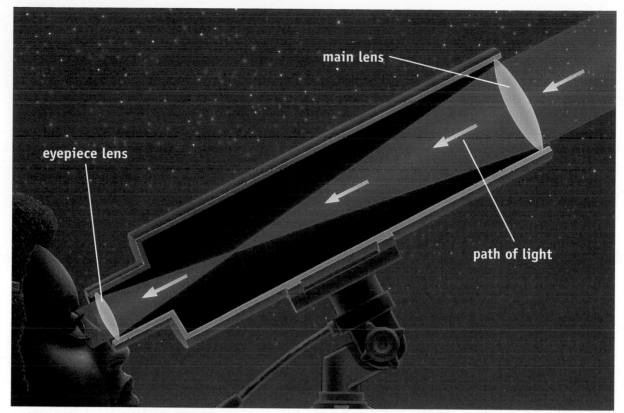

main lens

eyepiece lens

path of light

A simple telescope ▲

device that looks like two small telescopes side by side, will give you a much clearer picture than what you'd get with your unaided eyes.

A telescope works like a pair of eyeglasses. Both telescopes and eyeglasses use lenses, curved pieces of glass that can make objects look larger than they really are. If you wear eyeglasses, you look through lenses every day. Some kinds of telescopes use curved mirrors that make objects look larger. You may have seen a mirror like this in a fun house at an amusement park.

◀ **Large telescopes are often placed in buildings called observatories.**

An astronaut visits a space probe that landed on the Moon. ▶

Probing Deeper

A space probe is a machine that travels alone through space to study what is there. Because it can get closer to the Moon and even land on it, a space probe gives a better view than a telescope does. Like a robot, a space probe does tasks that people order it to do. Some probes take photographs. Others dig into the Moon's surface to study soil.

Astronomers have also learned a lot about the Moon from human space missions. Later, you'll read about the mission in which people first walked on the lunar surface.

(The term *lunar* is used when referring to things about the Moon. This word comes from the Latin name for the Moon, which is *luna*.)

Star Light, Star Bright

The brightness of the Sun makes it harder to study than the Moon.

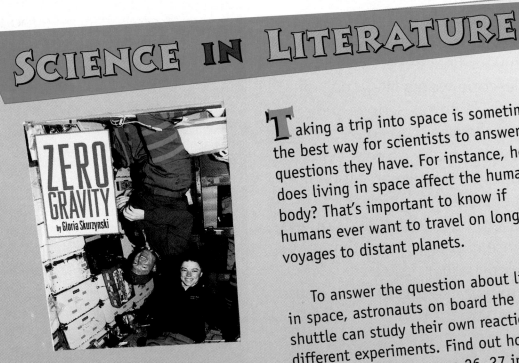

SCIENCE IN LITERATURE

ZERO GRAVITY
by Gloria Skurzynski
Bradbury Press, 1994

Taking a trip into space is sometimes the best way for scientists to answer the questions they have. For instance, how does living in space affect the human body? That's important to know if humans ever want to travel on long voyages to distant planets.

To answer the question about living in space, astronauts on board the space shuttle can study their own reactions to different experiments. Find out how they do this by reading pages 26–27 in the book *Zero Gravity* by Gloria Skurzynski.

▲ **A U.S. space station where astronauts studied the Sun**

You shouldn't look directly at the Sun, since it can hurt your eyes badly. Looking at the Sun through an ordinary telescope can blind you. So astronomers use different equipment to get a close view of the Sun. For example, their telescopes have built-in cameras that take pictures of the Sun. People can then look at the photos without harming their eyes.

The Sun, like the Moon, can be viewed more closely with a space probe than with a telescope. Yet even machines can't get *too* close to the Sun, since its heat would destroy them! ■

INVESTIGATION 1

1. Describe two ways in which the Moon differs from Earth.

2. Imagine that you took a walk on the Moon. Do you think your footprints would stay visible a long time? Or would they soon disappear? Explain your answer.

INVESTIGATION 2

WHAT IS BEING ON THE MOON LIKE?

Imagine you live in the future and your home is on the Moon. How would your life be different than it is now? How would it be the same? In Investigation 2 you'll discover what living on the Moon might be like.

Activity
Lunar Olympics

Would you be a better gymnast or weight lifter on the Moon? Find out!

MATERIALS

- tape
- meterstick
- heavy book
- string
- bathroom scale
- *Science Notebook*

Procedure

1. Find out how high you'd be able to jump on the Earth. Stand and face a wall. Reach up and place a small piece of tape on the wall at the highest spot you can touch. Then jump up and see how high you can place a second piece of tape.

2. Ask a group member to help you use a meterstick to **measure** the distance between the two pieces of tape. **Record** the result in your *Science Notebook*. The distance between the pieces of tape is the height you can jump on Earth.

Step 1

B18

3. To learn how high you could jump on the Moon, **multiply** the height you can jump on Earth by six. **Record** this number.

4. Find out how many books you could lift on the Moon. Place a heavy book on the floor next to a table. Tie a string around the book. Then with your elbow on the table, lift the book as shown.

5. Use a scale to **measure** the weight of the book. **Record** the result.

6. To find out how much you could lift on the Moon, take the weight of the book on Earth and **multiply** it by six. **Record** the result.

Step 4

Analyze and Conclude

1. Look at the information you've recorded that describes what you could do on the Moon. With members of your group, **hypothesize** what sports would be fun to play there. **Discuss** what would be different about each sport on the Moon. How might you want to change each sport's playing field or set of rules?

2. **Hypothesize** why you'd be able to perform so much better on the Moon than on Earth. **Discuss** what's different about the Moon that would make this improvement possible.

INVESTIGATE FURTHER!

EXPERIMENT

Find out how far you could throw a ball on the Moon. First, throw a ball as far as you can on a playing field. Have another group member measure the distance you threw it. Then, to find out how far you could throw the ball on the Moon, multiply the distance you threw it on Earth by 2.5.

Activity
A Moon Outing

What things would you pack for a picnic on the Moon? In this activity you'll decide.

Procedure

1. Begin two lists in your *Science Notebook*. Title them "Things I Could Use on the Moon" and "Things I Could Not Use on the Moon."

2. Pretend you're going on an outdoor picnic on the Moon. Place each item at right on one of your lists.

3. Make a third list entitled "Things I Would Need on the Moon." Include things that aren't on the other two lists. Explain why you think you would need each one.

Analyze and Conclude

1. Look at your list of things that cannot be used on the Moon. For each item, **hypothesize** why the item wouldn't work on the Moon.

2. Based on all three of your lists, **infer** what conditions on the Moon are most important in deciding what you should bring there. **Discuss** your conclusions.

Which things could be done on the Moon? ▼

baseball and bat
bathing suit
bicycle pump
drums
fan
fishing pole
flashlight
insect repellent
kite
playground slide
playground swings
shovel
slingshot
sunglasses
umbrella
yo-yo

Spacesuits

An astronaut is a person trained to go into space. When astronauts visit the airless Moon or take a "walk" in space, they have to wear spacesuits. A spacesuit is a set of clothing worn in space that can be tightly sealed to protect the person who wears it. Inside, each suit supplies everything a human being needs to survive.

Because of all the equipment it contains, each spacesuit weighs more than 100 lb on Earth. The same suit on the Moon would weigh only a fraction of what it does on Earth. ■

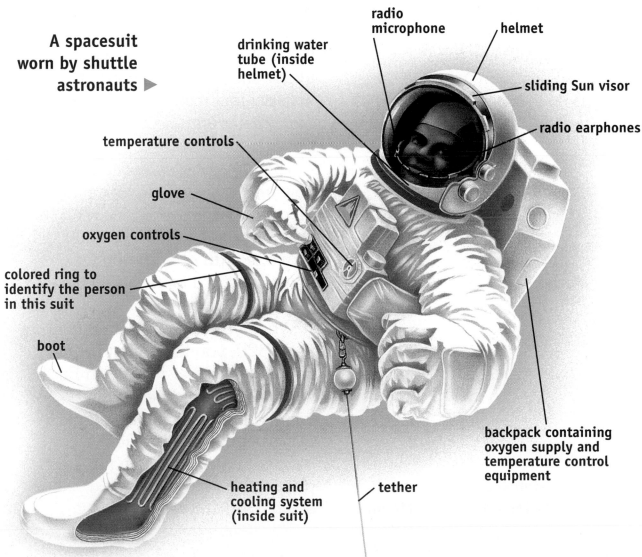

A spacesuit worn by shuttle astronauts ▶

radio microphone

drinking water tube (inside helmet)

helmet

sliding Sun visor

radio earphones

temperature controls

glove

oxygen controls

colored ring to identify the person in this suit

boot

heating and cooling system (inside suit)

tether

backpack containing oxygen supply and temperature control equipment

Getting Around on the Moon

Do you ever fly in your dreams? If so, when you awaken, it may take you a minute to realize that you can't keep right on flying out of bed! Why can't you just soar off the ground? It's because of **gravity** (grav'i tē), a pull that every object has on every other object. The force of gravity keeps people and objects on the ground. It holds your pencil on your desk. It holds you in your chair. In space, it even holds the Moon in its place near Earth.

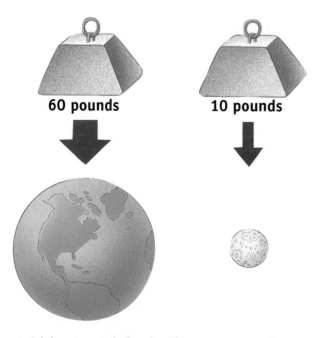

60 pounds   **10 pounds**

▲ **Objects weigh six times as much on Earth as they do on the Moon.**

Jumping on the Moon

Remember when you took part in the "Lunar Olympics" activity on pages B18 and B19? You figured out that you could jump six times higher on the Moon than you can on Earth.

On the surface of Earth, gravity is six times stronger than on the surface of the Moon. That's because Earth has more mass than the Moon. Mass is the amount of material that makes up an object. The greater an object's mass, the stronger its gravity.

The force of gravity determines how much you weigh. Since the Moon's gravity is only one-sixth that of Earth, on the Moon you'd weigh only one sixth of what you weigh now. But you'd look exactly the same.

When you took a Moon outing on page B20, you found that some objects you use every day on Earth would have to be used differently on the Moon. Imagine what a lunar playground would be like! You'd have an easier time going up in a playground swing, but you'd slide down a slide more slowly.

Astronaut Buzz Aldrin jumps down from his ship in the Moon's low gravity. ▼

▲ **Astronaut Aldrin conducts experiments on the Moon.**

Moonwalkers

In 1969 two Americans, Neil Armstrong and Edwin "Buzz" Aldrin, became the first people to walk on the Moon. To learn about the Moon, they took photos, collected rocks and soil, and performed experiments. They had to go through a lot of training to learn how to do these jobs in only one sixth of the gravity they were used to on Earth.

The astronauts' visit to the Moon wasn't all work. They had a lot of fun hopping around like kangaroos in the Moon's low gravity. They had to be careful how they moved, though. What goes up must come down, even on the Moon! ■

INVESTIGATION 2

THINK IT WRITE IT

1. Describe the conditions on the Moon that require astronauts to wear spacesuits.

2. Explain why an astronaut on the Moon can carry something that weighs as much as the astronaut does.

INVESTIGATION 3

WHAT IS THE SUN LIKE?

You see the Sun in the sky every day. You depend on its light to see other things. But you can't see the Sun itself very well, because looking directly at it can hurt your eyes. In this investigation you'll find out what the Sun is like up close.

Activity

Big Star, Small Earth

How big is the Sun? How far away is it? Compare Earth and the Sun in this activity.

MATERIALS

- paper model of the Sun
- drawing paper
- metric tape measure
- tape
- string
- *Science Notebook*

Procedure

1. Imagine that the Sun is the size of the model. Draw a circle to show how big you think a model of Earth should be. **Measure** the width of your circle and **record** the measurement in your *Science Notebook*.

2. **Compare** your estimate with those of other group members. **Discuss** why you think your estimate makes sense.

3. Your teacher will tell you what size your Earth model should really be. **Record** the correct size. On a sheet of paper, **draw** a circle the size your teacher told you. Label this circle *Earth*.

Step 1

4. Have a member of your group hold the Sun model at one end of a large open area. **Discuss** how far away the Earth model should be, based on the sizes of your models. Take your Earth circle and stand that distance away from the Sun circle. Have another group member **measure** the distance between the two models. **Record** the result.

5. Tape to the Earth model one end of a piece of string that is 59 m long. Tape the string's other end to the Sun model. Hold the models 59 m apart. This is how far apart Earth and the Sun would be if they were actually the sizes of the models.

Step 5

INVESTIGATE FURTHER!
....

EXPERIMENT

How big would a Moon model be in this activity? How far away would the Moon model be from the Earth model? Recall what you learned in Investigation 1 to help you answer these questions. Draw a Moon model on the same sheet of paper as your Earth model. Then check your estimates by turning back to pages B11 and B13.

Analyze and Conclude

1. How close was your drawing in step 1 to the size of the Earth model in step 3? What can you **infer** from this about the size of the real Sun?

2. How close was your guess in step 4 to the distance between the Earth and Sun models in step 5? What can you **infer** about the real distance between Earth and the Sun?

Activity
Making Sunspots

Dark spots on the Sun were first observed more than 400 years ago. In this activity you'll make a model of sunspots.

Procedure

1. To **make a model** of sunspots, first sprinkle iron filings onto a paper plate so that they thinly cover the surface.

2. Have one group member hold the plate level above a table. A second group member should hold a horseshoe magnet under the raised plate so that both ends of the magnet touch the plate's bottom.

3. Gently move the magnet around under the plate until all the iron filings have been collected.

4. **Observe** the plate from above. **Draw** a picture of what you see in your *Science Notebook*. Show where the filings are.

Analyze and Conclude

1. **Compare** your drawing of the iron filings with the photograph of sunspots on page B30. Make a list of things that look the same.

2. **Hypothesize** what might cause similar shapes to form in the iron filings and on the surface of the Sun.

Step 2

Sun Power

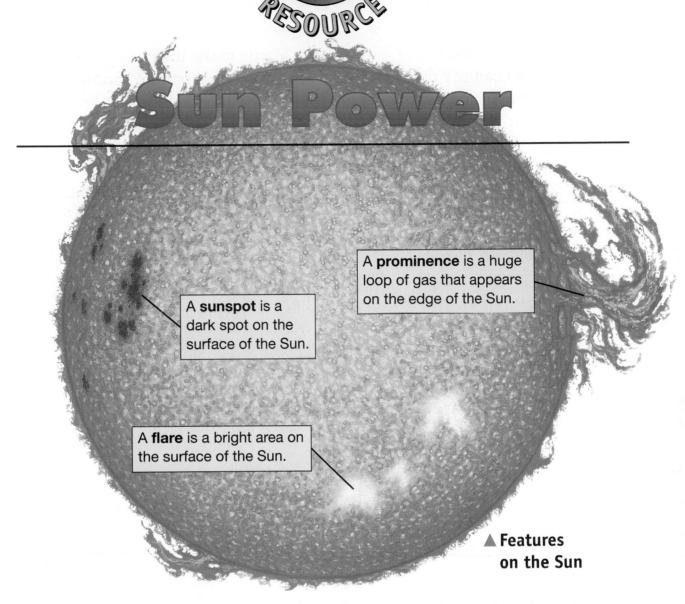

A **sunspot** is a dark spot on the surface of the Sun.

A **prominence** is a huge loop of gas that appears on the edge of the Sun.

A **flare** is a bright area on the surface of the Sun.

▲ Features on the Sun

It's hot enough to melt any metal. It's so far away that its light takes eight minutes to reach your eyes. If it were a hollow ball, more than 1 million Earths could fit inside it. Do you know its name? It's the Sun!

Our Star

Like the twinkling dots that we see in the night sky, the Sun is a star. Compared to other stars, the Sun isn't very large. But to us it looks much bigger than the others because it's by far the closest star to Earth.

And, as you learned in the activity on pages B24 and B25, the Sun is huge compared to Earth!

A **star** is a ball of hot gases that gives off energy. Every day you experience two forms of energy given off by the Sun. You see its light, and you feel its heat.

The Sun is *very* hot. The temperature on its surface is about 5,500°C (9,900°F). When scientists speak about the surface of the Sun, they mean the top of the main body of its thickest gases.

Features on the Sun

Astronomers can see different features that come and go on the surface of the Sun. There are dark spots known as sunspots and bright spots known as flares. There are huge loops of gas known as prominences. The picture on page B27 shows what these features look like.

In the activity on page B26, you moved a magnet to make iron filings form a pattern. When you did this, you made a model of a region of sunspots. A sunspot region acts like a magnet, with north pole spots and south pole spots. These spots appear dark because they are cooler than surrounding areas of the Sun.

You Can't Live Without It

What are your favorite foods? Whatever your answer is, those foods come from the Sun. How is this so?

Almost all living things depend on the Sun for their food. ▶

Plants make their own food. To do this, they use sunlight. Some animals eat these plants. Other animals eat animals that eat plants.

Without sunlight, plants could not make food and they would die. The animals that eat plants—and the animals that eat those animals— would starve.

Almost all living things depend on the Sun for their food, as well as for heat and light. Life on Earth could not exist without it! ■

Solar Storms

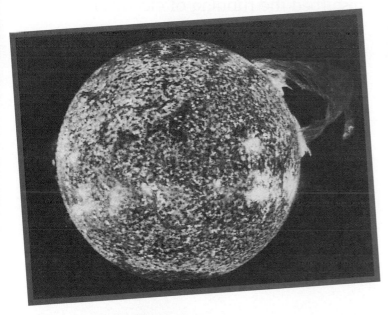

▲ **A solar prominence**

SCIENCE
TECHNOLOGY
& SOCIETY
You have probably seen electrical storms on Earth. What are some signs of such a storm? They include dark clouds, lightning, and thunder. The Sun also has storms— not storms of snow, wind, or rain, but storms of energy. These are called magnetic storms because they are created by the pull of magnetic forces in the Sun.

Suppose you asked an astronomer to name some signs of a solar magnetic storm. (The term *solar* is used to refer to things related to the Sun.) The astronomer would say that sunspots, flares, and prominences are signs of solar storms.

Fireworks From Space

Do you think that storms on the Sun can affect things on Earth? You bet they can! On many nights, a beautiful display of light can be seen in the sky near Earth's North and South poles. These two shimmering, colorful displays are called the northern lights and the southern lights. Solar storms produce these "fireworks." During the storms, invisible particles are given off by the Sun. When these particles reach Earth, they cause gases in Earth's atmosphere to glow.

The northern lights, as seen from the ground ▼

Earth. The high-energy particles disturbed the running of electrical equipment. The result was a power blackout across Quebec as well as other problems all over the world.

A major flare like this one can harm astronauts if it catches them during a space flight. But smaller solar storms often give astronauts a spectacular view of the northern and southern lights—as seen from space! ◼

Dangers of Solar Storms

People who live in the Canadian province of Quebec will long remember ten days in March 1989. During that period, light bulbs suddenly went out. Elevators came to a halt between floors. Because televisions and radios went silent, it was hard to find out what was going on.

A giant solar flare had sent high-energy particles and radiation streaming out of the Sun toward

The northern lights, as seen from space ▶

INVESTIGATION 3

1. List several ways in which the Sun affects Earth.

2. In the sky, the Sun and the Moon appear to be about the same size. Describe their real sizes compared with Earth's. Which of the two objects is farther away from Earth?

REFLECT & EVALUATE

WORD POWER

astronomer   meteorite
atmosphere   prominence
crater   star
flare   sunspot
gravity   telescope

 On Your Own
Review the terms in the list. Then use as many terms as you can in a paragraph that describes the Moon and the Sun.

 With a Partner
Use terms in the list to make a word-search puzzle. Print the terms in a column on graph paper. Arrange the terms so that one column of their letters forms another term from the list. See if your partner can find the hidden term and tell what it means.

BUILD YOUR PORTFOLIO

Make a poster that shows why the Sun is important to life on Earth. Illustrate your poster and add captions to explain each illustration.

Analyze Information

Study the drawing. Then use the drawing as you describe the nature and features of the Sun.

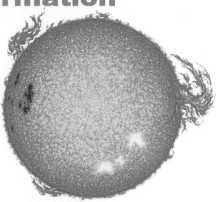

Assess Performance

Design and carry out an experiment to discover what type of crater would be produced by an object that falls at an angle onto the surface of the Moon. Compare your results with those of others. How are craters like this different from craters produced by objects that fall straight down?

Problem Solving

1. If an object on the Moon weighs 42 pounds, how much would that same object weigh on Earth? Why?

2. What are some reasons that life can exist on Earth but not on the Moon? How are astronauts on the Moon provided with the things they need to stay alive?

3. Suppose you want to send one space probe to the Sun and another to the Moon. Which probe must travel a greater distance? Which probe's target object is larger?

CHAPTER 2

MOTIONS OF EARTH AND THE MOON

"Twinkle, twinkle, little star, how I wonder what you are."
Writers of poems, stories, and songs often describe what they see in the sky. Why are the Sun, Moon, and stars so interesting to writers and their readers?

Look to the North

More than 100 years ago in the United States, some people helped enslaved African Americans escape to freedom. One who helped was a one-legged man named Peg Leg Joe. He taught them a song that was called "Follow the Drinking Gourd." A gourd is a type of vegetable. People dipped dried, hollowed-out gourds into water and drank from them. Peg Leg Joe's song about the gourd, however, held a secret message for the slaves.

An arrangement of stars in the night sky looks somewhat like the shape of a drinking gourd. Two of these stars point to the North Star. In this chapter you'll learn why the North Star is always found in the north. The secret message in the song was, "Follow the stars to the north." How did this help people travel to freedom?

Coming Up

◄ Following the "drinking gourd" to freedom

HOW DOES EARTH MOVE EACH DAY?

Have you ever wondered why the Sun seems to move across the sky during the day? Or why the Moon and stars seem to change position overnight? In this investigation you'll explore changes in the sky that help explain how Earth moves.

Activity

A Shadow Stick Sundial

How does the Sun appear to move throughout the day? Watch a shadow to find out.

MATERIALS

- goggles
- straight stick or rod
- large sheet of paper
- black marker
- clay
- flashlight
- *Science Notebook*

SAFETY

Wear goggles during this activity. Never look directly at the Sun.

Procedure

1. On a sunny day, go outdoors with a straight stick or rod and a large sheet of paper. Using the stick, punch a hole in the center of the paper and then into the ground, as shown.

2. Locate the shadow of the stick on the paper. Use a marker to draw a line down the middle of the shadow. Make your line the same length as the shadow. Label your line with the time of day.

3. Repeat step 2 every hour for as long as you can. You have now made a sundial.

Step 1

4. When the Sun's shadow is shortest, the shadow is pointing north. Label *north* on your drawing. **Infer** the other three directions. Then label *south*, *east*, and *west* on your drawing.

5. Go indoors and re-create your sundial, using a base of clay to hold the stick in position. Have your teacher darken the room.

6. Move a flashlight around your drawing until you can re-create each shadow that you drew outside. For each shadow, **observe** whether the flashlight is to the north, south, east, or west of your drawing. Note whether you have to hold the flashlight high or low.

7. In your *Science Notebook*, **draw** a copy of your sundial. Add a little picture of the Sun to show where you had to put the flashlight to re-create each shadow.

Step 5

Analyze and Conclude

1. Is the Sun high or low in the sky when the shadows are the longest?

2. **Infer** in what direction the Sun appears to move across the sky throughout the day.

3. **Suggest a hypothesis** that would explain the way the Sun appears to move. Do you think the Sun really moves that way? What else might explain what you've observed?

A sundial ▶

Activity
Making a Star Clock

Before people had clocks, they used the stars to tell time. In this activity you'll build your own star clock and use it to see how stars move during the night.

- -

Procedure

1. Cut out the star clock's wheel and base.

2. Place the wheel on top of the base and fasten them together with a paper fastener through their centers, as shown.

3. The wheel tells the date and the base tells the time. Set the mid-November point on the wheel next to the 6:00 P.M. point on the base.

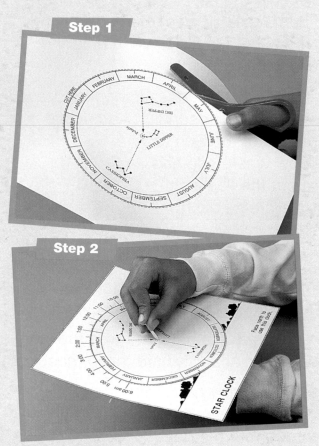

Step 1

Step 2

4. The star clock now shows you the positions in the sky of the Big Dipper, Little Dipper, and Cassiopeia (kas ē ō pē′ə) at 6:00 P.M. in mid-November. **Draw** the positions of these star groups in your *Science Notebook*. Include the star Polaris (pō lar′is). Label your drawing *6:00 P.M.*

5. Use your star clock to **predict** how the Big Dipper, Little Dipper, Cassiopeia, and Polaris would look at the following times during the rest of that same night in mid-November: 9:00 P.M.; 12:00 midnight; 3:00 A.M.; 6:00 A.M. **Draw** and label each of your predictions.

People have imagined seeing pictures among the stars. What do you see when you look at these star groups? ▶

Analyze and Conclude

1. Study all five drawings. **Describe** how the Big Dipper moves during the night. Then **describe** how the Little Dipper and Cassiopeia move.

2. What did you observe about the position of the star Polaris during the night?

3. How long would it take the Big Dipper to circle the sky one complete time?

4. **Infer** how people could have used the Big Dipper to tell time.

5. Real stars appear to move the same way the stars on your star clock do. **Discuss** with your group what might cause these star motions. **Hypothesize** what might be happening that would make the stars appear to move.

INVESTIGATE FURTHER!

EXPERIMENT

Imagine that you are a sailor on the ocean. How could you use Polaris to help you keep your ship on course? Christopher Columbus knew about Polaris and observed it at night. How would this star have helped Columbus find the Americas?

The Rotating Earth

We say that the Sun rises in the east, sets in the west, and moves across the sky in between. When we say this, we are describing what we see. We aren't describing what really happens, though!

The Sun doesn't really move across the sky. It just *looks* like the Sun is moving because *Earth* is moving.

Around and Around We Go

You can't feel Earth's movement. To you, the ground feels perfectly still. Your home seems to stay in the same place day and night. Yet you are a passenger riding on the surface of a spinning Earth.

Scientists call this spinning motion **rotation** (rō tā′shən). The picture on the next page shows several impor-
tant things about how Earth rotates. Notice the line that runs through Earth's North and South poles in the picture. This make-believe line is called an **axis** (ak′sis). Earth spins like a top on its axis.

It takes 24 hours for Earth to spin all the way around—that is, to make one whole rotation. That's why there are 24 hours in one day.

As Earth rotates, one side of Earth faces the Sun while the other side faces away from the Sun. When your side of Earth faces the Sun, it's day-time. When your side of Earth turns away from the Sun, it's nighttime.

Look at the picture on the facing page. Find the arrow that shows the direction of Earth's rotation. Find the spot that's marked, "Pretend you are

The Sun always sets in the west because of Earth's rotation. ▼

here." Picture yourself standing in that spot looking at the sky. As Earth rotates once a day from west to east, you'll see the Sun, the Moon, and the stars seem to move across the sky from east to west.

The North Star

There's one star that hardly seems to move at all. Its name is Polaris. Notice that Polaris lies almost exactly over Earth's North Pole. That's why Polaris is known as the North Star.

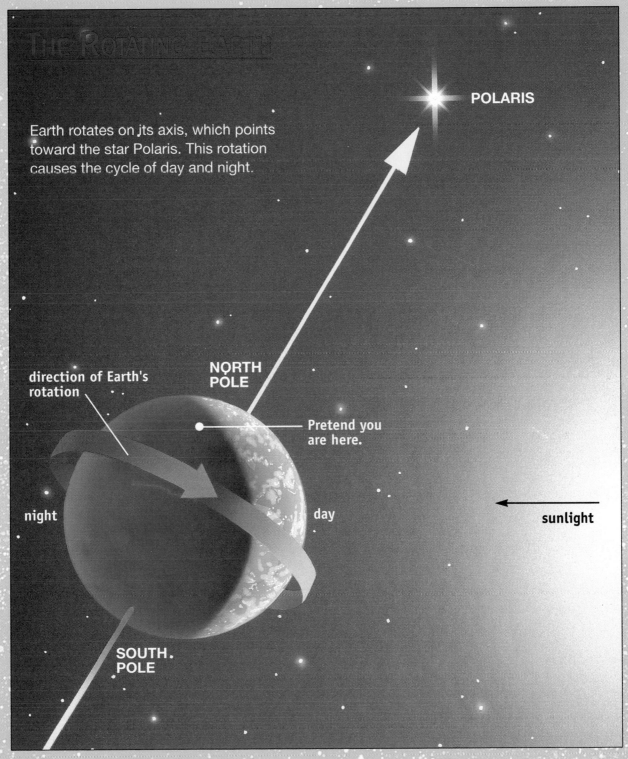

THE ROTATING EARTH

Earth rotates on its axis, which points toward the star Polaris. This rotation causes the cycle of day and night.

POLARIS

direction of Earth's rotation

NORTH POLE

Pretend you are here.

night

day

sunlight

SOUTH POLE

All the other northern stars seem to spin around Polaris as Earth turns. You saw this effect in the star clock you used in the activity on pages B36 and B37.

If you lived in Australia or southern Africa, you'd see all the southern stars seem to spin around a point in space directly above the South Pole. Unfortunately, there's no bright star right at that spot that people can call the South Star.

Italian clock

Chinese sundial

Find Your Way Home

The drawing below shows where you can find Polaris in the sky. It's in the star pattern called the Little Dipper. Find Polaris at the end of the dipper's "handle."

You can find Polaris by imagining a line from the two "pointer" stars in the Big Dipper. ▼

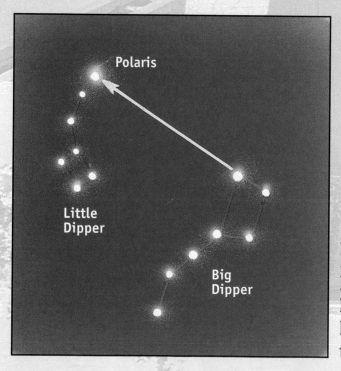

Polaris

Little Dipper

Big Dipper

If you can locate Polaris, what direction can you find? North, of course! And if you know which way is north, you can then figure out all the other directions.

For hundreds of years, sailors have used Polaris to find their way home and steer different courses. Campers often use Polaris to find directions. Even the most modern spaceships still steer by the stars.

Telling Time

Have you ever been outdoors playing and noticed that the Sun seemed to be very low in the sky? Did you think then that it was getting late and that you'd better hurry home? If you've ever had something like this happen, you've been using the Sun to tell time.

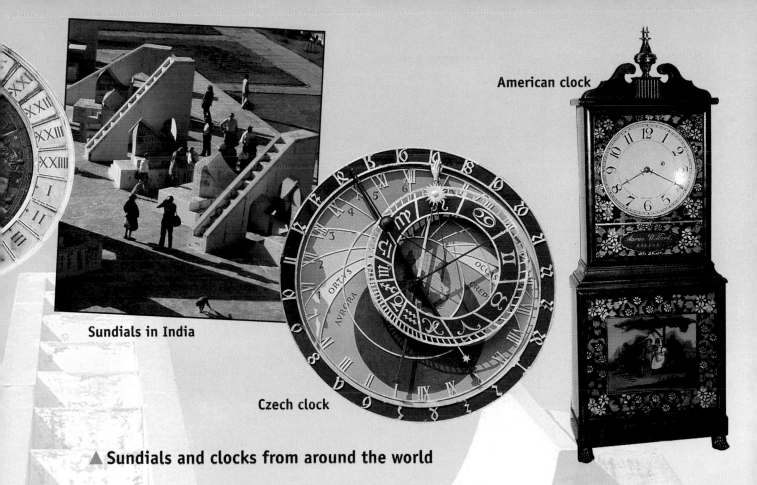

American clock

Sundials in India

Czech clock

▲ **Sundials and clocks from around the world**

Earth's 24-hour rotation is the basis for the way we tell time. Before there were clocks, everyone used to tell time by the motion of the Sun and the stars across the sky. During the day, many people used sundials like the one you made in the activity on pages B34 and B35. A sundial is a device that tells time by tracking shadows that the Sun makes. The shadows change as the Sun seems to move across the sky.

Even after people started to build clocks, they still had to check their work against the Sun and stars. Today's clocks keep very exact time, but scientists still check them against objects in the sky. There'd be a lot of confusion if our clocks didn't match the way Earth moves! ■

THINK IT WRITE IT

INVESTIGATION 1

1. Describe how Earth moves during the course of a day.

2. Just before you go to bed at night, you see a certain star in the east. The next morning, just before dawn, you see the same star in the west. Explain what happened to make the star's position seem to change.

INVESTIGATION 2

HOW DOES EARTH MOVE THROUGHOUT THE YEAR?

Does Earth's rotation on its axis explain the length of the year? Or does Earth also move in other ways? To find out, observe some more ways in which the Sun and the stars appear to move.

Activity

MATERIALS

• *Science Notebook*

Sun Paths

Does the Sun follow the same path across the sky every day of the year? Find out!

- -

Procedure

1. Look at the pictures. They show the Sun's path across the sky on four different days. Use the pictures

March

June

to answer the following questions. **Record** your answers in your *Science Notebook*.

2. Name the month in which the Sun appears highest in the sky. Name the month in which it appears lowest.

3. Name the month in which the Sun follows the longest path across the sky. Name the month in which it follows the shortest path.

Analyze and Conclude

1. **Hypothesize** what effects the changing path of the Sun would have throughout the year. How would the height the Sun reaches and the length of its path affect conditions on the ground?

2. **Infer** which month is the hottest in the place shown in the pictures. **Infer** which month is the coldest. Explain your answers.

3. **Infer** whether the four months pictured all have the same number of hours of daylight. If not, which month has the longest day? Which has the shortest? Give reasons for your answers.

4. Do the motions of Earth that you've learned about so far explain why the Sun's path across the sky would change as it does in these pictures? **Hypothesize** what might cause such changes.

September

December

Activity

Constellations Through the Year

Does Earth move in some way besides rotating on its axis? This activity will help you find out.

MATERIALS

- lamp
- stool
- drawings of the constellations Leo, Scorpius, Pegasus, and Orion
- *Science Notebook*

SAFETY

Don't touch the lamp. You could burn yourself. Use caution when walking around the lamp cord.

Procedure

1. Place a lighted lamp on top of a stool. This represents the Sun.

2. Have four group members each hold one of the four drawings that your teacher will provide. These drawings show different constellations (kän stə lā′shənz), or star patterns.

3. The four group members should stand as shown. Have a fifth group member pretend to be Earth and stand anywhere inside the circle.

4. The constellation Leo can be seen from the United States in spring-time. **Discuss** where Earth would have to stand inside the circle to see the picture of Leo. Remember that stars can be seen only at night. Then have Earth stand where you think it should be. Make sure that Earth can see Leo.

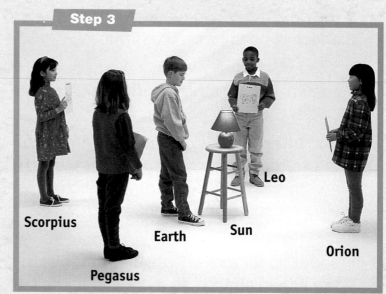

Step 3

Scorpius · Pegasus · Earth · Sun · Leo · Orion

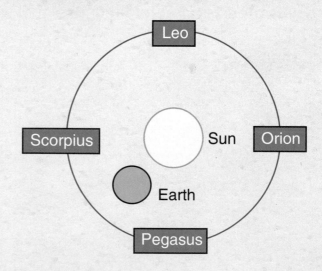

Leo · Scorpius · Sun · Orion · Earth · Pegasus

◀ **The constellation Scorpius**

▲ **The constellation Orion**

5. In your *Science Notebook*, **draw** a picture to show where Earth, the Sun, and each of the constellations are located. Draw the scene as if you were looking down on it from above. Label Earth, the Sun, and each constellation. Label the whole drawing *spring*.

6. The constellation Scorpius can be seen in the summer. Decide where Earth should stand to see Scorpius. Try it out, then **draw** a picture as you did in step 5. Label the new picture *summer*.

7. Pegasus can be seen in fall. Orion can be seen in winter. Decide where Earth should stand to see these constellations. **Draw** pictures labeled *fall* and *winter* that show these positions.

8. Look at your four drawings to remember where Earth stood to see the constellations in spring, summer, fall, and winter. Take turns walking from one position to the next until everyone has been to all four.

Analyze and Conclude

1. Based on your findings, **infer** how Earth moves during the year in relation to the Sun.

2. Explain how Earth's motion causes different constellations to be seen in different seasons.

INVESTIGATE FURTHER!

RESEARCH

Look up the names of the four constellations in this activity. Find out where each name came from and what it means. Then, with a parent's permission, go outside on a clear night and try to find the constellation or constellations that can be seen at this time of year.

Earth Moves Around the Sun

Native Americans who lived on the Great Plains did what you did in the activity "Sun Paths," on pages B42 and B43. They observed that the Sun's path changes during the year. These people used their observations to make medicine wheels—calendars of stone that track the changing path of the Sun across the sky.

Sky calendars such as medicine wheels show that changes in the Sun's path follow a regular pattern. The pattern takes about 365 days to complete—and then it begins again. Our yearly 365-day calendar is based on the same pattern that the Native Americans observed.

Earth Circles as It Spins

Scientists too learn things by observing the Sun. They've figured out that the Sun's changing path shows something about Earth's motion.

A Native American medicine wheel ▼

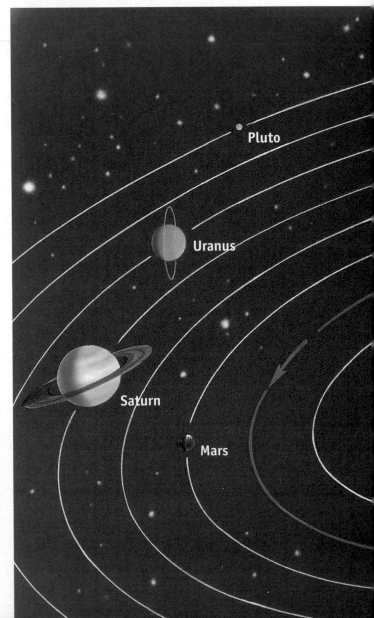

Pluto

Uranus

Saturn

Mars

As it rotates on its axis, Earth also **revolves** (ri välvz′) around the Sun. This means that it travels around the Sun along its own path, called an **orbit** (ôr′bit), that's shaped roughly like a circle. It takes Earth a year to complete one revolution. In Chapter 3 you'll learn why this motion makes the Sun's path across the sky appear to change over the course of a year.

Remember the activity on pages B44 and B45? The person who pretended to be Earth saw a different **constellation**, or nighttime star pattern, at each season of the year. That too is a result of Earth's revolution around the Sun.

As Earth rotates, its night side faces away from the Sun. As Earth revolves around the Sun, that night side looks toward different parts of space at different times of the year. For that reason we see different constellations.

You might once have thought the night sky looked boring—that all the stars appeared the same. But in fact, because of rotation and revolution, the sky changes all the time! ∎

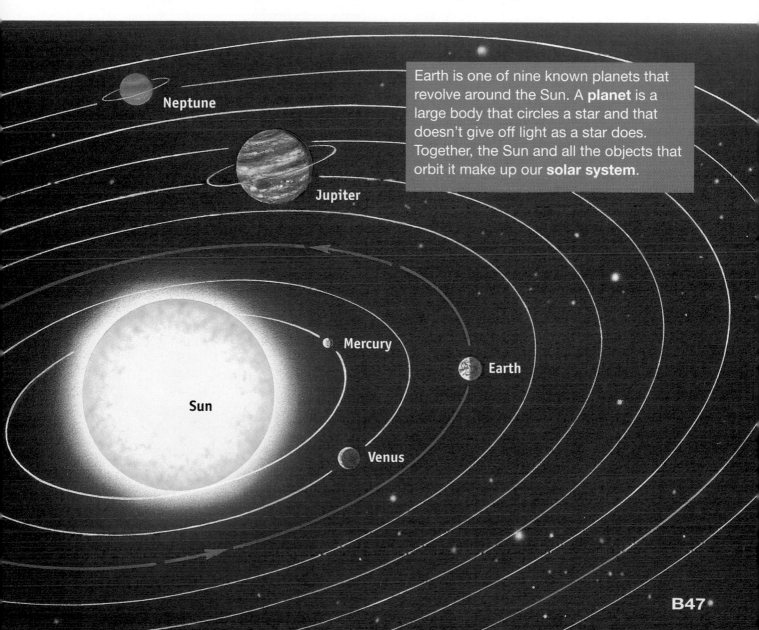

Neptune

Jupiter

Earth is one of nine known planets that revolve around the Sun. A **planet** is a large body that circles a star and that doesn't give off light as a star does. Together, the Sun and all the objects that orbit it make up our **solar system**.

Mercury

Earth

Sun

Venus

Earth and Sun
Ideas Through Time

People didn't always know that Earth revolves around the Sun. It took human beings a long time to figure out this fact. After all, we don't feel our planet moving through space. All we can tell from Earth

Aryabhata I, a mathematician in India, says that Earth rotates on its axis. This explains better some of the ways the Sun and stars appear to move. But Aryabhata still thinks the rotating Earth stays in one spot.

497

Most ancient societies—including those in China, Egypt, and India—think that Earth is flat and unmoving. The Sun and stars are thought to move across the dome of the sky.

3000 B.C.

A.D. 145

Ptolemy, an astronomer in Egypt, makes famous the hypothesis that Earth is round and that the Sun and other sky objects revolve around this unmoving Earth. Ptolemy's model is the one that most scientists accept for more than 1,000 years.

is that the Sun and stars appear to move across the sky.

It's not surprising that early societies thought Earth was standing still. Most of them thought that the Sun and stars revolved around Earth.

Through the years, however, different scientists developed better ways to explain the movements they saw in the sky. They formed different hypotheses about Earth's relationship to the Sun. Some of those scientists and their ideas are shown in this time line. ∎

900

Al-Battani, an Arabian astronomer, takes more careful measurements of the positions of the Sun, stars, and other objects in the sky. He realizes that Ptolemy's model doesn't fit all the movements he observes, but he doesn't propose a new hypothesis.

1543

Nicolaus Copernicus, a Polish astronomer, challenges Ptolemy's hypothesis. He says that the Sun is at the center of the solar system and that Earth is just one of many planets revolving around the Sun. It takes a long time for people to accept this idea, but today it forms the basis for all modern space science.

INVESTIGATION 2

1. Describe how Earth moves during the course of a year. Why is a year about 365 days long?

2. Explain why the constellation named Taurus the Bull is visible in November but not in May.

INVESTIGATION 3

HOW DOES THE MOON MOVE?

You've seen that the length of a day comes from Earth's rotation on its axis. You know that the length of a year comes from Earth's revolution around the Sun. Now you can investigate changes in the sky that occur over the course of a month.

Activity

Moon Phaser

What makes the Moon change its appearance over the course of a month? In this activity you'll use models to find out.

Procedure

1. Your teacher will turn off all the lights in a room except for one bright lamp or flashlight. This light will be a model of the Sun.

2. Stand in front of the Sun model. Hold a white plastic-foam ball at arm's length in front of you, as shown. This ball will be a model of the Moon.

Step 2

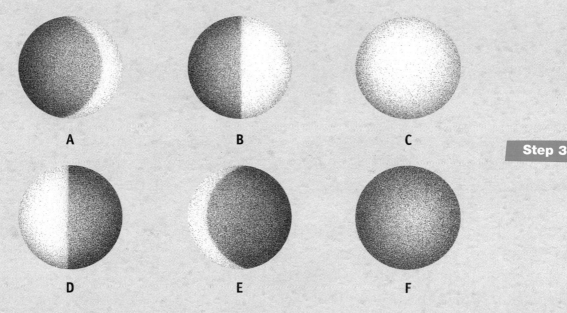

A   B   C

Step 3

D   E   F

3. Move the Moon model around. Try to re-create the way the model looks in each of the lettered pictures above. You can turn around in place as much as you wish, but stay in the same spot in front of the Sun model.

4. In your *Science Notebook*, **make a drawing** that shows where the objects in this activity are when the Moon ball looks to you like picture *A*. Draw the scene as if you were looking down on it from the ceiling. Show the top of the Moon model, the top of the Sun model, and the top of your head. Label all the objects you draw, and label your completed drawing *A*.

5. Repeat step 4, making five more drawings that show the positions of the objects when the Moon model looks like each of the other pictures: *B, C, D, E,* and *F*.

Analyze and Conclude

1. The light in this activity represents the Sun. The ball represents the Moon. Identify the object that you represent.

2. Based on your experiment, **infer** one way that the Moon moves in space.

UNIT PROJECT LINK

Imagine that your Moon base is on the Moon model in this activity. Draw a dot on the Moon ball to show where your base is. Then do step 3 of the activity again. What happens to your base as you re-create each picture? As you learn more about how the Moon moves, think about what the days and nights would be like at your Moon base.

Your Changing View of the Moon

In the way that they move, Earth and the Moon are very much alike. Earth rotates on its axis and revolves around the Sun. In a similar way, the Moon rotates on its axis and revolves around Earth.

The Same Old Face of the Moon

There's one special thing about the way the Moon rotates and revolves. It has to do with the time it takes for one complete rotation and one complete revolution.

For Earth, those two time periods are very different. It only takes 24 hours for one rotation, but it takes about 365 days for one revolution. The Moon, however, takes the same amount of time to rotate once on its axis as it takes to revolve once around Earth—about 27 days.

The same side of the Moon always faces Earth (*below*). You never see the Moon's far side (*inset*).

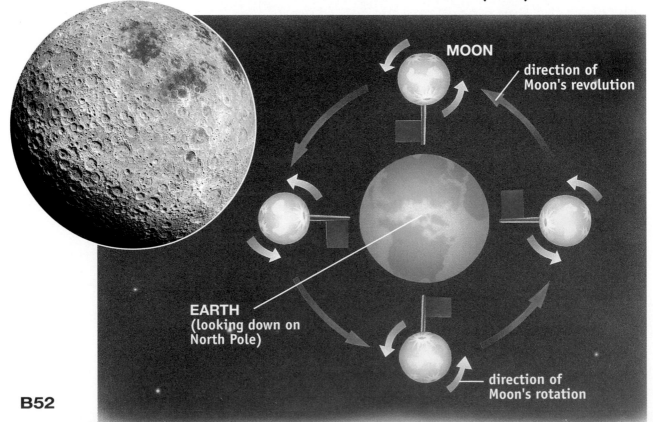

MOON

direction of Moon's revolution

EARTH
(looking down on North Pole)

direction of Moon's rotation

To see what effect this has, look at the drawing. You can tell by the little flag in the picture that the Moon has rotated exactly once in the same time that it's revolved around Earth exactly once. But the flag has stayed facing Earth all that time!

That's what happens with the real Moon. The same side of it always faces Earth. Only astronauts have ever seen the far side of the Moon with their own eyes. Other people can only look at the far side in pictures sent back by space missions.

Going Through Phases

If you were asked to draw a picture of the Moon, what would you draw?

Would you show a Moon that looks like a full circle or only part of a circle? If you think about it, you'll realize that these are both correct ways to draw the Moon. Sometimes the Moon is full, but at other times it looks like a crescent—a thin slice of a circle.

The changing shapes of the Moon that can be seen from Earth are known as **phases** of the Moon. You produced phases yourself in the activity on pages B50 and B51.

Phases of the Moon occur because the Moon, like Earth, has day and night. As the Moon circles Earth, people on Earth see different amounts of the daylit half of the Moon.

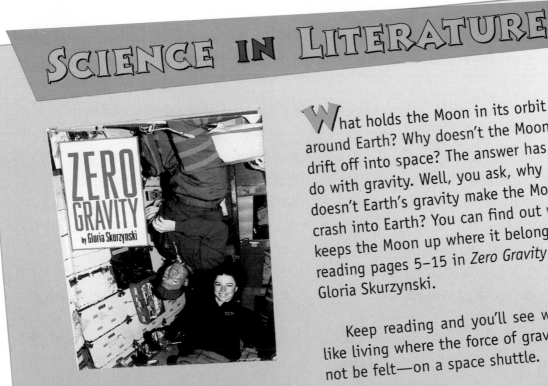

SCIENCE IN LITERATURE

ZERO GRAVITY
by Gloria Skurzynski
Bradbury Press, 1994

What holds the Moon in its orbit around Earth? Why doesn't the Moon just drift off into space? The answer has to do with gravity. Well, you ask, why doesn't Earth's gravity make the Moon crash into Earth? You can find out what keeps the Moon up where it belongs by reading pages 5–15 in *Zero Gravity* by Gloria Skurzynski.

Keep reading and you'll see what it's like living where the force of gravity cannot be felt—on a space shuttle.

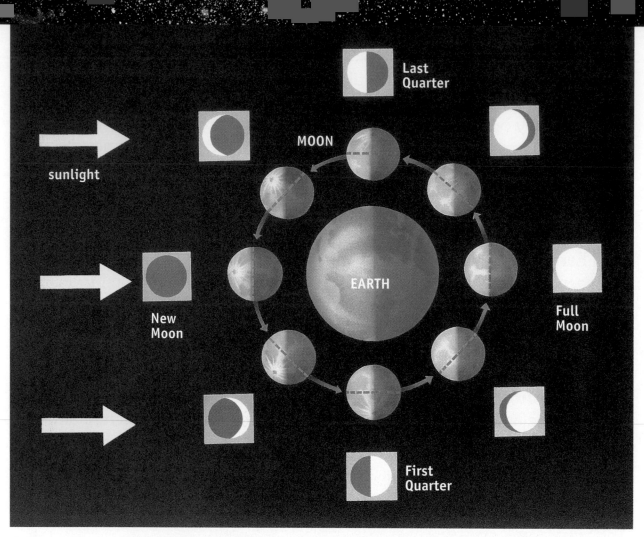

▲ The phases of the Moon; what you see from Earth is shown in each box.

Sometimes you see only a tiny sliver of that half. When the Moon is full, you see the entire daylit half.

You can understand phases better by looking at the drawing. Picture yourself standing on Earth to view the Moon in each position shown.

One thing you'll notice in the drawing is something called a new Moon. Have you ever seen a new Moon? In fact, it's almost impossible to see. That's because a new Moon occurs when the side of the Moon facing Earth receives no sunlight at all.

By the Light of the Moon?

When your grandparents or great-grandparents were teenagers, a popular song talked about dancing "by the light of the Moon." Can people really do anything by the light of the Moon? Not exactly.

It should be clear to you now that the Moon doesn't produce any light of its own as the Sun does. You can only see the Moon because sunlight bounces off its surface into your eyes. So even on a moonlit night, you're really dancing by the light of the Sun! ■

The Moon: Fiction and Fact

GLOBAL views

For thousands of years, people have seen pictures in the Moon. The ancient Chinese saw a rabbit and a toad. Some Europeans saw a crab. The Vikings saw a boy and girl in the Moon who they said were kidnapped when they went to get a pail of water. The boy and girl were Jack and Jill.

In the United States, people talk about "the man in the Moon." But many cultures, including the Maori (mä'ō rē) people of New Zealand, see a woman in the Moon instead.

It was once thought that the full Moon could cause strange behavior. The words *lunacy*, *loony*, and *moonstruck* come from this belief!

Look for the imaginary pictures in each Moon. ▼

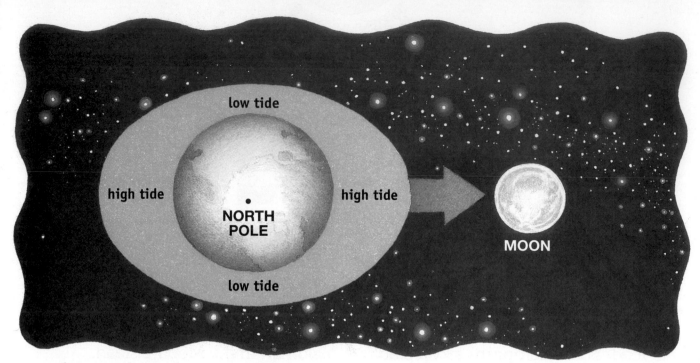

▲ **The Moon's gravity causes Earth's tides.**

The Real Power of the Moon

The Moon really does affect some things on Earth—the tides. Tides are the rising and falling of ocean water along coastlines.

Tides are caused by the gravity of the Moon. As Earth rotates on its axis, different sides of Earth face the Moon. The Moon's gravity pulls on the oceans on the side of Earth closest to the Moon, causing a high tide. At the same time, a second high tide occurs on the side of Earth that is farthest from the Moon. This high tide occurs because the solid Earth is pulled toward the Moon and away from the water on Earth's far side.

In between the two high tides are two low tides, as shown in the picture. During each 24-hour rotation of our planet, a given place on Earth will have two high tides and two low tides. That's a lot of changes caused by one faraway object! ■

═══════════════ **INVESTIGATION 3** ═══════════════

1. Describe how the motions of the Moon cause its phases.

2. Is it correct to call the far side of the Moon the dark side? Why or why not?

REFLECT & EVALUATE

WORD POWER

axis   orbit
revolve   phases
rotation   planet
constellation
solar system

 On Your Own
Review the terms in the list. Then use as many terms as you can in a paragraph that describes Earth's motion.

 With a Partner
Mix up the letters of each term in the list. Provide a clue for each term and challenge your partner to unscramble the terms.

BUILD YOUR PORTFOLIO

Make a poster showing the phases of the Moon. Label at least four of the phases. Include a drawing that shows how the positions of the Sun, the Moon, and Earth cause one of these phases.

Analyze Information

Copy this drawing. Label each star pattern. Label the star Polaris. Draw arrows to show how the stars appear to move. Tell which stars, if any, hardly seem to move at all.

Assess Performance

Make a model that shows how Earth and the Moon move. Use three balls of different sizes. Show what happens daily, monthly, and yearly in your model.

Problem Solving

1. Imagine that you are stranded on an island. How can you use the Sun to determine the directions north, south, east, and west? How can you use the Sun to tell time?

2. How do stars in the sky change throughout the night? How do they change throughout the year? What does observing the stars tell you about the way that Earth moves?

3. When the Moon is full, where is it located in relation to Earth and the Sun? Explain how the positions you describe would cause you to see a full Moon.

CHAPTER 3

EFFECTS OF EARTH AND MOON MOTIONS

In the Northern Hemisphere the longest day of the year is usually June 21. On this day the Sun follows its longest and highest path across the sky. What would you do to celebrate this day?

A Sun-Sational Day

June 21 usually has the shortest night of the year in the Northern Hemisphere. In many parts of the world, people stay awake all through this shortest night. The Hopi people of Taos, New Mexico, race up a mountain to meet the Sun as it rises, singing

There! There!
Beautiful white-rising has dawned
Beautiful yellow-rising has dawned
There! There!

On June 21 people in Scandinavia build giant bonfires to stand for the Sun's great light and heat. In northern Mexico beautiful head coverings are worn. In this chapter you'll find out more about the Sun and the ways it affects Earth.

Coming Up

◀ A Mexican headdress that celebrates the Sun

WHAT CAUSES SEASONS?

What kinds of things do you like to do in the summertime? Can you do the same things in winter? For most people on Earth, there are differences between the seasons—often big differences! In this investigation you'll find out how Earth's shape and movements cause the seasons.

Activity

Lined-Paper Sunlight

Why is it warmer during the summer in most places than it is during the winter? Find out what rays of sunlight have to do with the answer.

MATERIALS
- sheet of lined paper
- tape
- string
- construction paper
- scissors
- *Science Notebook*

Procedure

1. Place a sheet of lined paper on a table. Tape the paper in place.

2. Using a string, as shown, draw a large circle on construction paper. Then cut out the circle.

Step 2

3. This circle is a model of Earth. Label your model as shown in the diagram.

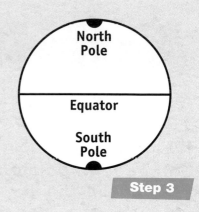

Step 3

4. Place the circle on top of the lined paper as shown below. Imagine that the lines on the paper are rays of light from the Sun. Draw an arrow to show where the sunlight is coming from. **Observe** how the rays of sunlight strike different parts of your model Earth. **Draw** a picture of your model in your *Science Notebook*.

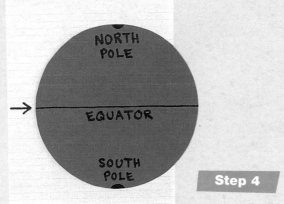

Step 4

5. Turn your model Earth so that the North Pole is tilted to the right, as shown. **Draw** how the Earth model and the Sun's rays look now.

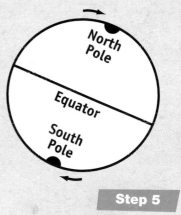

Step 5

Analyze and Conclude

1. Compare the drawings you did for steps 4 and 5. In each drawing, where are the Sun's rays closest together as they hit the ground? Where are they farthest apart? Where do the rays hit the ground straight up and down? Where are they slanted?

2. How might the distance between the rays of sunlight on the ground affect the temperature on your model Earth? **Infer** from your model how the angle at which sunlight hits the ground might affect the temperature on the real planet Earth.

3. Predict where on Earth it would be hottest and coldest in each of your drawings.

Activity
Earth Tilts!

What does Earth's revolution around the Sun have to do with changes in the seasons? Find out in this activity.

Procedure

1. Press small balls of clay onto the North Pole and South Pole of a globe. Stick a toothpick into each piece of clay to represent Earth's axis.

2. Use a lamp as a model of the Sun. Place the lamp so that it shines on the globe.

Step 1

3. Locate the drawing of Polaris that your teacher has taped high up on a wall or ceiling. Position the globe so that its axis tilts, with the North Pole pointing toward the Polaris drawing.

Step 3

To Polaris

4. **Observe** which parts of your model Earth are now getting the most sunlight. **Record** these observations in your *Science Notebook*.

To Polaris

Step 5

5. Make your Earth model revolve around your Sun model, but always keep the North Pole pointing toward Polaris. At each of the four points shown in the picture above, **observe** and **record** which parts of Earth get the most sunlight.

Analyze and Conclude

1. Locate your home state on the globe. Where was the globe in its orbit around the Sun when your state got the most sunlight? Where was the globe when your state got the least sunlight?

2. Make signs that say *spring*, *summer*, *fall*, and *winter*. Then **infer** where the globe would be in its orbit during each of these seasons in your home state. Place the signs in those parts of the room.

UNIT PROJECT LINK

Make a sky scene for your Moon base model. On large sheets of paper, draw what you'd see in the daytime sky from your base. Include the Sun, Earth, and stars. Show the day and night parts of Earth. Show the tilt of Earth's axis. What season is it in the United States on the Earth that you've drawn?

The Reason for Seasons

Remember when you used a construction paper circle and a sheet of lined paper to make a model of sunlight hitting Earth? In that activity on pages B60 and B61, you saw that different parts of Earth get different amounts of sunlight. If Earth were flat, this wouldn't be the case!

Results of Roundness

Different parts of our planet get different amounts of sunlight because Earth is round. The parts that get the least light are the North Pole and the South Pole. The parts that get the strongest light are near the equator (ē kwāt'ər). The **equator** is an imagi-

nary line that circles Earth halfway between the two poles.

How hot or cold a place is depends mainly on the angle at which sunlight strikes that place. The more direct sunlight a place gets, the warmer the place is. Sunlight strikes the equator pretty much straight on, so it's warmer there.

At the North Pole and the South Pole, however, sunlight always strikes the ground at an angle. This means that the light is spread out more thinly over a larger area, so it's colder there. Recall how the lined-paper light rays spread out at the surface near the poles of your Earth model.

Because Earth is round, sunlight strikes some parts of it more directly than others. ▼

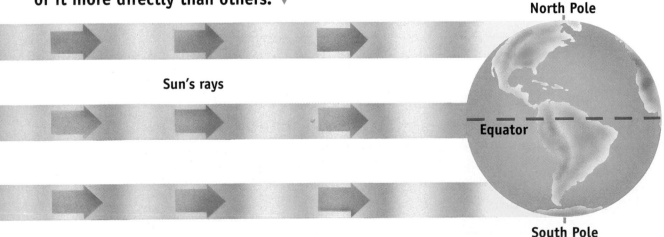

Sun's rays

North Pole

Equator

South Pole

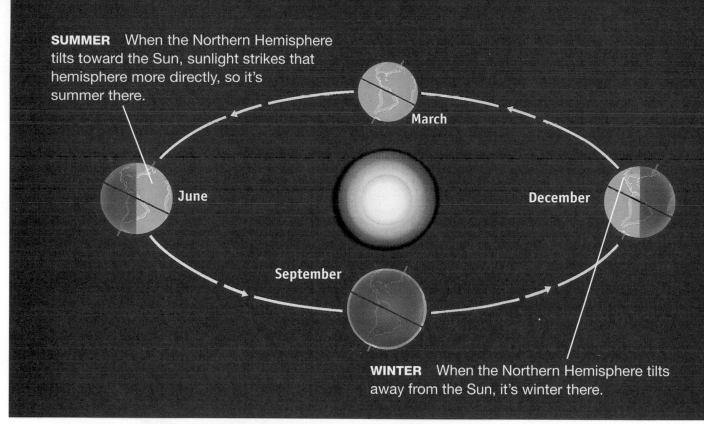

SUMMER When the Northern Hemisphere tilts toward the Sun, sunlight strikes that hemisphere more directly, so it's summer there.

March

June

December

September

WINTER When the Northern Hemisphere tilts away from the Sun, it's winter there.

▲ **Earth's positions at different times of the year**

Earth's Tilting Axis

Find the axis on each picture of Earth in the drawing above. Do you notice anything strange about the axis? It's tilted! You learned about this tilt when you did the activity on pages B62 and B63.

Having a tilted axis means that Earth slants a little to one side as it revolves around the Sun. Look at the drawing. Notice that, as Earth circles the Sun, the tilt always points in the same direction. The northern tip of the axis always points toward Polaris, the North Star.

The tilt of Earth's axis is what causes **seasons**—the four parts of the year. Spring, summer, fall, and winter are different from each other in most places on Earth. That's because the Sun's rays strike each place differently at different times of the year. Sometimes the rays strike the ground more directly. At other times they strike more at an angle.

The United States is in the Northern Hemisphere (hem'i sfir), the northern half of planet Earth. Use the drawing to tell what season it is in the United States when the Northern Hemisphere tilts toward the Sun.

When it's summer in the Northern Hemisphere, what season is it in the Southern Hemisphere? Use the drawing to check your answer.

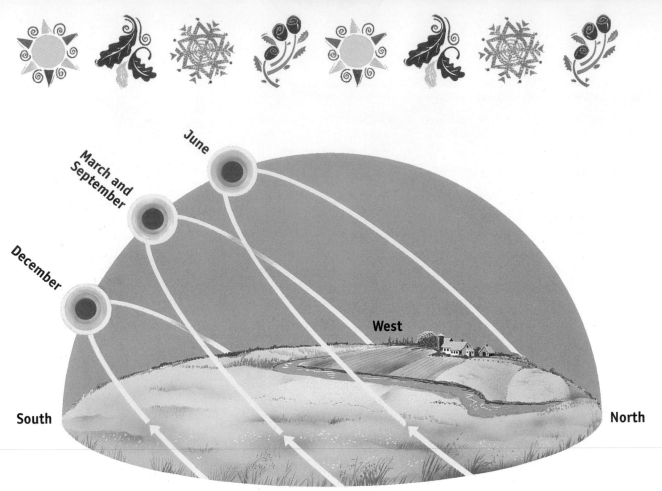

June

March and September

December

South

West

North

East

▲ **The Sun's apparent path across the sky at different times of the year**

Rising Up, Sinking Down

You know that the Sun seems to follow a changing path across the sky. And you know that Earth revolves around the Sun. As Earth revolves, the tilt of Earth's axis affects the Sun's apparent path across the sky.

In summer, because your part of Earth is tilted toward the Sun, the Sun's path appears highest in the sky. The summer Sun path is also the longest, as shown above. Because it's the longest, there are more daylight hours in the summer months.

During winter, the Sun's path appears lowest in the sky. This results in fewer daylight hours in the winter months. What a lot of changes happen because of one little tilt! ■

INVESTIGATE FURTHER!

....

RESEARCH

Find out how people in different countries celebrate the changing seasons. What do they do for the springtime planting or the fall harvest? How do they celebrate the winter day when the Sun's path stops sinking and starts to rise again? Find several examples from different cultures.

The First Calendar Makers

Do you know what day today is? Of course you do. In fact, you know what date, what month, and what year it is. That's because you use a calendar.

People have used calendars to keep track of time since they first began observing the Sun, Moon, and stars. Knowing the time of year has always been important, because farmers need to know when to plant their crops.

Ancient Sky Watchers

The Mayas of ancient Central America designed a calendar that was, for centuries, more accurate than any other in the world. They did this by developing very accurate ways of measuring the position of the Sun in the sky. They observed the Sun from observatories like the one pictured.

The Mayan calendar had 18 months of 20 days each. It also had an extra 5 days that weren't attached to any month.

Part of an ancient Mayan calendar ▼

A Mayan observatory in Mexico ▼

The Chinese also have a very ancient calendar. Their traditional calendar is very complicated because it's based mainly on the phases of the Moon, not on the Sun's position. A Chinese year usually has 12 months of 29 or 30 days each. Since this adds up to less than 365 days, a thirteenth month is added to some years to keep the calendar in line with Earth's revolution.

▲ **Each year in the Chinese calendar is named after an animal—for example, this dragon.**

Creating the Modern Calendar

Calendar makers face a difficult problem. Earth doesn't take exactly 365 days to revolve around the Sun. Instead, it takes about $365\frac{1}{4}$ days. If a calendar doesn't account for the

Julius Caesar, who helped create the modern calendar ▼

extra quarter-days, they add up over the years. Finally the calendar no longer matches the seasons.

When Julius Caesar became the ruler of ancient Rome, the Roman calendar was way out of step with the seasons. To correct this, Caesar decided that the year we now call 46 B.C. would have 445 days. After this "year of confusion," the Romans began using a new 12-month calendar that's the basis for the one we have today.

Most of the years in Caesar's calendar had 365 days. Every fourth year, however, was a *leap year* of 366 days. This made up for the extra quarter-day it takes Earth to revolve once around the Sun.

Since Caesar's time, small changes have been made in his calendar as astronomers have learned

to calculate more exactly the time it takes Earth to revolve around the Sun. Today, scientists can even figure out when to add an extra *leap second* to a year! In this way, they keep the calendar in line with Earth's real motion. ■

▲ **Modern calendar makers work at the Royal Observatory in Greenwich, England.**

SCIENCE IN LITERATURE

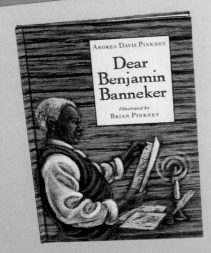

DEAR BENJAMIN BANNEKER
by Andrea Davis Pinkney
Illustrated by Brian Pinkney
Gulliver Books,
Harcourt Brace & Co., 1994

Young Benjamin Banneker grew up free in the 1700s when many other African Americans were slaves. As he worked on his parents' farm, he wondered about the Moon, the Sun, and the stars. He taught himself astronomy by observing the sky every night.

Benjamin Banneker wrote books that listed the positions of the Moon and the Sun throughout each year. He also predicted the start of each season. Find out what else Banneker wrote by reading *Dear Benjamin Banneker* by Andrea Davis Pinkney.

Near the Equator, Near the Pole

SCIENCE TECHNOLOGY & SOCIETY

Where do you live? Do you live on the East Coast or the West Coast of the United States? In the southwestern desert? Near the Rocky Mountains? On the Great Plains? If you live in the United States, the weather in your area is probably sometimes warm, sometimes cool.

As Hot as Summer

Suppose you lived near the equator in central Kenya in Africa. Look at the map on this page. Find the place where the line representing the equator runs through Kenya.

Kenyans wear lightweight clothing. ▼

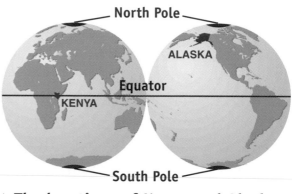

▲ **The locations of Kenya and Alaska**

Your life in Kenya would be quite different than it is in the United States. You wouldn't have four seasons with different temperatures. Living near the equator, you'd get direct sunlight all year round. It would therefore be very warm all the time.

In Kenya you'd wear shorts and light cotton shirts, and you wouldn't need a coat very often. You'd eat foods that grow well in warm lands, such as bananas and beans.

As Cold as Winter

Suppose that you lived among the Inuit (in'oo wit) people in northern Alaska. You'd never get direct sunlight that close to the North Pole. It would therefore be very cold all the time. You might ride on a snowmobile to get to school. Once you arrived, you'd probably get a hot breakfast to warm you up.

In northern Alaska you'd be in the Land of the Midnight Sun. This means that in the middle of summer, when the North Pole tilts toward the Sun, you'd have 24 hours of sunlight each day! But when the pole tilts away from the Sun in winter, you'd see hardly any sunlight. Imagine a day when the Sun didn't rise!

During the long, dark winter, some people develop an illness known as Seasonal Affective Disorder, or SAD. People with SAD become tired and unhappy. Bright

▲ **Inuit people wear heavy clothing.**

lights make them feel better by "fooling" their bodies into thinking there's more daylight! ■

The path of the Midnight Sun, which never sets ▼

===== INVESTIGATION 1 =====

1. Explain how Earth's movements cause the four seasons.

2. Suppose you're planning an expedition to the South Pole. What month would you choose to visit there? Explain the reasons for your choice. Describe the conditions you'd expect to find then.

WHAT ARE ECLIPSES?

Imagine you were living many centuries ago. Suppose that in the middle of a cloudless day the Sun suddenly started to disappear bit by bit. What would you think was happening? Such an event is called an eclipse. In this investigation you'll learn what causes two kinds of eclipses.

Activity

A Disappearing Act

Have you ever seen an eclipse? In this activity you'll observe eclipses of the Sun and the Moon and begin to think about how they happen.

MATERIALS
• *Science Notebook*

SAFETY //////
Never look directly at the Sun, even during an eclipse.

Procedure

1. Look at the two photographs. One shows a solar eclipse, an eclipse of the Sun. The other shows a lunar eclipse, an eclipse of the Moon. Each photo contains pictures that were taken 10 or 15 minutes apart. In this way, scientists recorded the changes that were taking place over time.

2. In your *Science Notebook*, **describe** what you see at each stage of the solar eclipse. Note what looks different about the Sun in these pictures from the way the Sun usually looks. **Observe** and **describe** how each stage of the eclipse looks different from the other stages.

B72

3. Repeat step 2 for the lunar eclipse.

4. Describe any differences you see between a solar eclipse and a lunar eclipse.

Analyze and Conclude

1. Hypothesize about what might cause the events shown in the solar eclipse photo. Think about the positions and motions of the Sun, Earth, and the Moon. **Discuss** your ideas with your group.

2. Hypothesize about what might cause the events shown in the lunar eclipse photo. **Discuss** your ideas with your group.

▲ Stages of a total solar eclipse

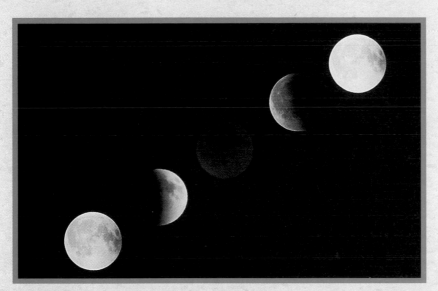

▲ Stages of a total lunar eclipse

Activity
Homemade Eclipses

What positions of the Sun, the Moon, and Earth result in an eclipse? In this activity you'll use models to re-create what you saw in pictures in the last activity.

Procedure

1. Place a bright lamp or flashlight on a table and point it out into the room, not toward the floor or ceiling. Turn off all other lights.

2. Pretend you are Earth, the lamp is the Sun, and a plastic-foam ball is the Moon. **Talk** with your group. Where should you position your model Moon so that you create a solar eclipse, like the one shown in the photograph on page B73? Try it out.

3. After your group agrees, **draw** in your *Science Notebook* the scene you created in step 2. Label the Sun, Earth, and the Moon.

Step 2

4. Now let a globe represent Earth. Place the globe where the lamp can shine on it. **Talk with your group** about where the Moon model should be to create a lunar eclipse, like the one in the photo on page B73. Try out the position you choose.

5. **Draw** the scene you made in step 4.

Analyze and Conclude

1. What are the positions of the Sun, Earth, and the Moon during a solar eclipse?

2. **Hypothesize** about what phase the Moon is in during a solar eclipse. Use the drawing from step 3 and the models to help you answer this question.

3. What are the positions of the Sun, Earth, and the Moon during a lunar eclipse?

4. **Hypothesize** about what phase the Moon is in during a lunar eclipse. Use your drawing and models to help you.

INVESTIGATE FURTHER!

EXPERIMENT

Why don't we see solar and lunar eclipses every month? Experiment with the lamp, globe, and Moon model to figure out why. Compare the positions that produce eclipses with the positions that produce a full Moon and a new Moon.

How an Eclipse Occurs

▲ **People view a solar eclipse, using safety glasses and special cameras.**

In 1991, astronomers from all over the world came to Mexico to visit an ancient Native American city called Monte Albán. Many of the scientists had traveled thousands of kilometers. They came to this place to observe in person what you saw in pictures on page B73—a total eclipse of the Sun.

The people who live around Monte Albán felt lucky that the eclipse could be seen from their home. Total solar eclipses are rare and each one can only be seen from a small area on Earth.

What's it like to observe a total eclipse of the Sun? One astronomer said, "You remember it for the rest of your life." A bright sunny day plunges into darkness. The temperature drops. Dogs may bark and roosters may crow. Daytime birds may stop singing. Flowers that only bloom at night may open. And most important of all, the Sun does its awesome "disappearing act"!

▲ Wolves and dragons were once said to cause eclipses.

Predicting Eclipses

People in the past didn't know what caused eclipses. They made up stories to explain them. Some Asian cultures said that the Sun disappeared because a dragon was trying to eat it. The Vikings of northern Europe saw that the Moon turned red during a lunar eclipse. They said this happened because a wolf bit the Moon and made it bleed.

From past observations, some ancient astronomers learned to predict when an eclipse would take place. Today, scientists know the exact movements of the Moon and Earth. They can tell just when an eclipse will occur—and predict it centuries in advance!

Goodbye Sun, Goodbye Moon

Recall the activity on pages B74 and B75. You learned that a **solar eclipse** occurs when the Moon, as it revolves, moves directly between the Sun and Earth. In this position the Moon blocks the Sun from our view.

During a total solar eclipse, features such as prominences are visible around the edges of the Sun.

A solar eclipse occurs when the Moon blocks the light of the Sun from reaching Earth. ▼

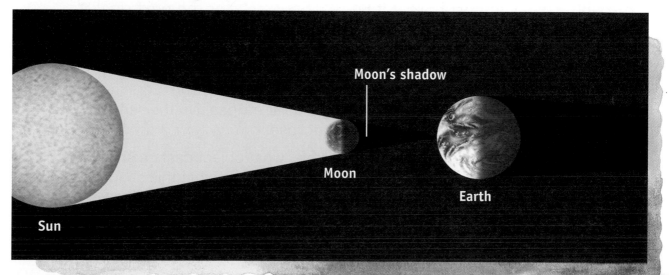

Moon's shadow

Moon

Earth

Sun

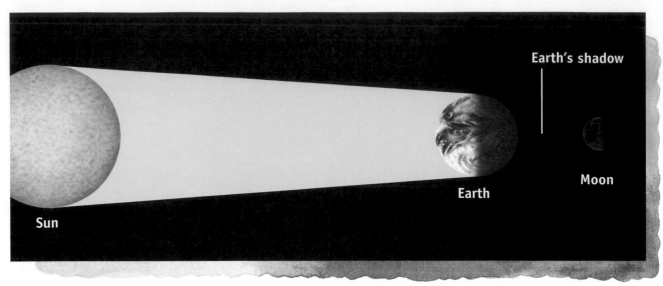

Earth's shadow

Moon

Earth

Sun

▲ A lunar eclipse occurs when the Moon moves into Earth's shadow.

It's usually hard to see features on the Sun because of the Sun's glare. This is one reason astronomers will travel far to see a solar eclipse.

An eclipse of the Moon works a little bit differently. A **lunar eclipse** occurs when the Moon moves into Earth's shadow. In this position, Earth blocks the Sun's light from reaching the Moon directly. A small amount of sunlight, however, does reach the Moon. That light bends around planet Earth by passing through Earth's atmosphere. Lit by this little bit of sunlight, the Moon looks red or copper-colored.

Eclipses don't happen very often because the Moon's orbit around Earth tilts a little. This makes it rare for the Sun, the Moon, and Earth to line up perfectly. Also, you have to be in just the right spot to see a total solar eclipse. If you're not in the right place, you'll see no eclipse or see only part of the Sun disappear.

But anyone on the night side of Earth can see a total lunar eclipse. So watch for the next one! ■

INVESTIGATION 2

THINK IT WRITE IT

1. Describe the positions of the Sun, Earth, and the Moon during a solar eclipse. Do the same thing for a lunar eclipse.

2. In a solar eclipse, what object casts a shadow on what other object? Explain what this shadow has to do with the fact that each solar eclipse is only visible from certain areas on Earth.

REFLECT & EVALUATE

WORD POWER

equator
lunar eclipse
seasons
solar eclipse

 On Your Own
Review the terms in the list. Then write one new thing you learned about each term.

With a Partner
Write a slogan or an advertisement for each term in the list. Do not use the term itself. Share the slogans with your partner. Challenge your partner to guess each term.

BUILD YOUR PORTFOLIO

Make a diagram that shows the positions of the Sun, the Moon, and Earth during a solar eclipse or a lunar eclipse. Label the parts of your diagram.

Analyze Information

Study the drawing. Then, for each numbered location, identify the seasons in the Northern and Southern hemispheres.

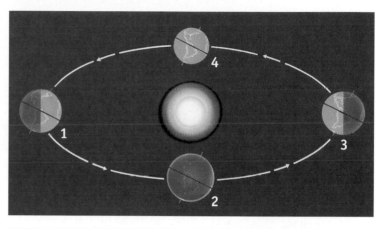

Assess Performance

Work with a partner to create a model of a solar eclipse or a lunar eclipse. Use a lamp or flashlight, a globe, and a plastic-foam ball. Explain your model to the class.

Problem Solving

1. When it's winter in the Northern Hemisphere, what season is occurring in the Southern Hemisphere? Why?

2. How does the tilt of Earth on its axis affect the amount of sunlight that the South Pole receives at different times of the year?

3. Describe how a solar eclipse differs from a lunar eclipse.

Throughout this unit you've learned about the Sun, the Moon, and Earth. How will you use what you've learned and share that information with others? Here are some ideas.

Hold a Big Event
to Share Your Unit Project

Write a story that takes place at your imaginary Moon base. Tell about an exciting event that might really happen someday on the Moon. Use the story to describe what life is like at your lunar base. Describe some of the conditions that people experience on the Moon. Tell about some of the buildings they live in and what they must do to survive. When your story is written, invite other classes, your parents, and your friends to see your Moon base model and hear its story.

Research

An almanac is a yearly book that includes information about the positions of objects in the sky. Find an almanac for this year. Look up when the Sun will rise and set on different days. Find out when the Moon will be in its different phases. Identify the days when the seasons will change. See whether any eclipses will occur this year. Use what you've learned to become a better observer of the sky.

Take Action

Can you find the Big Dipper and the Little Dipper in the night sky? Use your star clock to teach your family and friends how to find different star patterns. Show them the star Polaris and explain how to use that star to tell directions. Describe how you'd use the stars to tell time.

UNIT C

FORMS OF ENERGY

Theme: Systems

GET READY TO

OBSERVE & QUESTION
What is energy?

Think about all the different ways that you move. Energy is needed for all things, such as the waterslide car, to move. Energy is also needed for matter, such as the water, to change form. Where does energy come from to make things move or to cause a change in matter?

EXPERIMENT & HYPOTHESIZE
How can heat change materials?

Heat is a form of energy that can change matter. You know this if you've ever watched a fire burn a log. Using hot water and cold water in activities will help you investigate how matter is affected by heat.

INVESTIGATE!

RESEARCH & ANALYZE

As you investigate, find out more from these books.

- *Indoor Science* by Anita Ganeri (Dillon Press, 1993). When you rub a balloon on your hair, the balloon sticks to the wall. Why does this happen? It has something to do with energy. Read this book to find out about forms of energy.

- *The Mysterious Rays of Dr. Röntgen* by Beverly Gherman, (Atheneum, 1994). You know rays of light energy can pass through a glass window. But did you know that another kind of energy ray can pass through wood, flesh, and other non-metal objects? Read this book to find out about this energy ray.

WORK TOGETHER & SHARE IDEAS

What's your plan for an energy-efficient house?

Working together, you'll have a chance to creatively design and build a model of a house that uses energy wisely. Then you can display your model house, test its energy efficiency, and share your new knowledge with others.

CHAPTER 1

ENERGY

Energy is all around you. Notice anything that is
moving and you'll be seeing the result of some form of energy.
You've probably heard someone say that food gives
you energy. What is energy, anyway?

The Sunforce 1 Adventure

Sunforce 1 is a race car built by students of George
Washington University. The car is powered by energy from
the Sun. Sunforce 1 finished ninth out of 52 sun-powered
cars in the World Solar Challenge held in Australia.
The college students placed panels on the car to "catch the
sunlight." The panels changed the energy of sunlight into
electrical energy. The electricity powered the car's motor.

Ben Feldman and Stephane Thiriez are two of the
car's builders. They took turns driving the 3,013-
km (1,871-mi) course at a racing speed of
about 64 km/h (40 mph). They wanted to
show that cars powered by the Sun can
work. What other things can the energy of
sunlight do? Read on and find out!

Coming Up

Ben Feldman driving *Sunforce 1* at the World Solar Challenge

WHAT IS ENERGY?

Has anyone ever told you, "Eat your food so that you'll have energy (en'ər jē) to play" or "Turn out the lights, you're wasting energy"? In this investigation you'll find out what energy is by observing what it can do.

Activity

Energy to Burn

Get to know energy by using it and observing how it changes things.

Procedure

Put a ball of modeling clay on a sheet of foil where everyone in your group can see it. When your teacher brings you a wooden match, **observe** it. *Do not touch it.* **Record** all your observations in your *Science Notebook*. Now your teacher will strike the match and place it into the ball of clay. **Observe** the match as it burns. **Record** your observations.

Analyze and Conclude

1. **Infer** what caused the match to start burning.

2. Energy was used and given off as the match burned. What do you think energy is? **Record** all your ideas.

MATERIALS
- modeling clay
- aluminum foil
- safety match
- *Science Notebook*

SAFETY //////

Do not strike the match. Only your teacher should do this. Be sure all loose hair and clothing are tied back. Keep *well* back from the flame.

C6

Activity
Feel the Beat

Do you feel like running? Energy is needed for anything to move. Do this activity to see one way energy can cause motion.

MATERIALS
- drum with drumstick
- colored paper
- *Science Notebook*

Procedure

1. Beat a drum once with a drumstick. Quickly put your finger on the drum. Note what you feel. Have each group member try it. **Discuss** your observations. Then **record** them in your *Science Notebook*.

2. Make 10 to 20 pieces of confetti by tearing very tiny pieces of paper from a larger piece of paper.

3. Place the confetti on top of the drum.

4. **Talk with your group** and **predict** what will happen to the confetti as you beat the drum once. Be sure you can explain why you made the prediction you did. **Record** your prediction.

5. **Observe** the confetti as you beat the drum once. **Record** your observations.

Step 3

Analyze and Conclude

1. What did you feel as you were beating the drum? Where did the energy come from to make the drum feel this way?

2. What happened to the confetti as you were beating the drum? **Compare** your observations with your prediction.

3. **Infer** why this happened to the confetti.

Activity
Mystery Can

Here's a fun toy to make that will show you another way that energy can cause motion.

- -

MATERIALS

- scissors
- strong rubber band
- 2 plastic coffee can lids, each with two holes
- 2 washers
- coffee can with both ends removed
- *Science Notebook*

SAFETY //////

Be careful not to cut yourself on the edges of the can.

Procedure

1. Cut a rubber band so that you have one long piece. Thread it through the holes in one of the plastic lids from a coffee can.

2. Have a group member help you tie two washers to the rubber band. Study the diagram to help you.

3. Thread the rubber band through the holes in another lid and then tie the ends together as shown.

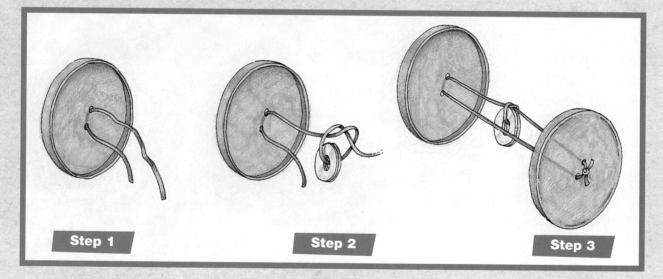

Step 1   Step 2   Step 3

4. Bend one plastic lid and push it inside a coffee can. Snap the other lid on the can.

5. Reach into the can and pull the bent lid through the can. Snap the lid in place.

6. **Talk with your group** and **predict** what will happen if you roll the can away from you across the floor. Be sure you can explain why you made the prediction you did. **Record** your prediction in your *Science Notebook*.

7. Now try rolling the can a few times. **Observe** what happens and **record** your observations.

Analyze and Conclude

1. What happened when you rolled the can? How did your group's prediction compare with the results?

2. **Infer** what was happening inside the can. How would you explain your observations?

3. Energy is needed to make things move. Where did the energy come from to start the can rolling? **Infer** where the energy came from after the can stopped rolling away from you.

INVESTIGATE FURTHER!

RESEARCH

Make a list of toys that move. Next to each toy listed, write what you think causes its motion. For example, a ball moves because you throw it. A wind-up toy moves because of a spring. Share your list with your classmates.

C9

Do You Have the Energy?

Imagine you are in the first seat of a car on a water ride at an amusement park. You are slowly being pulled up a big hill. Finally you're at the top. Swoosh! Your car rushes downward. Splash! It enters the water at the bottom of the hill. Water sprays you and your friends. The ride is fun because it moves very fast downhill. Energy is needed for motion to occur. In fact, energy is needed for lots of things to occur.

Energy Everywhere

Look around you. Notice how many things are in motion. Outside, cars whiz by on the streets. Children glide through the air on swings.

▲ **Is diving into a pool an example of energy of motion or stored energy?**

Inside your classroom, clock parts turn and bells clang. All these things need energy to move.

At this moment a heater may be warming the air in your classroom, or an air conditioner may be cooling the air. This morning you may have watched soft bread crisp into toast. These changes use energy, too. But what is energy? **Energy** is the ability to move something or cause a change in matter.

Everything around you is matter. **Matter** is anything that has mass and takes up space. The amount of matter in an object is its mass. An elephant has more mass than a grain of sand. So an elephant has more matter than a grain of sand.

Energy of Motion

When matter is moving, it has energy. When you throw a ball, the moving ball has energy. Energy made the confetti jump as you beat the drum in the activity on page C7.

Wind can move objects, such as tree branches, because moving air has energy. Moving water also has energy. The energy that moving matter has is called **energy of motion.** Look around your classroom and outdoors. What objects that you see have energy of motion?

Stored Energy

Although an object isn't moving, it can have the *ability* to move. Energy in matter that can cause that matter to move or change is called **stored energy**. A girl standing still on a diving board has stored energy. As she jumps off the diving board, she has energy of motion.

Energy can also be stored in fuels. Gasoline that makes a car move has stored energy. The food that you eat has stored energy, too.

C11

matter

Stored Energy Changes

If you store something, you know you can use it later. Energy that is stored can be used, too. When stored energy is used, it is changed to energy of motion.

Remember the activity on pages C8 and C9? As you rolled the can, the rubber bands inside wound up. As they wound up, they changed some of the can's energy of motion into stored energy. As the rubber bands unwound, the can moved and the stored energy became energy of motion again.

Although energy can be described as of energy of motion and stored energy, there are many forms of energy. Look at the pictures and read about different forms of energy.

FORMS OF ENERGY

▲ **HEAT** All matter is made of tiny particles that are constantly moving. The energy of motion of the tiny particles is **heat.** If you've ever washed your hands in hot water, you've felt the effects of heat energy!

ELECTRICAL ENERGY Have you ever touched a metal doorknob and received a shock? Shocks, lightning, and the electricity that runs through the wires of your house are examples of electrical energy. ▼

MECHANICAL ENERGY Mechanical (mə kan'i kəl) energy is the energy of moving objects. Mechanical energy moves the parts in machines. ▼

SOUND Sound is a form of energy that you can hear. Sound energy comes from particles that are vibrating, or moving back and forth rapidly. Sound moves in waves through matter such as air or water.

CHEMICAL ENERGY Chemical energy is stored in matter. Fuels such as gasoline, coal, and oil have stored energy. So do matches, wood, and food. Matter itself is not energy. Energy is stored in coal, for example, but coal is not energy. ▼

LIGHT Light is a form of energy that you can see. Light energy from the Sun moves in waves through space. Light energy also comes from electric lamps and burning matches, like the one you looked at in the activity on page C6. ▼

Everything you do is possible because of energy. Look around you. Are the lights on? Do you hear any sounds? Is anyone in the room moving? Think about all the ways you use energy. Energy really is everywhere! ■

━━━━━━━━━━━ **INVESTIGATION 1** ━━━━━━━━━━━

1. Use an example to explain how stored energy can change to energy of motion.

2. Think about all the things you do from the time you get up in the morning until you arrive at school. Write a short story about your activities and identify all the forms of energy you use.

INVESTIGATION 2

WHAT CAN HAPPEN TO ENERGY?

What do playing a video game, riding in a car, and baking brownies have in common? In this investigation you'll find out what they have to do with energy changes.

Activity
Sand Shake

A burning wooden match changes the stored chemical energy in wood to heat and light energy. In this activity observe another way that energy changes form.

Procedure

1. In your *Science Notebook*, **make a chart** like the one shown.

TEMPERATURE (°C) OF SAND		
Before shaking		
After shaking	**Prediction**	**Actual**

2. Fill a plastic jar about one-fourth full with dry sand.

C14

3. Place a thermometer in the sand. Wait one minute. **Record** the temperature of the sand on the first line of your chart.

4. Talk with your group and **predict** what the temperature of the sand will be after you shake the jar 200 times. Be sure you can explain why you made the prediction you did. **Record** your prediction on the second line of your chart.

5. Remove the thermometer. Place the lid on the jar. Shake the jar 100 times fast. Then have another group member shake the jar 100 times fast.

Step 3

Step 5

6. After shaking the jar, remove the lid and place the thermometer in the sand. Wait one minute. **Record** the temperature in your chart.

7. When your teacher tells you to, **record** your data on the chalkboard.

Analyze and Conclude

1. How did your prediction compare with your results? How does the class data compare with your data?

2. Hypothesize why the temperature changed. Tell why you think as you do.

UNIT PROJECT LINK

At the end of this unit, you'll make an energy-efficient model home. List the kinds of energy that will be used in your home. In your Builder's Notebook, draw diagrams to show how your house will be built to save energy.

Activity
Sun Power

Can light energy change to heat energy? Try this activity to find out.

Procedure

1. Fill a plastic jar halfway with sand. Place a thermometer in the sand. Wait ten minutes. **Record** the temperature of the sand in your *Science Notebook*.

2. **Talk with your group** and **predict** what the temperature of the sand will be after ten minutes in the sunlight. **Record** your prediction in your *Science Notebook*.

3. Place the jar of sand with the thermometer in sunlight. Wait ten minutes. **Record** the temperature of the sand in your *Science Notebook*.

Step 3

Analyze and Conclude

1. What happened to the temperature after the sand was in the sunlight?

2. What kind of energy change occurred? **Hypothesize** why you feel warm when you sit in the Sun.

Energy Changes Form

What do sweating in the hot Sun, listening to the radio, riding on a bus, and eating have in common? They all are examples of energy changing form.

Nothing Lost, Nothing Gained

Remember the burning match in the activity on page C6? When the match stopped burning, what do you think happened to the energy? It might be hard to believe, but the energy was not lost or used up. It just changed form.

Before your teacher struck the match, the chemical energy stored in it couldn't be used. As the match burned, its chemical energy changed to heat energy and light energy.

There are many ways in which energy can change form. And when energy changes form, heat energy is usually involved. On the next two pages, read about some ways that energy can change from one form to another. Look for energy changes in which heat energy is involved.

From Light to Chemical Energy

Plants use energy from the Sun to make food. Using light energy, plants change water and air to chemical energy in food.

From Chemical to Heat Energy

Coal, wood, and oil are used to heat homes. When these fuels are burned, they give off heat. Chemical energy is changed to heat energy. Look at the picture. What other form of energy is given off? ▶

From Chemical to Mechanical Energy

When gasoline is burned in a car engine, chemical energy is changed to mechanical energy. The mechanical energy moves the car. If you've ever felt the hood of a car after a drive, you know that heat energy is also given off.

From Electrical to Heat Energy

This stove uses electrical energy. The stove changes electrical energy to heat energy. What other kind of energy can you see? ▶

◀ From Electrical to Light Energy

A light bulb uses electrical energy. In the bulb the electrical energy changes to heat. The wire in the bulb gets so hot that it glows brightly.

From Light to Heat Energy

How does it feel to stand in sunlight? It feels warm, doesn't it? That's because energy from the Sun is absorbed, or taken in, by your body and changed to heat energy. That's also why the temperature of the sand you placed in sunlight increased in the activity you did on page C16. ▶

SCIENCE IN LITERATURE

THE MYSTERIOUS RAYS OF DR. RÖNTGEN
by Beverly Gherman
Illustrated by Stephen Marchesi
Atheneum, 1994

Light that you see is not the only form of energy from the Sun. The Sun gives off invisible energy rays, too. One hundred years ago a scientist in Germany worked night after night in his lab. Finally his hard work paid off. Wilhelm Röntgen had discovered one of these invisible rays.

Find out about the discovery of X-rays in *The Mysterious Rays of Dr. Röntgen* by Beverly Gherman. After you read, write a letter to Dr. Röntgen. Tell him how his discovery has affected people.

Using Energy Changes

Energy from the Sun is called **solar energy**. One way people use solar energy is to collect it in the form of light energy and change it to heat energy. This heat energy can be used to heat water. It can be used to heat homes.

The house below has a flat-plate solar collector on its roof. Read the steps to see how the solar collector helps provide heat for the house. ■

1 Sunlight is absorbed by the black metal plate. Heat builds up in the collector and is held in by the glass cover. The temperature inside the collector can reach as high as 94°C (200°F).

2 The heat energy is absorbed by water in pipes. The warmed water is pumped into a tank. The tank stores the hot water.

pump

tank

3 The tank may be connected to the pipes that carry water to the faucets in a home.

4 The hot-water tank may also be connected to a heating system. The hot water is pumped through radiators, warming the air in the house.

INVESTIGATION 2

1. Explain the energy changes that occur when you turn on a fan.

2. Think about the many ways that energy can change form at home or at school. Make a list of these changes. What form of energy is involved most often?

REFLECT & EVALUATE

WORD POWER

energy
energy of motion
heat
matter
solar energy
stored energy

 On Your Own
Review the terms in the list. Then use as many terms as you can in a paragraph that tells about energy in your life.

 With a Partner
Write each term in the list on one side of an index card and the definition on the other side. Use the cards to quiz your partner.

PORTFOLIO

Using pictures cut from magazines, make a poster that shows ten things that use energy. Write a caption for each picture that explains what forms of energy the object uses.

Analyze Information

Study the drawing. Then use the drawing to explain what will happen when the mouse eats the cheese. What forms of energy will be involved?

Assess Performance

Design and carry out an experiment to find out why the metal plate of a solar collector is black. You can use the following materials: coffee cans with lids, black paper, white paper, water, and thermometers. After your teacher reviews your plan, carry out the experiment. Compare your results with those of others.

Problem Solving

1. Explain what gasoline, a girl standing on a diving board, and food have in common.

2. Imagine you hear someone say that "Coal is energy." What's wrong with this statement? How would you correct it?

3. A battery in a flashlight contains stored energy. If the flashlight is left on, over time, the battery may "go dead." What happened to the energy that the battery contained?

2

HEAT AND TEMPERATURE

Imagine sleeping under snow and staying warm. Believe it or not, this is possible. In Alaska, people know all about staying warm. A person sleeping outdoors there, snuggled in a waterproof sleeping bag, would welcome snow. A layer of snow keeps the heat in, like a comfy blanket. How is this possible?

Mush On

Beverly Masek is a musher. A musher is a sled rider who drives a team of dogs over snowy ground. A native Alaskan, Beverly has raised nine generations of sled dogs. She has driven many of her dogs in the annual race called the Iditarod (ī dit'ər äd).

The Iditarod sled-dog race covers more than 1,600 km (1,000 mi) of Alaskan wilderness. For more than ten days, mushers and their dogs battle the bitter cold. How does Beverly Masek make it through this long, cold race? To keep herself warm, she dresses for the weather. She puts down straw for her dogs to sleep on. This keeps them from losing their body heat. And she knows how to use newly fallen snow as a blanket! In this chapter you'll find out more about keeping warm and staying cool.

Coming Up

◀ Beverly Masek makes sure her sled dogs are well rested and well fed during the Iditarod race.

WHAT IS HEAT AND HOW IS IT PRODUCED AND MEASURED?

You can live without electrical energy if you have to. You can also live without sound energy. But you can't live without heat energy. In this investigation you'll find out about heat energy.

Activity

Bottle Thermometer

Temperature is a measure of how hot or cold something is. It is measured with a thermometer. In this activity you'll see how a thermometer works.

Procedure

1. With your group, fill a clear plastic bottle with water. Add a few drops of food coloring to the water.

2. Wrap a small piece of modeling clay around a straw, about 5 cm from the end, as shown.

3. Put the shorter end of the straw into the bottle of colored water. Seal the straw in place with the clay.

4. Use a dropper to add more water to the straw until the water level is halfway up the straw. Use a grease pencil to draw a line on the straw at the level of water.

MATERIALS
- goggles
- clear plastic bottle
- water
- food coloring
- modeling clay
- metric ruler
- clear plastic straw
- dropper
- grease pencil
- 2 plastic bowls
- ice cubes
- timer
- *Science Notebook*

SAFETY
Wear goggles. Clean up any spills.

Step 2

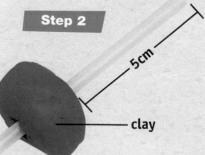

straw

5 cm

clay

C24

5. **Talk with your group** and **predict** what would happen to the water level in the straw if you put your bottle thermometer into a bowl of ice water and then into a bowl of warm water. Be sure you can explain why you made the predictions you did. **Record** your predictions in your *Science Notebook*.

6. Put the bottle thermometer into a bowl of water. Add ice to the water. Wait three minutes. Then mark the straw at the level of the water. **Record** your observations.

Step 6

7. Now put the bottle thermometer into a bowl of warm water. Wait three minutes. Mark the straw at the level of the water. **Record** your observations.

Analyze and Conclude

1. Describe what happened to the water in the bottle thermometer when you cooled it. What happened when you warmed it? How did your predictions compare with your results?

2. **Infer** whether warm water takes up more space or less space than cool water. How do your observations support your inferences?

3. **Hypothesize** how your bottle thermometer is similar to a real thermometer.

INVESTIGATE FURTHER!

EXPERIMENT

Predict what will happen if you place the bottle thermometer in sunlight. Try it. Mark the straw to show your results each time. Share your results with your classmates.

Activity

A Hot Topic

What can you do to make heat energy? Here's a way you may not have thought of before.

Step 2

Procedure

1. **Talk with your group** and **predict** what will happen to the temperature of a washer and a pencil eraser after they are rubbed back and forth on a sheet of paper. **Explain** why you made the predictions you did. **Record** your predictions in your *Science Notebook*.

2. Hold a washer to your cheek. **Record** whether the washer feels warm or cool. Rub the washer back and forth quickly on a sheet of paper. Do this for about 15 seconds. Hold the washer to your cheek. **Record** how the washer feels now.

3. Repeat step 2, using a pencil eraser. **Record** your observations.

Analyze and Conclude

1. How did the washer feel before and after it was rubbed on the paper? How did the eraser feel before and after it was rubbed on the paper? How did your results compare with your predictions?

2. **Hypothesize** why different amounts of heat were produced. **Infer** how the roughness or smoothness of the surfaces may have something to do with what you feel.

Heat Waves

You put a slice of cold pizza into a microwave oven and "zap" it. In a minute, the crust is hot and the cheese is melted. To understand this change, you need to find out how heat changes matter.

Moving Particles

You know that everything around you is matter, even food. And you know that all matter is made of tiny particles too small to be seen. These tiny particles are always moving. They have heat energy.

Matter can be found as a solid, liquid, or gas. A solid has a definite shape and takes up a definite amount of space. In a solid the particles are

close together, so they can't move much. They vibrate, or move back and forth, in a small space.

A liquid does not have a definite shape, but it takes up a definite amount of space. In a liquid the particles are a little farther apart and move faster than the particles in a solid. Because the particles aren't held in place, liquids take the shape of the container they're in.

A gas doesn't have a definite shape or take up a definite amount of space. It takes the shape of its container and will move out of an open container. In a gas the particles are farther apart and move faster than the particles in a liquid.

Compare the arrangement and speed of particles in a solid, a liquid, and a gas. ▼

solid

gas

liquid

C27

Heating and Cooling Matter

Solids, liquids, and gases all have particles that move. When heat is added to matter, the particles in the matter move faster. The faster the particles of matter move, the more heat energy the matter has and the hotter it is. The more slowly the particles move, the less heat energy the matter has and the cooler it is.

Think back to the activity on pages C24 and C25. When heat was added to the bottle thermometer, the particles of water moved faster and farther apart. So the colored water took up more space and the level of colored water rose up the straw.

◀Turn to page H14 to learn how to use a thermometer.

Heat and Temperature

On page C26 you used your cheek to tell whether a washer or an eraser was warm or cool. Is your cheek a good thermometer? The bottle thermometer you made is a little better. But it doesn't measure exact temperature, either.

Temperature is a measure of how hot or how cold something is. You know that temperature is measured with a thermometer. But does a thermometer measure heat energy? It can't because heat and temperature are not the same thing.

Think back to a time when you were splashed by a drop of hot water. Now imagine how it would feel to be splashed by an entire cup of hot water. You could get a painful burn. The drop of hot water and the cup of hot water are the same temperature. But the cup of hot water has more heat energy than the drop.

Which one has more heat energy? ▼

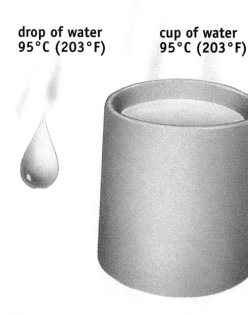

drop of water
95°C (203°F)

cup of water
95°C (203°F)

Making Matter Hot

Think back to the microwave oven that heated your pizza slice. A part inside the oven gives off invisible waves of energy called microwaves. The waves cause the tiny particles of water in the food to move faster, so your pizza gets hot.

Microwaves make particles in matter move faster. But there are other ways to do this. **Friction** (frik'shən) is a force that works against the movement of two objects when the objects touch. When two objects rub against one another, their particles move faster. When particles move faster, heat is produced.

Friction makes it hard for objects to move past or over each other. There is more friction if the surfaces that are rubbing are rough rather than smooth. When there is more friction, movement takes more effort and more heat is produced. That's why the rough eraser became warmer than the smooth washer when each was rubbed on paper in the activity on page C26. ■

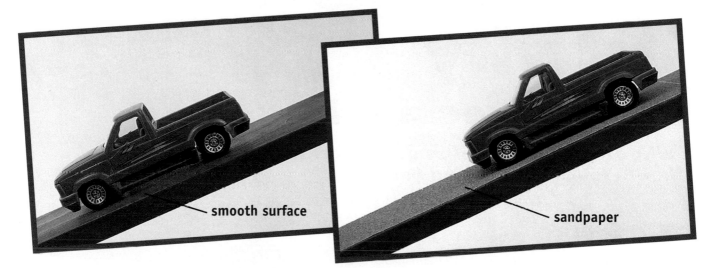

smooth surface

sandpaper

▲ **Why does the toy truck move faster on a smooth surface? On which surface will the toy truck's tires get warmer?**

INVESTIGATION 1

THINK IT WRITE IT

1. What are two ways to make matter warm? Explain what happens to particles of matter when they are warmed.

2. Draw pictures to show what happens to the particles of water in a bottle thermometer when heat is added and when it's taken away.

INVESTIGATION 2

HOW CAN HEAT MOVE?

Whether you are sitting in front of a campfire or soaking in a bathtub of warm water, you are gaining heat. How does heat move from the fire or warm water to you? In this investigation you'll find out.

Activity

Heat Takes a Trip

Why do the handles of some pots get too hot to touch safely? Find out.

MATERIALS

- hot water
- plastic jar
- metal spoon
- wooden craft stick
- plastic spoon
- timer
- *Science Notebook*

SAFETY ///////

Clean up any spills immediately.

Procedure

1. Suppose you place a metal spoon, a wooden craft stick, and a plastic spoon in hot water. With your group, **predict** what the dry end of each object will feel like after five minutes. **Record** your predictions in your *Science Notebook*.

2. Your teacher will pour hot water into a plastic jar. Place the metal spoon, wooden stick, and plastic spoon into the jar of hot water. Wait five minutes.

Step 2

C30

3. With the objects in the water, feel the dry end of each one. **Record** your observations.

Analyze and Conclude

1. Which object felt the warmest after five minutes in hot water? Which object felt the coolest?

2. **Compare** your predictions with your results. Were you surprised by the results? Explain.

3. Heat energy moves through solids. Some kinds of solids allow heat to move better than other kinds of solids. From your results, **infer** why pots are made of metal and why pot handles are often made of wood or plastic.

SCIENCE IN LITERATURE

INDOOR SCIENCE
by Anita Ganeri
Dillon Press, 1993

Why do houses creak at night? Why do doors get stuck? Why do pipes burst in winter? All these questions have something to do with heat. Look for the answers to these questions as you read *Indoor Science* by Anita Ganeri.

Indoor Science is a question-and-answer book. Use its table of contents or index to find the answers to other questions about how things work inside your home.

Activity
Side by Side

In this activity you'll play a game to model how heat moves through solids.

MATERIALS
- red paper (one sheet per student)
- plastic bag
- *Science Notebook*

- -

Procedure

1. Each student should get a sheet of red paper and crumple it into a ball. These balls are models of heat.

2. One student should collect all the paper balls and be the "heat source." The other students stand in a line, with arms touching, next to the "heat source." These students are models of the particles that make up a solid.

3. The heat source should pass paper balls (heat), one at a time, to the next student in line. That student should pass the heat to the next student and so on.

Analyze and Conclude

From the model, **infer** how a pan warms up when it's placed on a stove burner. **Record** your inference in your *Science Notebook*.

Step 3

Activity
Up and Down

Heat moves through solids, but how does it move through liquids and gases? Play this game to find out.

MATERIALS
- red paper (one sheet per student)
- plastic bag
- *Science Notebook*

Step 3

Procedure

1. Each student should get a sheet of red paper and crumple it into a ball. These red paper balls are models of heat.

2. Your teacher will take you to a flight of stairs. Each student should stand on a different step. Your teacher is the "heat source" and holds all the heat at the bottom of the stairs. You and the other students are models of the particles that make up liquids and gases.

3. Your teacher will hand a paper ball (heat) to the student on the bottom step. That student, carrying heat, moves to the top step. Everyone else moves down one step. Repeat this procedure, using all the red paper balls. This is a model of how heat moves through a liquid and a gas.

Analyze and Conclude

When air is heated, it rises. That's why each student went to the top of the stairs after gaining "heat." From the model, **infer** what happens to the heated air at the top of the stairs. **Record** your inference in your *Science Notebook*.

Activity
Heat Moves—No Matter

Objects can get warm even without tiny particles of matter to move the heat to them. Find out how by playing this game.

- -

Procedure

1. Each student should get a sheet of red paper and crumple it into a ball. These red paper balls are models of heat. One student will be the "heat source" and hold all the paper balls in a bag.

2. The heat source can't move from one place to another. The rest of the students should form a circle around the student who is the heat source. Then everyone should remain in place.

3. As a group, **decide** how the heat source will move the heat to the students in the circle. Remember that no one can move from one place to another. Only the paper balls (heat) can move from the heat source. When you've decided how to do it, try it.

Step 2

Analyze and Conclude

How did your class move the heat to the circle of students? How is this like the way energy from the Sun reaches Earth? How is it different? **Record** your ideas in your *Science Notebook*.

Heat on the Move

Imagine your hands are cold. To warm them, you wrap them around a cup of warm cocoa. How does the heat move to your hands?

A Touching Story

Remember the game you played in the activity on page C32? You and your classmates had direct contact with each other. **Conduction** (kən-duk'shən) is the movement of heat by direct contact between particles of matter. The pictures show the movement of heat by conduction through a metal pot.

❶ In solids the tiny particles of matter are touching each other.

❷ When the particles in the solid are heated, they move faster and bump into particles next to them.

❸ Then those particles start moving faster. After a while, all the particles in the solid are moving faster.

Heat energy always moves from an area of higher temperature to an area of lower temperature. That's why your cold hands are heated by a warm cup of cocoa.

CONDUCTION OF HEAT THROUGH A POT

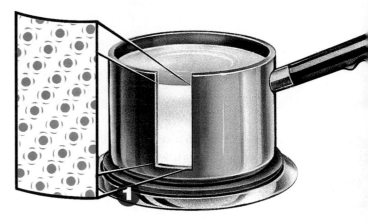

C35

▲ Air is a good insulator. That's why two doors help keep a house warm.

▲ Insulation helps keep heat from moving in and out of a house.

A Good Conductor

Some solids conduct heat more easily than other solids. A material that heat travels through easily is called a **conductor** (kən duk′tər).

Think back to the activity on pages C30 and C31. The metal spoon heated faster than the wood or the plastic. That's because metals are good conductors of heat energy. The wood and plastic did not heat as quickly. That's because these materials are not good conductors. An **insulator** (in′sə lā tər) is a material that does not conduct heat well.

Fluid Motion

Since the particles in liquids and gases are farther apart, they don't touch each other as often as the particles in solids do. Heat travels through liquids and gases by convection (kən vek′shən). **Convection** is the movement of heat through liquids and gases by the movements of particles.

Liquids and gases are called fluids (floo′idz). The particles in fluids are not close enough to pass energy from one particle to the next by conduction. When heat energy is added to a fluid, the particles near the heat move faster and farther apart. Then there are fewer particles in the warmer part of the fluid than in other parts. The warmer part of the fluid becomes "lighter" and moves upward. Read more about convection in the drawing on page C37.

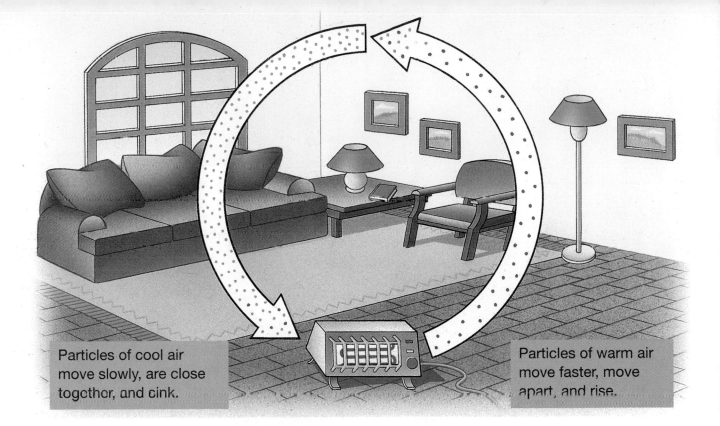

Particles of cool air move slowly, are close together, and sink.

Particles of warm air move faster, move apart, and rise.

▲ Follow the movement of air in this convection current. How is this like the game you played on page C33?

Direct Rays

Heat can also move without any matter to carry it. Think back to the activity on page C34. Imagine that there were almost no particles of matter between the heat source and the circle of students. That would be a model of the space between the Sun and Earth. There is almost no matter in space between the Sun and Earth. An area that has no matter in it is called a vacuum (vak′yo͞om).

The Sun gives off energy called radiant (rā′dē ənt) energy. Some of that energy is light energy, which you can see. But much of the energy is in the form of invisible waves.

These waves can travel through the near vacuum of space, where there is no matter to move heat. The movement of heat energy in the form of waves is called **radiation** (rā dē ā′shən). The Sun is not the only source of radiant energy. Any light that shines on you can warm you by radiation. ■

UNIT PROJECT LINK

Think about how to use insulation to control how heat travels in your model home. In your Builder's Notebook, draw pictures to show how insulation would work in your model home. Begin building your model home.

Keeping Warm!

SCIENCE TECHNOLOGY & SOCIETY

Look at the bird standing in the snow. How does it keep warm? If you look closely, you'll see that the bird's feathers are fluffed. The fluffed feathers trap air between them. Air is a good insulator. The trapped air and the feathers help keep the bird warm.

People aren't as lucky as birds. They don't have feathers. In cold winter weather it's important to hold in body heat. Wearing layers of clothing helps to trap air and keep heat in. But some kinds of clothing are better insulators than others.

▲ **How is this robin keeping warm?**

Look at the pictures of different materials and fibers used for winter clothing. Fibers are single, threadlike structures from which materials used for clothing are made.

Down feathers are small, soft feathers. Down jackets contain feathers from geese. Down feathers trap air, which is a good insulator.

▲ Cotton can be woven into a wafflelike pattern to trap air. This weave is used for thermal underwear.

C38

Wool is often used in making winter clothing. Wool fibers have a rough, scalelike surface that traps air.

Recycled plastic bottles can be stretched into thin strands of fiber. These strands trap air well when they're used to fill jacket linings. The recycled plastic fibers can also be woven into cloth. ▼

INVESTIGATION 2

1. What happens to the temperature of a bowl of hot soup that's left out on a counter for several hours? Explain why this happens.

2. Houses are often built with insulating materials between the outside and inside walls. Explain why this is done.

INVESTIGATION 3

HOW CAN HEAT CHANGE MATERIALS?

If you leave a carton of ice cream on a kitchen counter, it'll soon melt into a soupy mess. What does heat have to do with this change? In Investigation 3 you'll see how heat changes matter.

Activity

Wet or Dry

Find out why a dry swimsuit feels warmer than a wet one.

Procedure

Place two thermometers, one labeled *A* and one labeled *B*, side by side. In your *Science Notebook*, **record** the temperature reading of each. Lay a wet cloth over the bulb of thermometer *A* and a dry cloth over the bulb of thermometer *B*. After 15 minutes, **record** each temperature again.

Analyze and Conclude

1. Did either cloth take heat from its surroundings? How do you know?

2. **Infer** why you feel cooler in a wet swimsuit than a dry one.

MATERIALS
- 2 thermometers, labeled *A* and *B*
- 2 squares of cotton cloth
- water
- timer
- *Science Notebook*

SAFETY //////
Be careful when handling glass thermometers. Clean up any spills immediately.

wet cloth

dry cloth

C40

Activity

A Sweet Activity!

When a solid mixes with a liquid and disappears, the solid is said to dissolve. How does heat affect this change?

MATERIALS
- goggles
- cold water
- metric measuring cup
- 2 clear plastic cups
- spoon
- sugar
- warm water
- *Science Notebook*

SAFETY
Wear goggles for this activity. Clean up any spills immediately.

Procedure

1. Pour 100 mL of cold water into a clear plastic cup. **Talk with your group** and **predict** how many spoonfuls of sugar will dissolve in the cold water. **Record** your prediction in your *Science Notebook*.

2. Add sugar, one level spoonful at a time, to the cold water and stir until the sugar dissolves. **Count** and **record** the number of spoonfuls of sugar you add until no more sugar will dissolve.

3. Repeat steps 1 and 2, using warm water. **Record** your results.

Step 2

Analyze and Conclude

1. Which dissolved more sugar, the cold water or the warm water? **Compare** this result with your prediction.

2. **Infer** how heat changes the ability of water to dissolve sugar. How do you know?

Adding and Subtracting
Heat

You know that heat moves from warmer matter to cooler matter. Ice cream melts in a warm kitchen because heat energy from the warm air moves to the cold ice cream.

Melt Away

When energy is added to a solid, such as frozen ice cream, its particles move faster and farther apart. When the particles move fast enough, the solid melts. **Melt** means to "change from a solid to a liquid."

Solids melt at different temperatures. Some solids, such as ice cream, melt at room temperature. Chocolate will melt in your hand. And iron melts at 1,530°C (2,786°F).

Ice cream melts at room temperature. ▼

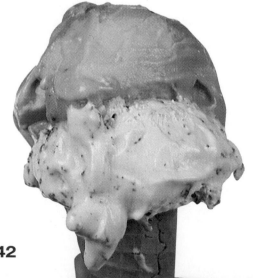

▲ **What causes the clothes to dry?**

Up, Up, and Away

When heat is added to liquid water, the particles move faster. If enough heat is added, the particles will move fast enough to escape from the liquid. Then the water changes to a gas called water vapor. **Evaporate** (ē vap′ə rāt) means "to change from a liquid to a gas." Evaporation took place in the activity on page C40. As the liquid water in the cloth absorbed heat from the air, the water changed to a gas.

Out of Thin Air

Have you ever seen water droplets form on the outside of a pitcher of cold juice? Water vapor from the air condensed (kən denst′) on the pitcher. **Condense** means "to change from a gas to a liquid." The particles of water vapor near the pitcher moved more slowly as they cooled. They came closer together and changed to liquid on the glass.

▲ Why won't the iron feel cold when it freezes?

Recall the example of melting iron on page C42. If the temperature of liquid iron goes below 1,530°C (2,786°F), the iron will become solid. This change is another example of freezing.

Well Mixed

Heat energy helps matter mix. When a solid mixes with a liquid and becomes invisible, it is said to dissolve. In the activity on page C41, you found that more sugar dissolves in hot water than in cold water. The particles in hot water move faster and farther apart, so more sugar dissolves.

▲ Where do the drops come from?

Liquid to a Solid

If enough heat is taken away from a liquid, it will freeze. **Freeze** means "to change to a solid." When liquid water loses heat energy, the particles of water move more slowly and come closer together. When the particles are close together and move slowly back and forth, the water has formed solid ice.

Which will dissolve more sugar? ▼

▲ **Why are bridges built with air spaces at one end?**

The Story Expands

Particles of matter move faster and farther apart when heat is added. Matter expands, or takes up more space, when it's heated.

When heat is taken away, most matter contracts, or takes up less space. As heat is taken away, particles move more slowly and move closer together. As they move closer, the matter gets smaller.

Water is an exception to the rule that matter contracts when heat is taken away. Water is different because water expands when it freezes.

Changing Forever

When heat is added to some kinds of matter, those kinds of matter change forever. Think about an egg. It looks quite different before you cook it than it does after you cook it. Other materials, such as wood, change to ash when they're burned. You can't change a cooked egg back into a raw egg any more than you can change ash back into wood. ■

Heat changes some matter forever. ▶

INVESTIGATION 3

THINK IT WRITE IT

1. List and describe five different ways that matter can change when heat is added or subtracted.

2. Infer and explain why sidewalks are made with spaces between the sections of concrete.

REFLECT & EVALUATE

WORD POWER

condense   freeze
conduction   friction
conductor   insulator
convection   melt
evaporate   radiation
temperature

 On Your Own
Review the terms in the list. Then write one new thing you learned about each new term.

 With a Partner
Write a clue for each term in the list. Then challenge your partner to write the correct term for each clue.

Make a labeled drawing to show how a thermometer works.

Analyze Information

Study the drawings. Then identify which drawing shows a solid, which shows a liquid, and which shows a gas. Now use the drawings to describe the differences between a solid, a liquid, and a gas.

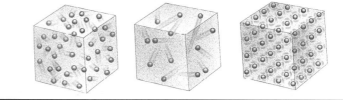

Assess Performance

Design models that can be used to explain the differences in the movement of heat by conduction, convection, and radiation. After your teacher has reviewed your design, make your models. Compare your models with those of your classmates.

Problem Solving

1. Think about how heated air and cooled air move. Use this information to describe where in a home—ceilings, floors, or walls—heating and air conditioning vents should be placed for the greatest efficiency.

2. What could you do to a container of water to make salt dissolve in the water more quickly?

3. During cold weather, would a home that has windows made up of two panes of glass separated by a space filled with air be warmer—or cooler—than a home that has windows made up of only one pane of glass? Explain.

C45

USING AND SAVING ENERGY

Every time you flip on a light or switch on the TV in your home, you use energy. Family members use energy when they cook a meal or wash clothes. How else is energy used in your home?

Energy Detective

There may be robbers in your home! They may be stealing energy. These energy robbers are hard to catch. You have to know where to look.

You need Anthony Fornarotto, energy detective! He knows how to spot things in your home that are robbing you of energy. The energy detective can find places where heat is escaping or track down lights and machines that use too much energy.

Anthony Fornarotto is really a home energy surveyor (sər vā′ər). He inspects homes and suggests ways to save energy.

In this chapter you'll explore energy—how people use it and how it can be saved. Then you can be an energy detective.

Coming Up

◀ Anthony Fornarotto, energy detective, explains how heat escapes around doors.

INVESTIGATION 1

WHAT ENERGY SOURCES DO PEOPLE USE?

Everything you do requires energy. Where does all this energy come from? What's good and bad about the energy we use? Find out in Investigation 1.

MATERIALS

•*Science Notebook*

Activity

Energy Count

How many ways do you use energy? Can you figure out where the energy comes from?

- -

Procedure

1. In your *Science Notebook*, **make a chart** with headings like the one shown.

Ways I've Used Energy Today	Where the Energy Comes From

2. Talk with your group and **record** in the first column of your chart all the ways you've used energy today.

3. In the second column of your chart, **record** where you think the energy comes from for the activities you listed in the first column. For example, if you wrote *Listened to the radio* in the first column, then you might write *batteries* in the second column. If you don't know where the energy comes from, it's okay to guess.

4. **Compare** your chart with those of other groups.

Analyze and Conclude

1. Where does the energy you use most often come from? **Compare** your results with those of other groups.

2. Look again at your chart. Suggest another way of doing each activity that would use only energy from your body instead of another energy source.

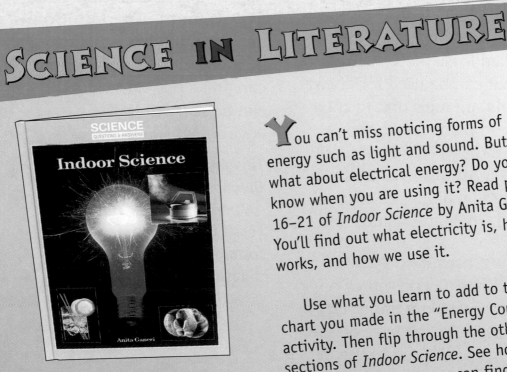

SCIENCE IN LITERATURE

INDOOR SCIENCE
by Anita Ganeri
Dillon Press, 1993

You can't miss noticing forms of energy such as light and sound. But what about electrical energy? Do you know when you are using it? Read pages 16–21 of *Indoor Science* by Anita Ganeri. You'll find out what electricity is, how it works, and how we use it.

Use what you learn to add to the chart you made in the "Energy Count" activity. Then flip through the other sections of *Indoor Science*. See how many uses of energy you can find in the pictures.

The Fossil Fuel Story

If you've ever been to a museum, you may have seen large skeletons of dinosaurs. Dinosaur bones are fossils (fäs′əls). A fossil is the remains of a plant or animal that lived many years ago.

Energy From the Past

It might surprise you to learn that long-dead plants and animals give us energy today. How is this so? Most of the fuels (fyoo′əlz) that people use are called fossil fuels. A **fuel** is a material that can be used for energy. **Fossil fuels** are fuels that formed from decayed plants and animals that lived long ago. We burn fossil fuels to get most of the energy we use. The three main types of fossil fuels are oil, coal, and natural gas.

Good News and Bad News

Fossil fuels are a good source of energy for three main reasons. First, as you can see from the table on the next page, fossil fuels can be used in different ways to supply energy. Second, there is a fairly large supply of fossil fuels right now. Third, at the present time, fossil fuels tend to be less costly than other sources of energy.

Using fossil fuels has drawbacks, or problems. One drawback has to do with what happens when fossil fuels are burned. Think about a burning match. Besides light and heat, a burning match gives off smoke. When we burn fossil fuels, smoke and other gases go into the air and cause air pollution (pə loo′shun). **Air pollution** is any harmful, unwanted material in the air. Air pollution can make people sick and can be harmful to the environment.

This dinosaur, *Ouranosaurus*, lived 140 million years ago. Fossil fuels began forming long before dinosaurs were alive. ▶

Another problem with fossil fuels is that they take millions of years to form. So although we have a large supply right now, it *is* limited. If we don't find and use other energy sources, our fossil fuel supplies will continue to become smaller and smaller. Then the cost of these fuels will rise greatly. What other energy sources will we use in the future? The next resource may give you some of the answers to this question. ■

FOSSIL FUELS

Type of Fuel	Uses
Oil — Oil, also called crude oil, is a mixture of materials. When crude oil is refined, gasoline, diesel fuel, jet fuel, and fuel oil are separated from the mixture.	• To power cars, trains, ships, trucks, and airplanes • By power plants to make electricity, in furnaces to heat buildings, by industry to run machines • As raw materials in making plastics
Coal	• By industry to run machines • By more than three fourths of electric power plants in the U.S. • In furnaces to heat buildings
Natural Gas	• By industry in the same ways that coal and oil are used • In furnaces to heat buildings • In many homes for stoves, water heaters, and clothes dryers

An Alternative Story

Coal, oil, and natural gas have been the major sources of energy worldwide for more than 100 years. But other energy sources may one day replace fossil fuels as the world's major source of energy. Four such alternative (al tʉr'nə tiv) energy sources are described in the table below and on the next page.

Energy From Sunlight

You know that solar collectors use sunlight to heat water for homes and businesses. Solar energy can also be used to power calculators, cars, outdoor lights, and ships. These machines use devices called solar cells. A solar cell changes energy from sunlight into electrical energy.

Alternative Energy Sources	Uses	Benefits	Drawbacks
Solar energy	• Heats water • Heats houses • Produces electricity • Runs small appliances • Runs calculators	• Causes no air pollution • Won't run out	• Not always sunny • Expensive to build solar power plants • Doesn't produce enough power for large cities
Wind energy	• Produces electricity • Moves sailboats • Pumps water • Grinds grain	• Causes no air pollution • Won't run out	• Wind doesn't always blow • One wind farm doesn't produce enough power for a large city

Sunlight can also be used as an energy source in a power plant to produce electricity. The picture in the table shows a solar power plant in California called Solar One. It supplies electricity to a town of 6,000.

Energy From the Wind

Wind has been a useful source of energy for hundreds of years. Windmills grind grain and pump water in many places in the world. But the power of the wind can also be used to produce electricity.

The picture in the table shows a wind farm in California. Machines, called wind generators, change the energy of wind to electricity.

Energy From Moving Water

Energy from water sounds great, since water seems so plentiful. But water must be moving to be a source of energy. In the picture of the hydroelectric (hī drō ē lek'trik) power plant shown in the table, moving water from the waterfall turns generators. The generators produce electricity.

Energy From Matter

Nuclear (nyo͞o'klē ər) energy comes from a fuel called uranium (yo͞o rā'nē əm). A handful of uranium can provide as much electrical energy as 390 barrels of oil. But nuclear energy produces harmful wastes. ■

Alternative Energy Sources	Uses	Benefits	Drawbacks
Water energy	• Produces electricity	• Causes no air pollution • Won't run out • Lakes can also be recreational areas	• Dams can't be built everywhere • Dams flood animal and plant homes • Moving water not found everywhere
Nuclear energy	• Produces electricity • Powers ships and submarines	• Causes no air pollution • Small amount of fuel produces large amount of energy	• Produces dangerous radioactive waste, which must be safely stored • Power plants costly to build

No Smoke in "Smoky City"

GLOBAL views

The people of Iceland don't burn coal or oil. The ground there doesn't hold those fuels.

Crackling wood fires don't heat the homes of the people. The forests that once dotted this cold country were cut down for firewood long ago.

However, the people of Iceland *do* stay warm. And they stay warm even on the coldest, darkest, longest nights of winter. What's more, they stay warm without burning anything!

Impossible? No. The Icelanders have a *very* special heat source—Earth itself!

Steam and hot water come out of the ground in many places in Iceland. ▼

The Hot Earth

Iceland sits on a part of Earth's surface that has all sorts of cracks and holes in it. Hot rock, both solid and melted, lies beneath the cracks and holes.

Sometimes melted rock flows out of the ground like rivers of fire. Other times it shoots out of great sputtering

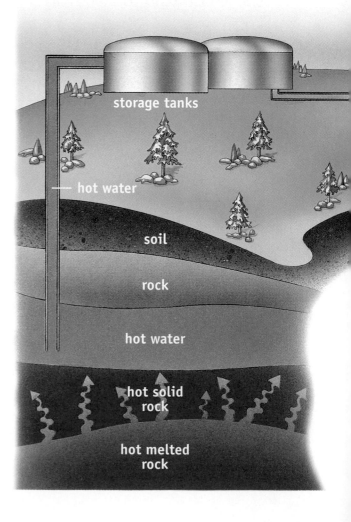

storage tanks

hot water

soil

rock

hot water

hot solid rock

hot melted rock

volcanoes. In some places, hot rocks warm pools of water, which give off steam. People can bathe in the warm pools, even on the iciest winter days. But Icelanders can't keep warm all winter by sitting in these natural bathtubs. So how do they stay warm?

Using Earth's Heat

The people in one small town in Iceland solved the problem of staying warm about 70 years ago. They drilled deep into the ground, where they found water that was a sizzling 84°C (183°F). They ran pipes into the hot water and pumped it into

their homes. The Icelanders used Earth's heat to keep warm.

Heat from Earth is called geothermal (jē ō thʉr′məl) energy. Geo- means "earth." *Thermal* means "having to do with heat." So geothermal energy is heat from Earth.

Today almost the entire capital of Iceland is warmed by geothermal energy. The first people to settle there saw steam coming from the ground and thought it was smoke. They named their city Reykjavik (rā′kyə vēk), which means "smoky city." However, there is no smoke in Reykjavik because almost no one there burns coal or oil. ◼

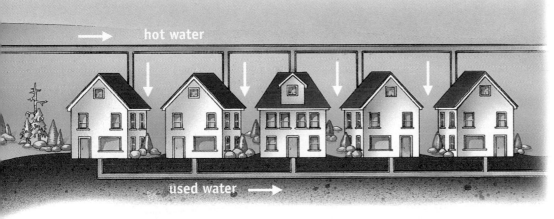

hot water

used water

◀ **Geothermal energy can be used to heat many homes.**

INVESTIGATION 1

1. List different energy sources people use. Which one do you think is best? Explain.

2. Pretend the people in your town or city use oil to heat their homes. You are told that fossil fuels have run out as an energy source. Make a plan for your town to get energy in another way. Explain how it could be done.

HOW CAN PEOPLE SAVE ENERGY?

Scientists say that people should use energy wisely and try to save it, especially the energy that comes from fossil fuels. Why should we save energy? How can we save it? Find out in this investigation.

Activity

MATERIALS

• calculator
• *Science Notebook*

Saving Fuel

Find out how much energy a car, a van, and a bus use. Then decide how energy can be saved.

- - - - - - - - - - - - - - - - - - -

Procedure

Your group is planning a trip to the zoo for 40 people. The zoo is 100 miles away. There are three ways to get to the zoo—by car, van, or bus. Study the data in the table. **Calculate** which way will use the least amount of fuel. **Record** your choice in your *Science Notebook*.

Vehicle	Number of Seats	Miles per Gallon of Fuel
Car	4	25
Van	8	20
Bus	40	10

Analyze and Conclude

1. Explain your group's choice for getting to the zoo.

2. How can taking a bus save energy? Why might some people choose *not* to take a bus?

Activity
Keep It Cool

Heat energy moves from warmer matter to cooler matter. How can you slow down this movement? How can this help save energy?

Procedure

1. Pretend that an ice cube is an air-conditioned house. In an air-conditioned house, you want to keep the cold air in and the warm air out.

2. Talk with your group. Make a plan to keep an ice cube from melting. You can use any or all of the materials listed.

3. Use a ruler to **measure** how wide the ice cube is. **Record** the width in your *Science Notebook*. Try your plan.

4. Wait 10 minutes. Then remove any materials from around your ice cube. **Measure** and **record** how wide it is. **Compare** this size with the size you recorded in step 3.

5. Share your results with your classmates.

Step 3

Analyze and Conclude

1. Which group's ice cube had the smallest change in size after 10 minutes? What did that group do to keep the ice cube from melting?

2. Hypothesize how using certain materials in the walls of a house can reduce energy use.

Old King Coal

During the 1800s, coal was "king." Some people even called it King Coal. It was called king because coal was the main source of energy in countries that had industry. Coal was burned to run steam engines in factories and on trains. It was used to heat homes and to make steel.

Today in the United States, coal is used mostly to produce electricity. In fact, three fourths of the electricity produced in this country has coal as an energy source. Where does coal come from?

We're Swamped!

The coal we use today formed from swamp plants that died as long as 360 million years ago! This was long before dinosaurs lived.

How do swamp plants turn into coal? There are four main stages in the process. Each stage produces a different material, as shown on the next page.

Old Fossils

Oil and natural gas formed in much the same way as coal. Millions of years ago, mud and sand slowly covered the remains of tiny living things in the sea. The weight of more mud and sand changed the layers of remains into oil and natural gas.

When the fossil fuels that we use today were forming, dinosaurs came and went. Coal, oil, and natural gas are indeed old fossils.

UNIT PROJECT LINK

Look back at your list of the many kinds of energy that people use at home. Think of ways people can conserve, or save, each kind of energy. In your Builder's Notebook, draw pictures with labels to show how these energy-saving ideas would work in your model home.

How Coal Forms

Imagine that it's 360 million years ago. Earth is covered by swamps. When the swamp plants die, they fall to the swamp floor. Read what happens next.

1 PEAT Layers of sand and soil cover the plant matter. Over time the plant matter forms peat. Peat is a hard, brown plant material. Peat is the first step in the formation of coal.

2 LIGNITE Over millions of years, layers of rock form over the peat. The weight of these layers changes the peat to lignite (lig′nīt).

3 BITUMINOUS COAL Layers of rock form over the lignite, increasing the weight and pressure. The lignite changes to bituminous (bi tōō′mə nəs) coal.

4 ANTHRACITE Extreme heat and pressure cause the bituminous coal to change to anthracite (an′thrə sīt), or hard coal. Anthracite is as hard as rock.

C59

Energy Wise

How old will you be 30 years from now? Some scientists predict that at the present rate of use, we'll run out of oil in about 30 years. Scientists think that natural gas will last a little longer—about 60 years. For coal their prediction is for even longer than that—about 225 years. These predictions assume that new supplies of fossil fuels will not be discovered. But even if new supplies are found, oil, natural gas, and coal will not last forever.

Burning Up the Future

As you know, most machines today get their energy from the burning of fossil fuels. Think back to the activity you did on pages C48 and C49. What energy source did you use most often? It's likely that the energy source came from fossil fuels.

Fossil fuels are the major energy source burned in power plants that produce electricity. Most of the heat used to warm buildings comes from burning fossil fuels. Cars, trains, and planes burn fossil fuels for energy, too. Burning destroys these fuels. And once they're gone, they're gone forever.

Reasons to Save Energy

Scientists advise that there are several reasons for reducing our use of fossil fuels. One reason is that we might run out of fossil fuels before other energy sources can be found or developed. By reducing our use of energy from fossil fuels now, we can make them last longer.

A second reason for reducing the use of fossil fuels is to decrease air pollution. Burning fossil fuels puts

Take Short Showers. Energy is used to make hot water. The less hot water you use, the more energy you save.

Wash Only Full Loads in Washing Machines and Dishwashers. Less energy is used washing one full load than washing two smaller loads.

C60

smoke, soot, and harmful gases into the air. This kind of air pollution can make people sick and hurt the environment. The less we rely on fossil fuels for energy, the less air pollution we will produce.

A third reason for reducing our use of fossil fuels is to save money. The cost of these fuels will rise steadily as they become more and more scarce. So the less energy everyone uses, the more money we'll all save.

How to Do It

What can be done to keep fossil fuels around longer? If you save energy, you save fossil fuels. Look at the ways to save energy shown below and on the next page. How many ways can energy be saved around your home and when you travel?

SAVE ENERGY AT HOME

Insulate Your House.
Encourage a family member to make sure your home is insulated. In the activity on page C57, you learned how insulation slows down energy use.

Turn Out Lights.
When no one is in a room, turn out the lights.

In Winter, Turn Down the Temperature Setting for the Heating Unit.
Turn up the temperature on air-conditioning units during summer.

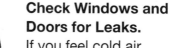

Check Windows and Doors for Leaks.
If you feel cold air coming into your house near a window or door, tell an adult. The leak can be plugged with a material called caulk.

Use Fluorescent (floo-res'ənt) **Light Bulbs.**
Fluorescent light bulbs use less energy than standard bulbs and last longer.

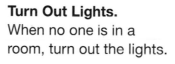

Close the Refrigerator Door Quickly.
Energy is needed to remove the heat that rushes in.

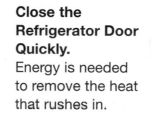

SAVE ENERGY ON THE GO

Car-pool.
If four students get together and car-pool, gasoline will be saved.

Use Public Transportation.
You found out in the activity on page C56 that taking a bus saves fuel. If there is bus service near your home, suggest to family members that they use it.

Drive the Speed Limit.
The faster a car moves, the more fuel it uses. Encourage your family to drive slowly. It'll save fuel and money.

Walk If You Can Instead of Riding in a Car.
You'll save energy, and you'll get exercise.

INVESTIGATION 2

1. Explain why coal, oil, and natural gas are called fossil fuels.

2. Give at least two reasons why saving energy is wise. Make a list of ways you plan to save energy.

REFLECT & EVALUATE

WORD POWER

air pollution
fossil fuels
fuel

 On Your Own
Review the terms in the list. Then use as many terms as you can in a paragraph about using and saving energy.

 With a Partner
Mix up the letters of each term in the list. Provide a clue for each term and challenge your partner to unscramble the terms.

PORTFOLIO
Make a poster showing all the ways your family, your school, and the people in your town can save energy.

Analyze Information

Study the drawing. Then use the drawing to explain how energy is being wasted.

Assess Performance

Design an experiment to find out which insulating materials can keep a vial of warm water warm the longest. After your teacher approves your plan, carry out your experiment. Use your findings to explain how insulation keeps warm air inside a house in the winter.

Problem Solving

1. In many parts of the world, wood is burned as a fuel. How is burning wood similar to burning fossil fuels? How is it different?

2. You work for the power company in your town. Your company wants to use alternative energy sources to produce electricity. What three alternative energy sources would you suggest the company use? Why?

3. Describe three things you can do at home to help your family save fossil fuels. Explain how each activity will use less fossil fuels.

Throughout this unit you've investigated questions related to forms of energy and saving energy. How will you use what you've learned and share that information with others? Here are some ideas.

Hold a Big Event
to Share Your Unit Project

Display your group's model house. To test its energy efficiency, place an ice cube inside the house. Set a lamp 46 cm (18 in.) from the house. Turn the lamp on and time how long it takes for the ice cube to melt. The longer the ice cube takes to melt, the more energy efficient your house will be in summer. Invite other classes and family members to visit your classroom to see your project. Don't forget to display your Builder's Notebook with your model house.

Experiment

List ideas for saving electricity at home. Ask the people in your home to follow your energy-saving ideas for one month. Then ask an adult to help you read next month's electric bill. How does this bill compare with bills from earlier months?

Research

Visit an appliance store. Ask a salesperson to explain to you what an energy-efficiency rating is. Look at the ratings on different brands of the same appliance, like a refrigerator. Which appliance saves the most energy?

Take Action

Do an energy audit. Make a list of ways to be more energy efficient in your classroom and around your school. Place energy-saving tips on signs to remind everyone to be thoughtful about energy.

UNIT D

EARTH'S WATER

Theme: Systems

GET READY TO

OBSERVE & QUESTION

Where are sources of fresh water found?

Think about where the water you use every day comes from. Is it brought by pipes from a far-away reservoir like the one shown? Does it come from a well drilled deep in the ground? Or does it come from some other source?

EXPERIMENT & HYPOTHESIZE

What things in water can be harmful?

Building a model of a water-filtering system will help you investigate how water that is dirty and unsafe is made clean and safe for drinking.

INVESTIGATE!

RESEARCH & ANALYZE

As you investigate, find out more from these books.

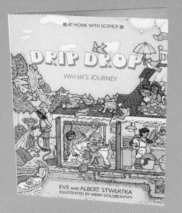

- **DRIP DROP Water's Journey** by Eve and Albert Stwertka (Julian Messner, 1991). Have you ever wondered how water comes out of your faucet, and what happens to water that goes down the drain? This book will tell you.

- **Cloudy With a Chance of Meatballs** by Judi Barrett (Aladdin Books, 1978). Can you imagine what would happen if the water cycle changed into the food cycle? Read this book to find out what happens when food falls from the sky.

WORK TOGETHER & SHARE IDEAS

What's your plan for a water supply system for Waterville?

Working with classmates, you'll have a chance to design and build a model of a town called Waterville. In a group you'll plan

- where the water for your new town will come from.

- how the water will be made safe.

- how the water will be moved to the buildings.

- how to care for and conserve the water.

Then you can display your model town and share your new knowledge with others.

WATER, WATER, EVERYWHERE

Water has many uses. You drink it. You cook with it. You use it to wash dishes and clothes. Farmers depend on it to make their crops grow and to keep their animals healthy. Industry has many needs for it. Where do we get all this water?

• •

Florida's Precious Water

Nicole Duplaix is a writer. She writes articles on science topics for magazines. One of her favorite topics is the huge swampy area in Florida called the Everglades.

The lakes and rivers of the Everglades supply water to homes, farms, and industries in southern Florida. As a science writer, Duplaix alerts people to things that are harming the area's water supply.

Duplaix interviews scientists and public officials who have ideas about how to protect the Everglades. Her articles help readers learn ways to protect this valuable water source. Someday you might write a science article about the water supply in your area. What would you tell your readers?

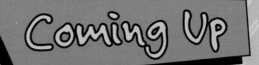

Coming Up

◄ The lakes and rivers of the Everglades supply water to people, as well as to wildlife, such as this roseate spoonbill.

WHERE IS WATER FOUND ON EARTH AND WHY IS WATER IMPORTANT?

What makes Earth a great place to live? Water! Our planet is the only one that is known to have liquid water. In fact, Earth is sometimes called the water planet. You'll find out why as you investigate.

Activity

The Water Planet

Which covers more of Earth's surface—land or water? In this activity you'll make an estimate of how much water covers Earth.

MATERIALS

- metric ruler
- paper plate
- colored markers
- map of the world
- tracing paper
- scissors
- *Science Notebook*

SAFETY

Be careful when using scissors.

Procedure

1. Using a ruler, **draw** two lines on a paper plate to make four equal sections as shown in the drawing. This is your pie graph.

2. Look at a map of the world. **Talk with your group** and **estimate** what part of Earth's surface is covered with water—$\frac{1}{4}$, $\frac{1}{2}$, or $\frac{3}{4}$. **Record** your estimate in your *Science Notebook*.

3. Color one or more sections of your pie graph to show your estimate.

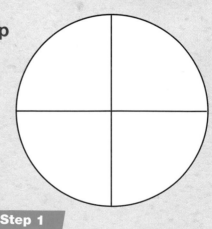

Step 1

4. Now check your estimate. Lay tracing paper over a map of the world and then trace the water and land areas. Cut out the shapes. Write *water* on the pieces that are water and *land* on the pieces that are land.

5. Lay the cutouts of land and water on a table. Think of a way to arrange them to **compare** the amount of water to the amount of land. **Record** how you did it.

Analyze and Conclude

1. Look at all the pie graphs made by your class. What fraction of water do most of the graphs show?

2. **Compare** your estimate with what you found in step 5.

3. **Infer** why Earth is called the water planet.

INVESTIGATE FURTHER!

RESEARCH

What fraction of your state is covered by water? Look at a map to help you make an estimate. Make a pie graph to show your estimate.

Activity
Dry Up!

A carrot is a living thing. Does a carrot have water in it? You'll find out by doing this activity.

Procedure

1. Use a balance to **measure** the mass of a carrot slice. **Record** its mass in your *Science Notebook*.

2. Place the carrot slice in a pie pan.

3. Put the pan in a sunny, dry place for one day.

4. The next day, turn the carrot slice over. Let it remain in the sun for another day.

5. The following day, again **measure** the mass of the carrot slice. **Record** your result.

Step 1

Analyze and Conclude

1. **Compare** the mass of the carrot in steps 1 and 5. What can you **infer** caused the difference?

2. A carrot is a plant. **Make an inference** about whether there is water in other plants. Give reasons for your inference.

3. **Infer** whether there is water in human beings. Explain your reasoning.

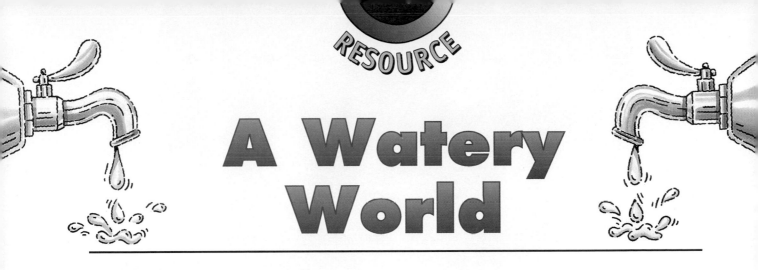

A Watery World

We live in a watery world. Think back to the activity on pages D6 and D7. You found out that Earth is covered by more water than land. In fact, about three fourths of Earth is covered by water.

Water on Earth

Pretend that all the water on Earth could be poured into 100 cups. Of the 100 cups, 97 would be filled with salt water, water that contains salt. Most of this salt is table salt, the kind used to flavor food. The salt comes from rocks and soil carried by rivers and streams into the ocean. Because of the large amount of salt, you'd become sick, or even die, if you drank a lot of sea water. Your body cannot use salt water for its functions.

If 97 of the 100 cups contain salt water, that leaves 3 cups of fresh water. Fresh water is water that people and animals can drink. But of these three cups of water, two are frozen into ice. These two cups of ice represent water frozen in icecaps, glaciers, and icebergs. That leaves only one cup of fresh water for all the living things on Earth to use.

EARTH'S WATER

97 cups salt water

Ice   Liquid

3 cups fresh water

▲ From space, Earth looks blue because of all the water.

Water is the most common substance on Earth. But large bodies of water such as oceans and rivers are not the only places water is found. When you did the activity on page D8, you found out that a carrot has a lot of water in it. In fact, *all* living things contain a large amount of water. Nearly two thirds of your body is water. Look at the drawing below. How much water makes up an elephant, a potato, and a tomato?

Using Water

Like air and soil, water is a natural resource. A **natural resource** is a useful material from Earth. All living things need water to stay alive. A healthy person might live for more than a month without food, but the same person could survive only about three days without water.

While you need water just to survive, you use water in many different ways. Look at the pictures on the next page to see some uses of water.

WATER IN LIVING THINGS

3/4 Water

2/3 Water

4/5 Water

9/10 Water

WATER USES IN THE UNITED STATES

▲ **INDUSTRY** Water is used as a source of power and to make many products. This machine is cooled by water.

HOMES You use water every day. You use water when you bathe, cook, clean, and water plants. ▼

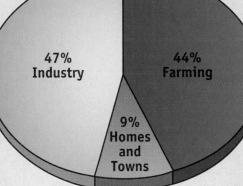

47% Industry

44% Farming

9% Homes and Towns

▲ **FARMING** Water is used for livestock and to grow crops. In dry places, farmers must irrigate their fields.

TOWNS Water is used to put out fires, treat sewage, and clean streets. ▼

━━━━━ **INVESTIGATION 1** ━━━━━

THINK IT WRITE IT

1. Earth is called the water planet, yet finding enough drinking water for everyone on the planet is sometimes a problem. Explain why.

2. Pretend you are a water-use detective. List four ways that people use water. Why is water so important?

HOW DOES NATURE MOVE WATER?

Think about this: If all water runs downhill to the ocean, why doesn't the ocean overflow? You'll find out where the water goes in this investigation.

Activity

Disappearing Act

Water disappears from an uncovered cup. How does temperature affect this change?

MATERIALS

- metric measuring cup
- water
- 2 plastic cups
- grease pencil
- *Science Notebook*

SAFETY

Clean up any spills immediately.

Procedure

Pour 100 mL of water into two plastic cups. Mark the level of the water on each with a grease pencil. Put one cup in a warm place and the other in a cool place. With your group, **predict** in which cup the water level will change the most. **Record** your prediction in your *Science Notebook*. After two days, **record** your observations.

Analyze and Conclude

1. How did the amount of water in the cups differ after two days? **Compare** this to your prediction.

2. **Hypothesize** what happened in this activity.

Activity

Water Ups and Downs

Liquid water disappears from a cup and goes into the air. Find out how you can get the liquid water back again.

Procedure

1. Mold a pan-shaped cover from aluminum foil for a plastic jar. Make sure the cover fits tightly over the jar's opening.

2. Remove the foil cover and place it off to one side.

3. Now have your teacher add hot tap water to the jar until it is one-third full.

4. Put the foil cover back on the jar. Secure the cover with a rubber band. Quickly place a few ice cubes in the foil cover. Watch closely! **Observe** what happens on the underside of the foil. **Record** your observations in your *Science Notebook*.

Step 4

Analyze and Conclude

1. You've **made a model** of Earth. The warm water represents a lake or an ocean. The air above it represents the air around Earth. The air high above Earth is cold. The ice on the foil cover cooled the air higher in the jar. Based on your observations of your model, **hypothesize** how water gets into the air.

2. **Infer** whether water on Earth might go into the air faster during the day or at night. Explain why you think so.

Nature Recycles

What constantly changes yet always stays the same? If you don't know, you're about to find out!

Think back to the last time you had a drink of water. Some of that water could have been the same water a dinosaur drank! The same amount of water has been on Earth for millions of years. But the form, or state, of water is always changing.

States of Matter

Water, like all the things around you, is matter. Air, milk, books—all are matter. And matter exists in one of three basic states—as a liquid, a solid, or a gas.

A **liquid** has no definite shape, but it takes up a definite amount of space. Look at the pictures below. The colored water takes up space, but it doesn't have a particular shape. It takes the shape of the container that holds it. All liquids do this.

A **solid** has a definite shape and takes up a definite amount of space. You know that you can't "pour" a sneaker into a jar. This is because solids can't change shape.

A **gas** is a state of matter that has no definite shape and takes up no definite amount of space. A gas spreads out to fill the container that holds it, and the space a gas takes up varies with the size of the container.

How are liquids and solids different? ▼

You might have seen someone inflating a helium (hē′lē əm) balloon. Helium is a kind of gas. When helium or any gas is released into a balloon, it spreads out and fills the entire balloon, as you can see in the drawing to the right.

Amazing Water

Water is the only substance that can be found in nature as a solid, a liquid, and a gas. How can you change the state of water? Think about the activity on page D12 in which you placed water in a warm place. You saw that it seemed to disappear faster than water in a cooler place. But the water didn't really disappear. It changed state. The water changed from a liquid to a gas. When liquid water changes to a gas, that water is said to **evaporate** (ē vap′ə rāt).

To change the state of water, you have to add or take away heat energy. If you put water in a freezer, the water turns to a solid called ice. The freezer *takes away* heat energy from the water.

When you boil water, you are *adding* heat energy to water. Heating changes liquid water to a gas. When water is a gas, it is called **water vapor**. You can't see water vapor, but there are times when you can feel it. On some warm days in summer, the air seems heavy and wet and your skin feels "sticky." On such days there's a lot of water vapor in the air. When the air feels cool and dry, there is less water vapor in the air.

To change the state of water, you have to add or take away heat energy. ▼

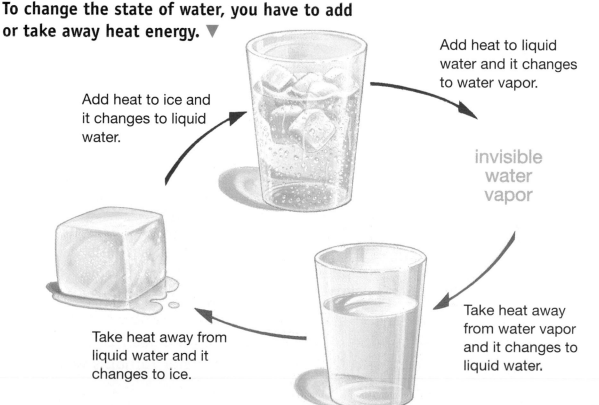

Add heat to ice and it changes to liquid water.

Add heat to liquid water and it changes to water vapor.

invisible water vapor

Take heat away from water vapor and it changes to liquid water.

Take heat away from liquid water and it changes to ice.

THE WATER CYCLE

PRECIPITATION When water drops in clouds get bigger, they become heavy and fall to Earth as rain. If the air is cold enough, the drops may form hail, sleet, or snow. The liquid or solid forms of water that fall to Earth are kinds of **precipitation** (prē sip ə tā′shən).

WATER ON THE GROUND Some water from rainfall soaks into the ground. Some flows downhill and collects in lakes, rivers, and oceans. Some falls directly into these bodies of water.

When you add ice to a glass of lemonade, droplets of water often form on the outside of the glass. Water vapor in the air near the cold glass loses heat energy as the water vapor comes into contact with the cold glass. The water vapor changes to liquid water on the glass. When water vapor changes to liquid water, it is said to **condense**. In the activity on page D13, you saw water condense on the underside of the aluminum foil. How did the ice cubes on top of the foil help water condense?

A Never-Ending Cycle

Remember the riddle that appeared on page D14? It asked, "What constantly changes yet always stays the same?" Do you know the answer yet?

It's water! The "constant changes" referred to in this riddle are changes in the state of water. These changes are part of something called the water cycle. The **water cycle** is the path that water follows as it evaporates into the air, condenses into clouds, and returns to Earth as rain.

Look at the drawing of the water cycle. Why is this path called a cycle? As you look at the picture, read what is happening in the different parts of the water cycle.

You've seen how water constantly changes. Water—that amazing substance—can change from a solid to a liquid to a gas and back again. Yet it always stays the same. No matter how often it changes from one state to another, water remains water.

WATER CONDENSES   When water vapor in the air cools, it condenses back into tiny droplets of liquid water. When there are many droplets together, they form clouds.

WATER EVAPORATES   The sun warms the water. The heat energy causes water to evaporate and rise into the air as invisible water vapor.

SCIENCE IN LITERATURE

CLOUDY WITH A CHANCE OF MEATBALLS
by Judi Barrett
Illustrated by Ron Barrett
Aladdin Books, 1978

What would happen if the water cycle changed into a food cycle? That's exactly what happened to the town of Chewandswallow in Judi Barrett's tall tale *Cloudy With a Chance of Meatballs*.

Instead of rainfalls and snowfalls, Chewandswallow's weather is made up of falling pancakes, milk, and sandwiches. Does that sound great? Read the story and decide if Chewandswallow's weather is the kind that you'd enjoy.

The Salty Problem

SCIENCE TECHNOLOGY & SOCIETY

What if the rain stopped and never fell again? You can imagine how dry everything would be. Suppose rainwater was your only source of fresh water. If it never rained, you would have quite a problem, wouldn't you?

Look at the map. Cape Verde, a group of islands off the western coast of Africa, has had almost no

rain since 1968! That's long before you were born. So where do the people of Cape Verde find fresh water to drink?

Fresh Water From Salt Water

Many islands, like the ones of Cape Verde, often don't have sources of fresh water. But they are surrounded by oceans, which are salt water. You know that people can't drink salt water without becoming ill. But can it be used as a source of fresh water?

Think about the water cycle. When salt water evaporates, only the water changes into water vapor, not the salt. Evaporation of salt water is part of the process of desalination (dē sal ə nā'shən). In desalination, salt is removed from ocean water to produce fresh water. One way this can be done is shown in the drawing on the next page.

It's very costly to desalinate ocean water. It takes a great deal of energy to pump the water through pipes and to heat it. But people who live on islands are happy to have fresh water—even if they must pay a lot in order to have it!

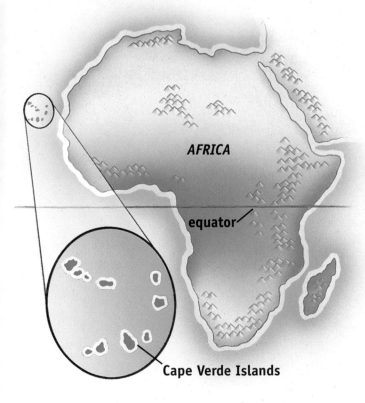

AFRICA

equator

Cape Verde Islands

▲ **Rainfall is scarce in Cape Verde.**

DESALINATION

1 Cold ocean water is pumped through coiled pipes.

2 The ocean water in the pipes goes to a heater, where the water is made very hot.

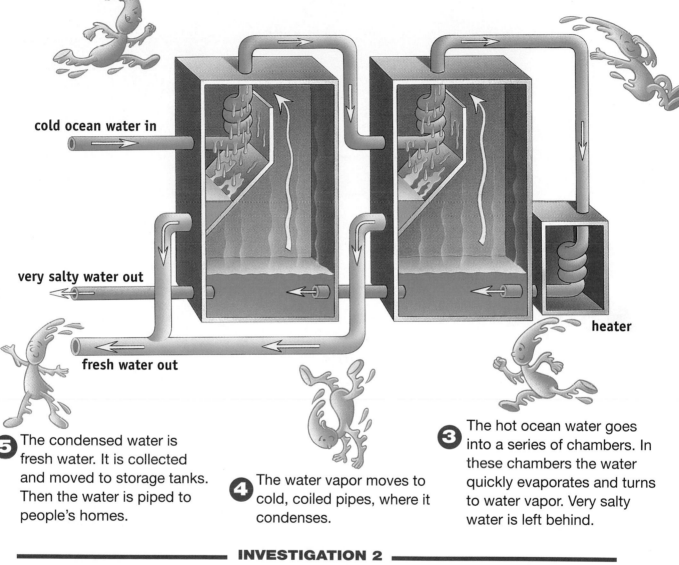

cold ocean water in

very salty water out

fresh water out

heater

5 The condensed water is fresh water. It is collected and moved to storage tanks. Then the water is piped to people's homes.

4 The water vapor moves to cold, coiled pipes, where it condenses.

3 The hot ocean water goes into a series of chambers. In these chambers the water quickly evaporates and turns to water vapor. Very salty water is left behind.

INVESTIGATION 2

1. If water runs downhill to the oceans, why don't oceans overflow?

2. Draw a picture of the water cycle. Then explain the changes a drop of water goes through as it moves through the cycle.

WHERE ARE SOURCES OF FRESH WATER FOUND?

Rain, snow, and other forms of precipitation bring fresh water to Earth. But how do we get fresh water where and when we need it? In this investigation you'll find out.

Activity

Well, Well

In many places the ground holds water like a sponge. In this activity, find out about one way people get that fresh water out of the ground.

- - - - - - - - - - - - - - - -

Procedure

1. Fill a small pie pan nearly to its top with sand.

2. Push a plastic cup, from which the bottom part has been cut off, into the sand. Use a plastic spoon to scoop the sand out of the cup. You've **made a model** of a well.

Step 2

Step 4

3. With your group, **predict** what will happen when you add water to the sand around the cup. **Record** your prediction in your *Science Notebook*.

4. Pour enough water into the sand around the well to soak the sand. Wait about five minutes and then look into your well. **Record** your observations.

Analyze and Conclude

1. In step 4, what did you see in the well?

2. **Infer** where the material in the well came from.

3. If each day you add water to the sand around your well, the sand will stay moist. The water you add is like rain. How does rain affect a well?

4. **Predict** what will happen to your well if it doesn't "rain" for a few days. Explain your prediction. Then **test** it.

INVESTIGATE FURTHER!

EXPERIMENT

Do this activity again, but this time use clay soil or topsoil instead of sand. Describe the results. Infer which of the materials you used works best with a well.

Activity
Soak It Up!

Do all kinds of earth materials hold fresh water equally well? In this activity you'll find out.

Procedure

1. Cover your work area with newspaper. Use the top part of a plastic soda bottle as a funnel. Place a piece of cheesecloth over the opening in the neck of the funnel as shown. Hold the cheesecloth tightly in place with a rubber band.

2. Place the funnel, neck down, in the bottom part of the bottle.

3. Fill the funnel halfway with gravel.

4. Pour 250 mL of water into a measuring cup. Now pour the water into the funnel. Wait one minute.

Step 1

Step 4

5. After one minute, move the funnel to an empty container. Pour the water from the bottom part of the bottle into the empty measuring cup. **Measure** the amount of water that passed through the gravel.

6. Make a chart like the one shown in your *Science Notebook*.

Earth Material	Water That Passed Through in One Minute (in mL)
Gravel	
Sand	
Soil	

7. Record your measurements in the chart. Empty the measuring cup and the funnel, and rinse off the cheesecloth.

8. Talk with your group about your results. **Predict** what will happen if you repeat the activity, first using sand and then using soil. **Record** your predictions.

9. Repeat steps 2 through 5 and step 7 using sand and then soil. **Record** all your measurements in your chart.

Analyze and Conclude

1. Through which material did the water pass the fastest? the slowest? **Compare** your predictions with the results.

2. Which material tested in this activity held water the best? How do you know?

3. From your observations, **infer** what can happen to rainwater when it falls on different kinds of ground.

UNIT PROJECT LINK

Imagine your company has been chosen to design a water system for Waterville, a planned community. What questions will you need to answer before selecting a source of water for the town? Study the brochure on Waterville, then choose a water source for the town.

Bring Water Home

Imagine coming home from school, feeling tired. But before you can rest, you have a chore to do. You have to take a bucket to the town well to bring water home. Most people living in the United States today are lucky—they've never had a reason to do such a chore.

But not all Americans have easy access to water. Every day, people who live in Fox Springs, Alaska, drive to a spring. A spring is a water source where water flows naturally from the ground. People fill containers with the spring water, then drive home. Some people have to drive 16 km (10 mi) every time they need water!

In many villages in Africa, it's easier to get water than it used to be. In the past, people hauled water in buckets or pails from rivers and lakes. Now most villages have wells where people can get fresh water.

▲ Lining up for spring water in Fox Springs, Alaska

▲ Getting water from a well in Mali, in Africa

▲ **Look for the white pipe coming from the roof of this house in Bermuda.**

On islands such as Bermuda, a rainstorm is a welcome event. The roofs of homes are built in such a way that the rainwater is collected. A pipe funnels the water to tanks under the homes. When it doesn't rain much, the people who rely on such systems must buy water.

Tunisia is a country in northern Africa. Parts of Tunisia are in the Sahara, a desert. Some people get their water from wells at an oasis. An oasis is an area in a desert where water is near Earth's surface.

▲ **An oasis in Tunisia, in Africa**

▲ **Burmese women filling water jugs from the Irrawaddy**

The Irrawaddy is a river that flows through central Burma, a country in Southeast Asia. The Irrawaddy supplies people with drinking water. The river water is also used for growing rice. Rice is a very important part of the diet of people in Burma.

More than 2 billion people on Earth do not have a plentiful, nearby source of fresh water. The next time you turn on a faucet, think about how lucky you are. ■

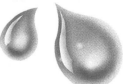

Getting to the Source

▲ **In Chicago, people use water pumped from Lake Michigan.**

You know that the water cycle brings fresh water to Earth in the form of precipitation. But where does rainwater and melting snow go? Rainwater and melting snow flow downhill and collect in rivers and lakes or soak into the ground. This water is the source of fresh water for cities.

On the Waterfront

Some cities are lucky enough to have a natural lake or a moving river nearby. A source of water that already exists on the land, such as a lake or a river, is called **surface water.** Cities that use surface water pump the water out of rivers and lakes, clean it, and send it to homes, schools, and businesses through a network of pipes. Chicago, Illinois; Pittsburgh, Pennsylvania; and St. Louis, Missouri, are cities in the United States that use surface water from nearby lakes and rivers.

Fresh Water From Far Away

Some cities have to go much farther away to find surface-water sources. New York City's water comes from lakes in the Catskill Mountains, more than 160 km (100 mi) away. The water from these lakes is piped to the city through huge tunnels that are as high as a basketball player standing on another player's shoulders!

Storing Surface Water

Some regions have built dams across moving rivers or streams. A dam is a barrier that stretches across a river or stream and blocks the water's movement. The place behind the dam where the water collects and is stored is called a **reservoir** (rez'ər vwär). The water collected in reservoirs by dams on the Colorado River is one source from which Los Angeles, California, gets its water. Phoenix, Arizona, also depends on this river for its fresh water.

Digging Deep

If there is no surface water nearby, people look underground. Water that soaks into the ground and fills the spaces between soil and rocks is called **ground water**. Remember how well earth materials held water

▲ The Glen Canyon Dam holds back surface water, forming Lake Powell.

in the activity on pages D22 and D23. An underground layer of rock where ground water collects is called an **aquifer** (ak'wə fər). Aquifers are important sources of water.

People drill wells into aquifers to obtain water. ▼

well

aquifer

To get water out of an aquifer, people often dig a well. A well is a deep, narrow hole that is dug into the ground, down to the level of ground water. You saw in the activity on pages D20 and D21 how a well works. Wells work because water will flow from soaked soil into holes. Sometimes electric pumps or windmills are used to pump water up the well. Miami, Florida; Honolulu, Hawaii; San Antonio, Texas; and Mexico City, Mexico, have dug wells into aquifers to get fresh water.

Some cities don't have surface fresh water or ground-water aquifers nearby. Santa Barbara, California, is one such city. Santa Barbara gets its supply of fresh water by desalinating water from the Pacific Ocean.

Which one of the sources of fresh water you've learned about is the source your city or town uses? See if you can get to the source. ■

▲ **A windmill can be used to pump ground water from an aquifer.**

INVESTIGATION 3

1. Describe three different ways in which towns and cities can get water for their people to use.

2. Imagine you are in charge of finding a water supply for your town. You live in an area that gets lots of rain, but there are no surface-water supplies nearby. Describe and draw a picture of what you would do to get water flowing to your town.

REFLECT & EVALUATE

WORD POWER

aquifer
condense
evaporate
gas
ground water
liquid
natural resource

precipitation
reservoir
solid
surface water
water cycle
water vapor

 On Your Own
Review the terms in the list. Then use as many terms as you can in a paragraph about how water changes states.

With a Partner
Use the terms in the list to make a word-search puzzle. See if your partner can find the hidden terms and tell you what each one means.

BUILD YOUR PORTFOLIO

Make a list of all the different ways that you use water. Then find or draw pictures of these ways and use them to make a poster.

Analyze Information

Study the drawing. Then describe how water moves through the water cycle.

Assess Performance

Design and carry out an experiment to find out how different sizes of containers affect evaporation. What do the results tell you about evaporation?

Problem Solving

1. Imagine that you're stranded at sea without drinking water. Suddenly a piece of an iceberg floats by. Explain why you should or shouldn't melt the ice for drinking water.

2. Imagine it's a cold day and water is boiling on your stove. Then you notice water droplets on the inside of the windows in the kitchen. Explain how the water got there.

3. You have a garden in a place where the soil is sandy and tends to dry out quickly. How can you make the soil better for a garden?

CHAPTER 2

WONDERS OF WATER

Have you ever cooled off under an open fire hydrant or a lawn sprinkler? Where does the water come from? How does water move through pipes? Next time you cool off under a sprinkler, think about how the water moved from its source to you.

• •

Rushing, Gushing Water!

OPEN HYDRANT

Water rushes up
and gushes,
cooling summer's sizzle.
In a sudden whoosh
it rushes,
not a little drizzle.
First a hush and down
it crashes,
over curbs it swishes.
Just a luscious waterfall
for
cooling city fishes.
—Marci Ridlon

In Chapter 2 you'll discover some of the wonders of water. You'll even find out how water gets to all the fire hydrants in town!

WHAT HAPPENS TO WATER IN PIPES?

What makes the water flow from a faucet? What might cause the water to trickle out? Find out what keeps the water flowing in your home and when water pipes might need to be fixed.

Activity
The Pressure's On

What makes water flow out of faucets? Something must be pushing it out. You'll find out what's pushing the water in this activity.

MATERIALS

- masking tape
- empty milk carton (1-pint) with three holes at different heights
- water
- large baking pan
- *Science Notebook*

SAFETY

Clean up any spills immediately.

Procedure

1. Place a piece of masking tape over three holes that have been made at the bottom of an empty milk carton.

2. Fill the carton with water and place it in a large baking pan.

3. **Talk** with members of your group and **predict** with them what will happen at each hole when the tape is removed. **Record** your predictions in your *Science Notebook*.

Step 1

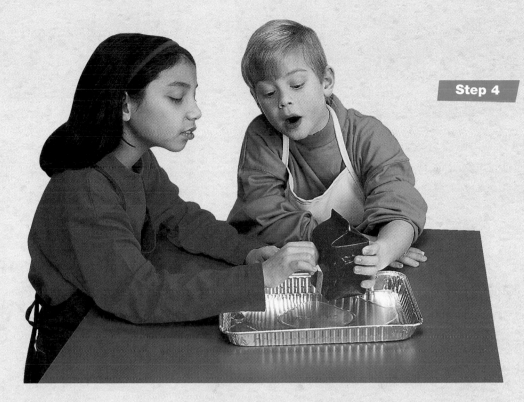

4. Have a partner hold the carton over the pan. Then peel back the tape from the side so that it uncovers all the holes at the same time. **Observe** each hole. **Record** your observations. **Compare** your predictions with your observations.

Analyze and Conclude

1. How are the streams of water different as they come from the holes?

2. **Hypothesize** what makes the water come out of the holes differently.

3. Imagine that your milk carton is a model of an apartment building. Each of the three holes is at a different floor. Suppose all the water faucets in an apartment building were turned on at the same time. From your observations, **infer** what the water flow would be like on each floor.

INVESTIGATE FURTHER!

EXPERIMENT

When a fire hydrant is opened, the water comes out with great force. Work outside with a partner. Using the materials in this activity, try to increase the distance a stream of water can reach. What did you do to increase the distance?

Activity
Tower Power

A water tower stores water for homes and businesses. Do this activity to see how a water tower affects the flow of water in pipes.

MATERIALS
- funnel
- plastic tubing
- masking tape
- pin
- metric ruler
- baking pan
- water
- *Science Notebook*

SAFETY
Clean up any spills immediately.

Procedure

1. Push a funnel into one end of a length of plastic tubing. You have **made a model** of a water tower.

2. Cover the other end of the tubing with masking tape. Wrap the tape around the tubing a few times to make sure no water can get out.

3. Carefully use a pin to make a small hole in the tape, as shown.

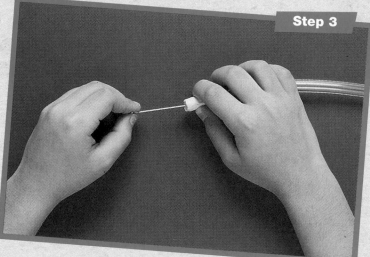
Step 3

4. **Talk with your group** and together **predict** what will happen when water is poured into the funnel. **Record** your prediction in your *Science Notebook*.

5. Hold the taped end of the tube about 30 cm above the funnel. Work over a pan or a sink.

6. Have a partner pour water into the funnel. At the same time, slowly lower and then raise the funnel. **Observe** how the water flows out of the pinhole in the taped end of the tubing. **Record** your observations.

Analyze and Conclude

1. How did your prediction compare with the result?

2. What did you do to make the water flow faster? What can you **infer** about the height of the model water tower and its effect on the rate of water flow?

3. **Hypothesize** why real water towers are sometimes placed on the roofs of buildings.

UNIT PROJECT LINK

How will water travel from its source to homes and businesses in Waterville? How will the water be cleaned so that it's safe to drink? Study the map of Waterville and the surrounding area. Then design a system to clean and transport water to the town. Construct a simple model to show the town's water system. Show how the water will get to homes and other places that use water.

Under a Lot of Pressure

The diver in the picture below is deep in the ocean. Why must a diving suit be worn? You may think it's so the diver can get air, but the main reason is to keep the diver from getting crushed by the water!

The water around the diver is pushing on the diver. In fact, the water is pushing on everything in the ocean. This pushing of water on a surface is called **water pressure**.

Putting on the Pressure

The amount of pressure on divers depends on how much water is above them. The deeper they dive, the more water pressure there is because there is more weight of water above them.

Imagine that you've placed your hand flat on your desk. Then someone puts a book on your hand. You would feel pressure. If more books were added, you'd feel more pressure because there was more weight. This happens because of gravity (grav´i tē). **Gravity** is a pull that every object has on other objects. As Earth's gravity pulls down on the book, the book puts pressure on

A diving suit protects this deep-sea diver from water pressure. ▼

your hand. In the same way, as Earth's gravity pulls down on the water, the water puts pressure on a diver.

You don't need a deep ocean to have water pressure. Any liquid puts pressure on the container it's in. Think back to the activity on pages D32 and D33 in which you watched water come out of three holes in a carton. The water pressure at the bottom of the carton was greater than the water pressure nearer the top. The greater pressure caused the water to come out of the bottom hole with greater force and at a faster rate than the water coming out of the holes above it.

Water Goes to Town

Has someone in your home ever run water or flushed a toilet while you were taking a shower? Did you feel the flow of water change? This happened because the water pressure in the pipes dropped, or became less. How does water under pressure get to your home?

You learned that towns and cities have different water sources. In some towns water is pumped under pressure through pipes to homes. In other towns water is pumped to a water tower and gravity is used to keep water flowing under pressure to homes. Read the steps on the next two pages to see how water is moved.

SCIENCE IN LITERATURE

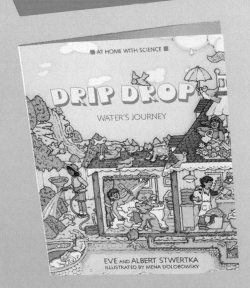

DRIP DROP
WATER'S JOURNEY
by Eve and Albert Stwertka
Illustrated by Mena Dolobowsky
Julian Messner, 1991

If you've been taking water for granted, or even if you haven't, you should read *Drip Drop* by Eve and Albert Stwertka. It's a book full of real science about the journey that water makes to reach your home. It's also a book in which cats and dogs have lots to say!

Read about pumps and pressure on pages 16–17. Then get an adult's permission to make the milk carton pump shown on page 16. It will help you understand how air can force water to rise up in pipes from underground.

HOW WATER IS MOVED TO HOMES

water source

1

pump house

2

water treatment plant

3

pumping station

1 First the water company must pump water out of a water source.

2 Then the water goes to a treatment plant to be cleaned. After the water is cleaned, it goes to a pumping station.

3 The pumping station pumps the water under pressure to large water pipes, or water mains. The large water mains have been placed beneath the streets of a town. In some towns, the water is pumped to a water tower.

fire hydrant

water main

high-pressure water pipe

Breaking Under Pressure

Water mains carry a lot of water under pressure. Sometimes water mains leak or break open. Perhaps you've seen water squirt out through a break in a hose. When a water main breaks, the same thing happens. Water leaks out, sometimes flooding roads and basements, and always wasting water. Buildings affected by the leaky water mains will have low water pressure or even no water at all.

The people who work at water companies know that pipes some-

times break. So they put valves in the pipes. A valve is used to stop the flow of water in a pipe. When you turn the water on in your home, you open a small valve. When you turn the water off, you close the valve. The valves in a water main work in the same way, but they are much larger than those in a faucet.

An Icy Problem

In very cold weather, the water flowing through pipes can freeze. Water expands, or gets larger, as it freezes. As it freezes and expands,

4 Running alongside the water mains are smaller pipes. These pipes lead to fire hydrants. In these pipes the pressure is even higher than it is in the water mains. This is why water comes gushing out of a fire hydrant with great force when it is opened.

high-pressure water pipe

4

valve

5 Water mains also branch off into smaller pipes, called submains, which lead to every street. Still smaller pipes branch off to every building.

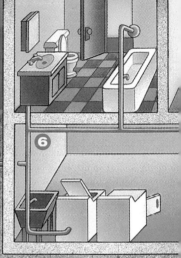

6

5 — submain

6 In buildings, more pipes branch off to every sink, tub, and toilet.

the water pushes outward against the pipes. The pressure of water that freezes in a pipe can cause the pipe to break.

The people who plan water systems know how far down in the ground the soil freezes in winter. They make sure that as many water pipes as possible are buried below that level. That way there is less danger of having the water freeze and break the pipes. ■

INVESTIGATION 1

THINK IT WRITE IT

1. Explain how a water tower works to keep water flowing.

2. Pretend you work for the water company in your town. People are complaining that they have no water pressure. Describe two different things that could be causing the problem.

HOW DOES DRINKING WATER VARY?

Selling bottled drinking water is a big business. There's lots of money to be made if a company can convince people that its bottled water is better than everyone else's. Isn't all water the same? Find out in this investigation.

Activity

Water Taste-Test

Does water from different sources taste different? Take the taste-test to find out.

MATERIALS
- marker
- small paper cups
- 3 water samples in 3 bottles, marked A, B, and C.
- *Science Notebook*

SAFETY /////

Clean up any spills immediately.

Procedure

1. Use a marker to write a different letter—*A*, *B*, or *C*—on each of three paper cups. Each person in your group should have his or her own set of cups.

2. Your teacher has prepared three bottles of water. Pour a small sample of water from bottle *A* into your cup *A*. Do the same with the other two samples, using cups *B* and *C*.

Step 2

3. Take a small sip of each sample.

4. With your group **rank** the samples 1, 2, 3, using 1 for the water sample you liked best, and so on. Keep sipping until you all agree. **Record** your group's ranking in your *Science Notebook*.

Analyze and Conclude

1. **Compare** your group's ranking with the rankings of other groups. Did most groups agree with your choices, or did they disagree?

2. **Tally** the results from your class. Which sample got the most first-place votes?

3. What can you **infer** about the source of each water sample? Do you think the samples came from the same source or from different sources? Explain your inferences.

4. Find out from your teacher where each water sample came from. Do the results surprise you? If so, explain why.

Activity

Hard and Soft Water

In this activity you'll find out how hard water and soft water differ.

Procedure

1. Label a vial *hard water*. Put 10 mL of hard water into it. Add one drop of dish soap. Put the lid on.

2. Label a second vial *soft water*. Put 10 mL of soft water into it. Add one drop of dish soap. Put the lid on.

3. **Predict** which vial will have the most suds after being shaken. **Record** your prediction in your *Science Notebook*.

4. Shake both vials back and forth the same number of times. **Observe** each vial and **record** your observations.

Step 4

Analyze and Conclude

1. What did you observe about hard water and soft water? How did your prediction compare with the results?

2. A water softener can change hard water into soft water. **Infer** why people sometimes buy water softeners for their homes.

3. Repeat this activity with a water sample from home. Do you have hard water or soft water?

A Matter of Taste

"Why does Grandma's water taste so different from our water?" asked Alisha.

"I don't know," said Mark. "Maybe Grandma flavors her water!"

Of course, Grandma doesn't flavor her water. But does Grandma's water really taste different?

No Taste

Most people think water has no taste, but it does. If you tasted water samples from many different places, you would find out that water from each region has its own flavor.

The taste of water depends on the chemicals (kem'i kəlz) and minerals (min'ər əlz) found in the water. Chemicals are added to water at treatment plants to kill germs. One chemical, called chlorine (klôr'ēn), not only kills germs but can also add a taste and smell to water. Drinking water that has a lot of chlorine in it may smell and taste like the water in a swimming pool.

D43

▲ **Streams dissolve lots of minerals.**

Having a Hard Time

Minerals in water come from the soil and rocks over which water passes. Moving water dissolves (di zälvz′) these minerals. When minerals **dissolve**, they mix with water and separate into very tiny parts that cannot be seen. Have you ever mixed sugar with water? As you stir the mixture, the sugar dissolves and you can no longer see it. Water dissolves minerals in much the same way. Even though we can't see these minerals, we can taste them.

When water contains large amounts of dissolved minerals, that water is called **hard water**. It's difficult to get things clean with hard water. That's because the minerals in hard water keep soap from dissolving easily. Recall that hard water made less suds in the activity on page D42. Other minerals in hard water—iron and copper, for example—produce stains. Hard water can stain clothing, sinks, and tubs.

Making It Soft

Water containing few minerals is called **soft water**. In some towns, the minerals are removed before the water reaches people's homes. In other towns, households treat their own water to remove the minerals before they use the water.

If water did not have any minerals, chemicals, or air in it, the water would be flat, or tasteless. **Distilled water** is water without any minerals or chemicals in it. It is pure water.

▲ **Dissolved minerals in water can leave stains in a sink.**

▲ **Water must be clean, clear, free of odors, and must taste good.**

Distilled water is made by evaporating water to separate it from minerals and chemicals. The water vapor is then condensed. Recall how the distilled water tasted in the activity on pages D40 and D41. Water companies hire people to taste water before it's sold to towns and cities. If the water doesn't have a good taste, what do you think the water companies do? They add some more chemicals and minerals to the water!

Water in different regions of the country will have different tastes, depending on the minerals and chemicals in the water. That's why water may have a different taste at Grandma's house than it does at yours. ■

INVESTIGATION 2

1. A cousin visits you from another town. She says your water tastes different from hers. Explain to her why this may be so.

2. Water that has no minerals and chemicals tastes as bad as water that has too many minerals and chemicals. Explain what this means.

WHAT THINGS IN WATER CAN BE HARMFUL?

What kinds of harmful things are in fresh water? How can water be made safe for drinking? You'll investigate these questions and find their answers.

Activity

Let's Clear This Up

Freshwater sources have soil, rocks, twigs, and other unwanted items in them. Find out how filtering water is an important step in cleaning water.

MATERIALS

- goggles
- plastic soda bottle, cut in half
- cheesecloth
- rubber band
- fine gravel
- sand
- plastic jar with lid
- spoon
- soil, twigs, leaves
- water
- *Science Notebook*

SAFETY

Wear goggles during this activity. Do not taste any materials used in this activity.

Procedure

1. **Make a model** of a water-filtering system. Use the top part of a plastic soda bottle as a funnel. With a group member, use a rubber band to attach a piece of cheesecloth to the end of the funnel.

2. Set the funnel in the bottom part of the bottle. Put a layer of fine gravel into the funnel. Then add a layer of sand over the gravel. The materials in the funnel are part of your filtering system.

Step 2

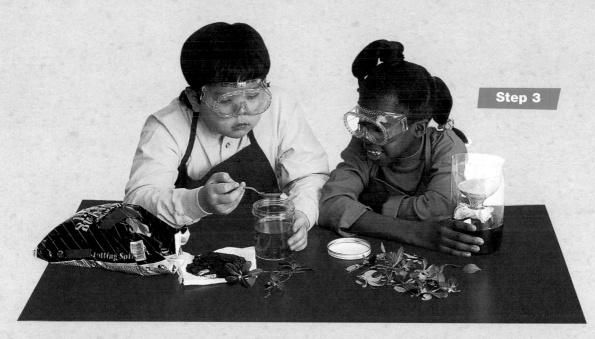

Step 3

3. Pour water into a plastic jar until it is three-fourths full. Add two spoonfuls of soil and a few twigs and leaves to the water. Screw the lid tightly on the jar. Shake up the mixture to make muddy water. This mixture is like the water that may be in a reservoir or river.

4. Talk with your group and **predict** what you will see if you pour the muddy water through the filter. **Record** your prediction in your *Science Notebook*.

5. Slowly pour the jar of muddy water through the filtering system in the funnel. **Observe** the material that passes through the funnel into the base of the plastic bottle. **Record** your observations.

Analyze and Conclude

1. **Compare** your prediction with your results.

2. Filtering is one step in making surface water safe for use in homes. **Hypothesize** how filtering changes muddy water.

3. How is what happens to the muddy water in your model of a water-filtering system like what happens to rainwater when it falls on the ground?

INVESTIGATE FURTHER!

EXPERIMENT

What other materials do you think could be used to filter water? Do this activity again using different materials in your funnel. See how clean you can make the water. **Caution:** Do not drink your filtered water. Share your results with your class.

Activity

Not As Clear As It Looks

Water may contain many living things. In this activity, you'll see why clear water may not be clean water.

- -

Procedure

1. Use a grease pencil to label a clear plastic cup *Tap Water*. Pour 50 mL of tap water into the cup. Label a second cup *Aquarium Water*. Pour 50 mL of aquarium water into this cup.

2. Fertilizer is food for living things. **Talk with your group** and **predict** what will happen to the water if you put fertilizer into each cup. **Record** your prediction in your *Science Notebook*.

3. Use a dropper to place 20 drops of liquid fertilizer into each cup, cover with clear plastic wrap, and secure with a rubber band. Place the cups in a window.

4. After two days, **observe** the water in each cup with a hand lens. **Record** your observations.

Step 3

Analyze and Conclude

1. What did you observe in each cup? How did your prediction compare with your results?

2. Changes to the water occurred because of the presence of tiny living things. **Infer** why they might be present in one cup but not the other.

MATERIALS

- goggles
- grease pencil
- 2 clear plastic cups
- metric measuring cup
- aquarium water
- tap water
- liquid fertilizer
- dropper
- clear plastic wrap
- 2 rubber bands
- hand lens
- *Science Notebook*

SAFETY

Wear goggles during this activity. Clean up any spills immediately. Wash your hands when you have finished this activity.

Wee Beasties!

 They're everywhere and they're multiplying! What are they? They're germs! But what are germs? People use the word **germ** when they're talking about tiny living things that can make them sick.

These protists are shown about 100 times larger than they actually are. ▼

Germs Everywhere

There are different kinds of germs. One group of germs includes protists (prōt'ists). Protists are neither animals nor plants, but they are alive. Many kinds of protists live in water and wet soil.

Another group of germs includes bacteria (bak tir'ē ə). Bacteria are neither animals nor plants. Bacteria live in soil, air, and water.

Protists are so small that they can't be seen with just the eyes. But bacteria are even smaller. About 500 bacteria could fit inside one protist! Fifty million bacteria could live in a single drop of pond water!

Anton's Discovery

If germs are too small to see, how have people learned about them? To find the answer, you need to know what happened more than 300 years ago. That is when "wee beasties" were discovered.

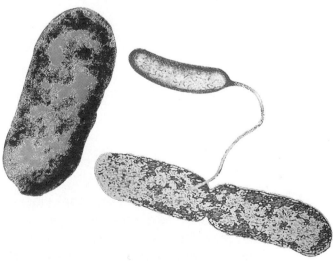

▲ **These bacteria are shown about 10,000 times larger than they actually are.**

In the second half of the 1600s, a young man named Anton van Leeuwenhoek lived in Holland. Anton was interested in improving microscopes (mī'krə skōps). A microscope is a device that has lenses that make very small things look bigger than they really are. Anton looked at many things through his microscopes.

One day, Anton looked at a drop of lake water through a microscope. He saw many tiny things moving around in the water. He called them "wee beasties" because they looked like little animals to him.

What a Treat

Today we know that the tiny living things Anton saw were *not* animals.

WATER TREATMENT PLANT

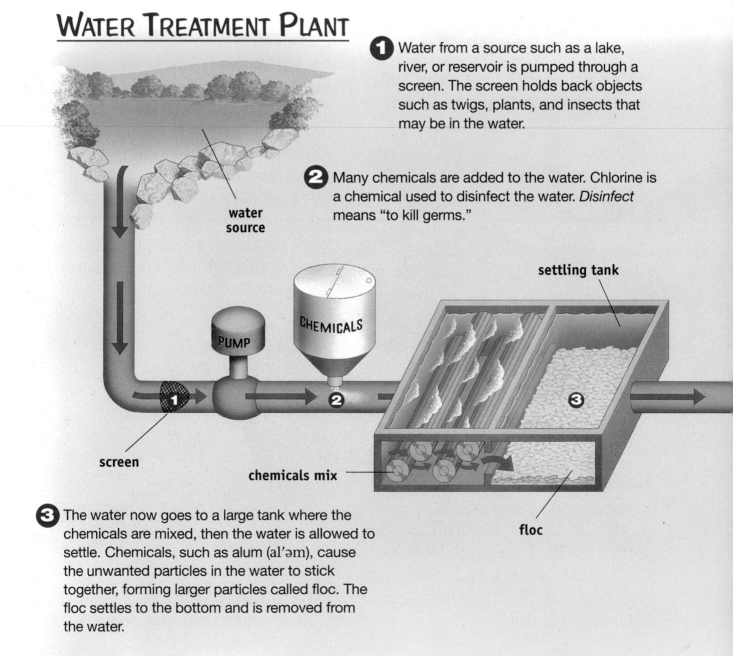

1 Water from a source such as a lake, river, or reservoir is pumped through a screen. The screen holds back objects such as twigs, plants, and insects that may be in the water.

2 Many chemicals are added to the water. Chlorine is a chemical used to disinfect the water. *Disinfect* means "to kill germs."

water source

settling tank

CHEMICALS

PUMP

screen

chemicals mix

floc

3 The water now goes to a large tank where the chemicals are mixed, then the water is allowed to settle. Chemicals, such as alum (al'əm), cause the unwanted particles in the water to stick together, forming larger particles called floc. The floc settles to the bottom and is removed from the water.

We know they were protists. We also know that protists and bacteria that live in fresh water can be harmful to people by causing illness.

Other unwanted living things in fresh water include algae (al'jē). Think back to the activity you did on page D48. After you added fertilizer to water, tiny living things grew and multiplied. These living things were algae.

To make fresh water safe for people to use, the water must first be filtered. After filtering, the water must be treated to kill unwanted, harmful living things. These things are done in a water treatment plant. Follow the steps in the process of water being filtered and disinfected (dis in fek'tid) at a water treatment plant in the drawing below.

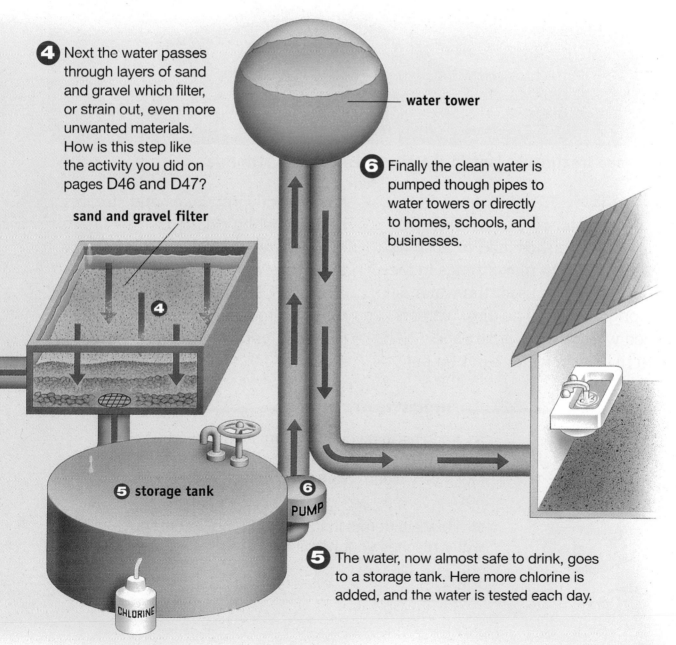

4 Next the water passes through layers of sand and gravel which filter, or strain out, even more unwanted materials. How is this step like the activity you did on pages D46 and D47?

sand and gravel filter

4

water tower

6 Finally the clean water is pumped though pipes to water towers or directly to homes, schools, and businesses.

5 storage tank

6 PUMP

CHLORINE

5 The water, now almost safe to drink, goes to a storage tank. Here more chlorine is added, and the water is tested each day.

▲ **Sewage treatment plant in the city of Palo Alto, California**

Waste Not, Want Not

Clean water is used to wash people, clothes, dishes, and to flush toilets. It is used to make things in factories. After it is used, the water is no longer clean. The dirty water is called waste water, or sewage (sōo'ij). Waste water can't be put back directly into lakes and streams. It must first be cleaned.

Waste water is cleaned in much the same way as drinking water is cleaned. Cleaned waste water can be returned to lakes and rivers, where it becomes part of the water cycle again. ■

=== **INVESTIGATION 3** ===

1. Imagine that you are hiking in the woods. You are very thirsty, and the water in a nearby pond looks very clean. Would you drink it? Why or why not?

2. How are germs in the water killed before the water reaches your home?

REFLECT & EVALUATE

WORD POWER

dissolve
distilled water
germ
gravity
hard water
soft water
water pressure

On Your Own
Review the terms in the list. Then write one new thing you learned about each term.

With a Partner
Write each term in the list on one side of an index card and the definition on the other side. Use the cards to quiz your partner.

Make a drawing to show how water moves through pipes to get to your bathroom sink. Show all the valves. Is there a main valve that can stop all the water coming into your home? Show it, too.

Analyze Information

Study the drawing. Two cracks have formed in the water tower. Compare how water will flow out of crack X and crack Y. Explain why the water might flow differently from each crack.

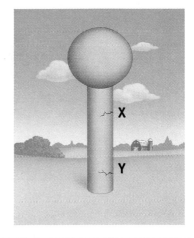

Assess Performance

Design an experiment to find out if the width of a water pipe can change the pressure of the water coming out of the pipe. After your teacher has reviewed your plan, carry out your experiment. Compare your results with those of others.

Problem Solving

1. Imagine you turned on your water faucet and only drips came out. List all the things that could be causing the problem. What could you do to solve the problem?

2. You are a water quality engineer at a water treatment plant. One day the water has an unpleasant taste. Explain what could have happened and what you would do.

3. Sometimes during a flood, people are advised to boil water before they drink it. Why does boiling the water makes it safer to drink?

CHAPTER 3

CARING FOR OUR WATER

"When the well's dry, we know the worth of water."
—Benjamin Franklin
Franklin said that more than 200 years ago.
Today, the need for clean water is greater than ever.
In this chapter you'll find out why it's important to protect
fresh water all over the world.

Saving Lake Victoria

Peter Ochumba is a scientist who studies East Africa's Lake Victoria. He takes water samples and gathers information about the living things in the lake. He also keeps track of activities near the lake that might affect the water.

Ochumba has found that fertilizers, pesticides, and wastes from factories have changed the lake. It has become murky and some fish have died.

Think about Lake Victoria as you explore the investigations in this chapter. Look for changes that might be made to bring the lake back to life.

◄ Peter Ochumba,
African scientist

D55

WHAT CAN HAPPEN TO CLEAN WATER?

Suppose you are very thirsty. You go to the water fountain and see a sign that says "Water Is Unsafe. Do Not Drink!" What can happen to clean water to make it unsafe to drink? In this investigation, you'll find out.

Activity

Not-So-Gentle Rain

When fuels are burned, substances can go into the air and change clean rainwater to acid rain. Find out how acid rain affects living things.

MATERIALS

- goggles
- 2 paper cups
- grease pencil
- pencil
- potting soil
- 20 radish seeds
- metric ruler
- dropper
- water
- dropper bottle with vinegar
- *Science Notebook*

SAFETY

Wear goggles during this activity. Clean up any spills immediately. Wash your hands when you have finished handling soil.

Procedure

1. Label one paper cup *Tap Water* and another paper cup *Acid Rain*. Use a pencil point to poke a hole in the bottom of each cup.

2. Add soil to both cups until they are three-fourths full. Drop 10 radish seeds onto the soil in each cup. Lightly cover the seeds with 1 cm of soil.

Step 2

3. Use a dropper to add plain tap water to the seeds in the cup labeled *Tap Water* to dampen the soil. Add the same number of drops of vinegar, an acid, to the seeds in the cup labeled *Acid Rain*.

Step 3

4. With your group, **predict** what will happen to the seeds in each cup. Explain why. **Record** your prediction in your *Science Notebook*.

5. Moisten your seeds whenever the soil feels dry. *Use the correct kind of liquid for each cup.*

6. **Observe** your seeds every day for two weeks. **Record** your observations. After two weeks, **compare** your observations to your predictions.

Analyze and Conclude

1. Did the seeds sprout in each cup? If so, in which cup did the seedlings grow best? **Hypothesize** what caused the differences.

2. **Hypothesize** how acid rain might affect the plants on which it falls.

INVESTIGATE FURTHER!

RESEARCH

Find out how much acid rain plants can be watered with and still grow. Set up another experiment, using week-old plants. Share your results with your classmates.

Water Worries

You have been hired to solve the mystery of a polluted (pə lo͞ot'əd) river. A body of water that is **polluted** contains unwanted or harmful materials. Find out where the harmful materials, called pollutants, are coming from. How many ways are pollutants getting into the river?

SCHOOL

FERTILIZER

DUMP

SEPTIC TANK

How many of these causes of river pollution did you find?

FARMING CHEMICALS A farmer has been using fertilizers to grow better crops. The farmer has also been using chemicals to kill weeds and insects. When it rains, these materials are carried by the rain into the river.

FACTORY WASTES What happens to the waste water coming from the factory? Notice the smoke coming from the chimneys. Smoke can combine with moisture in the air to form **acid rain**. Recall what happened to plant growth in the activity on pages D56 and D57. What might happen to plants and animals in the river if acid rain falls into it?

YARD CHEMICALS Find the family doing yardwork. Fertilizers and chemicals used to kill insects and weeds can mix with rainwater and seep into the river.

LEAKING GAS TANK There's an old gas station, no longer in business, next to the factory. Gasoline is leaking from the underground tank that is cracked. Where will the gasoline go?

LEAKING SEPTIC TANK The school has an old septic tank buried underground. Septic tanks are containers that hold waste water from sinks and toilets. Old septic tanks often crack and leak. When they do, the waste water moves through the soil to the river.

OIL CHANGE Find the person changing the oil in a truck. If the oil is poured on the ground or down a drain, it will seep into the river.

TOWN DUMP Look at the town dump. Trash from the town is dumped into a hole in the ground. When it rains, the rainwater mixes with substances, such as battery acids, paints, and cleaners, in the trash. This polluted rainwater also flows into the river.

Salty-Water Worries

The pollution of rivers is only one of our "water worries." Oceans get polluted, too. People once thought that the oceans were so big that sewage or trash dumped into them wouldn't hurt them. But these things *have* harmed the oceans.

In the past, trash and sewage were hauled to and dumped into the oceans. It is now against the law in the United States to dump waste in the oceans. But trash and sewage are still dumped into oceans in many parts of the world.

Scientists have studied the oceans and found that sewage was the worst pollutant. Next came plastics, oil, and chemicals from factories and farms. These pollutants often flowed into rivers first, then they flowed out to the ocean. But these pollutants often washed back up on shore, making swimming at some beaches dangerous.

Over the years, many laws have been passed to prevent dumping of pollutants into rivers, lakes, and oceans. These bodies of water are much cleaner today than they were even a few years ago.

Running Dry

Cleaning up water pollution isn't our only water worry. Having

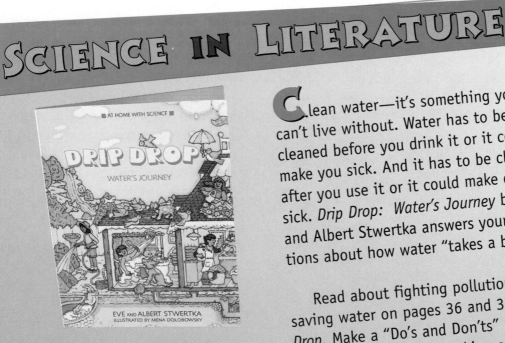

SCIENCE IN LITERATURE

DRIP DROP
WATER'S JOURNEY
by Eve and Albert Stwertka
Illustrated by Mena Dolobowsky
Julian Messner, 1991

Clean water—it's something you can't live without. Water has to be cleaned before you drink it or it could make you sick. And it has to be cleaned after you use it or it could make others sick. *Drip Drop: Water's Journey* by Eve and Albert Stwertka answers your questions about how water "takes a bath."

Read about fighting pollution and saving water on pages 36 and 37 of *Drip Drop*. Make a "Do's and Don'ts" poster to spread the word about taking care of Earth's water.

enough fresh water for everyone is also a worry. Will there always be enough water for all the ways people need water?

The worry about running out of water is very real in some parts of the United States. People who use water from the Ogallala Aquifer, shown below, are especially worried. Scientists estimate that the water remaining in the aquifer will last only about 40 more years. In the south-western corner of Kansas, the aquifer level has dropped about 60 m (200 ft) in the last 45 years. Plans to save water must be put into place now if there is to be fresh water in the future.

In Beijing, China, the ground-water level is dropping at such a fast rate that one third of the city's wells have gone dry. Two hundred major cities in China have water shortages.

▲ **In Rajasthan, India, drinking water is often scarce.**

During dry seasons, Madras, India, opens only one public water tap. To save water, the city opens the tap only between 4 A.M. and 6 A.M.

Water shouldn't be taken for granted. It should be treated as the valuable natural resource that it is. If we keep water supplies clean and use water wisely, we can have a future that is free from water worries. ■

Does the Ogallala Aquifer supply your state with water? ▼

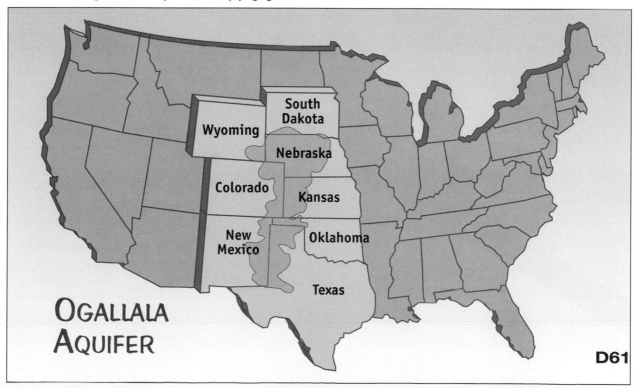

South Dakota

Wyoming

Nebraska

Colorado

Kansas

New Mexico

Oklahoma

Texas

OGALLALA AQUIFER

Industrial-Revolution
Pollution

Since people first lived in communities, they have been polluting their environment. But pollution has become much more serious in modern times. That's because there are so many more people on Earth today than ever before.

The time line shows some events of the past that have made people's lives easier. It also presents some of the harmful effects that these events have led to, such as water pollution. As you read the time line, look for things that people have done to stop pollution.

First Clean Water Act is passed by Congress. Cleanup of lakes and rivers begin.
1948

Thomas A. Edison invents the electric light bulb. Electricity is produced by burning coal and fuel oil. More air pollution and acid rain result.
1879

Industrial Revolution begins in England, moves to America. New machines are invented and many factories are built. The machines burn coal that pollutes the air, causing acid rain. More people move to cities, so more sewage and trash are released into rivers.
1750

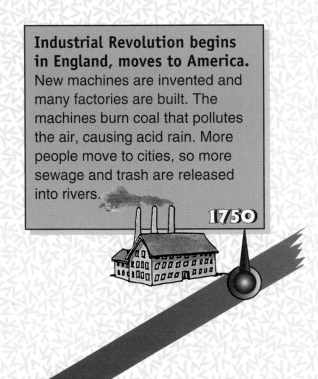

1859
E.L. Drake drills the first oil well in Pennsylvania. Oil is later refined to make products such as gasoline. When burned, gasoline puts pollutants into the air.

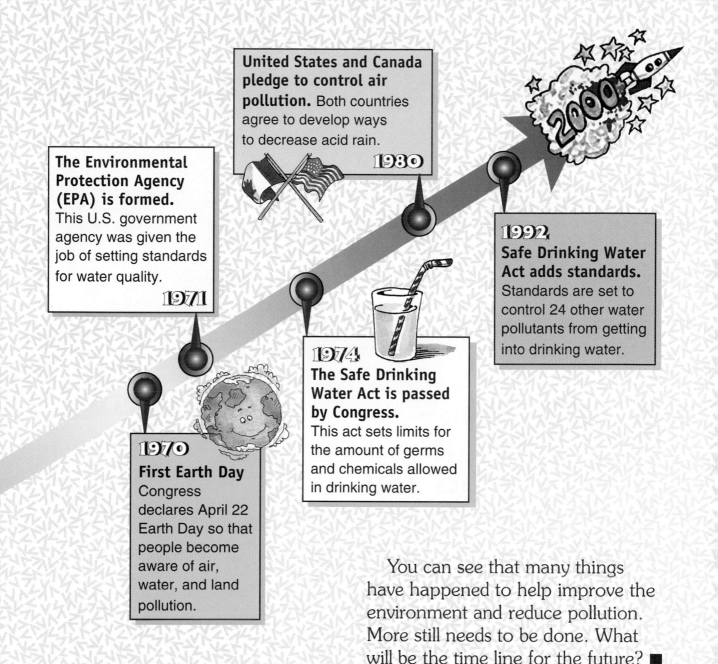

The Environmental Protection Agency (EPA) is formed. This U.S. government agency was given the job of setting standards for water quality.

1971

United States and Canada pledge to control air pollution. Both countries agree to develop ways to decrease acid rain.

1980

1992
Safe Drinking Water Act adds standards. Standards are set to control 24 other water pollutants from getting into drinking water.

1970
First Earth Day Congress declares April 22 Earth Day so that people become aware of air, water, and land pollution.

1974
The Safe Drinking Water Act is passed by Congress. This act sets limits for the amount of germs and chemicals allowed in drinking water.

You can see that many things have happened to help improve the environment and reduce pollution. More still needs to be done. What will be the time line for the future? ■

INVESTIGATION 1

1. What kinds of water worries could the people of your city or town be having?

2. Write a story about what life will be like 100 years from now. Tell whether there will still be water pollution and water worries. What solutions will have been found?

HOW DOES WATER POLLUTION MOVE FROM PLACE TO PLACE?

You saw in Investigation 1 that pollution dumped on land can end up in the water. In this investigation you'll see how water can move that pollution from place to place.

Activity

All Washed Up

Tides are the daily rise and fall of ocean water. If you've ever visited an ocean beach, you know what tides do. In this activity you'll make a model to see if tides add to pollution along coastlines.

MATERIALS

- goggles
- rocks, gravel, or sand
- large baking pan
- water
- metric ruler
- potting soil
- spoon
- cooking oil
- *Science Notebook*

SAFETY

Wear goggles during this activity. Clean up any spills immediately. Wash your hands when you have finished this activity.

Procedure

1. **Make a model** of an ocean coastline, using rocks, gravel, or sand. Put the material you have chosen in one end of a baking pan. Arrange the materials to look like a beach or rocky coast.

2. Pour water into the pan until the water is 1 cm deep. Sprinkle a little soil on your "ocean." Then add one spoonful of cooking oil.

HIGH TIDE

Step 3

3. **Talk with your group** and **predict** what effect moving the water up onto the "coast" will have on your coastline materials. Explain why you made the prediction you did. **Record** your prediction in your *Science Notebook*. Then slowly raise the ocean end of the pan until the water moves up onto the coast. Slowly lower the pan. Do this three or four times.

4. Now **observe** your coastline materials. Touch them. **Record** your observations.

Analyze and Conclude

1. How did your model represent the motion of tides on Earth?

2. What did you observe in step 4 when you looked at and touched your coastline materials? **Compare** this result with your prediction.

3. The materials you put into your ocean are a model of pollution from oil spills and the dumping of wastes. What can you **infer** from your model about how ocean pollution affects land?

Activity
Going My Way?

Tides move ocean water. "Rivers" of water called currents *also move through the oceans. How might currents move pollution from place to place?*

MATERIALS
- goggles
- cold tap water
- clear plastic aquarium
- dropper
- food coloring
- small jar with lid
- hot tap water
- *Science Notebook*

Procedure

1. Pour cold water into a clear plastic aquarium until the aquarium is three-fourths filled.

2. Put three drops of food coloring into a small jar. Carefully fill the jar with hot tap water. Screw on the lid.

3. Slowly place the jar upright on the bottom of the aquarium. Try not to disturb the water. **Talk with your group** and **predict** what will happen when you take the lid off the jar. Explain why you made the prediction you did. **Record** your prediction in your *Science Notebook*.

4. Slowly remove the lid of the jar. **Observe** and **record** what happens.

Step 3

Analyze and Conclude

1. What happened after you took off the lid? In which direction did the hot colored water move? In which direction did the cold water move?

2. You made a model of one way that water moves near coastlines. **Hypothesize** what would happen to pollutants that get swept into a current.

The Current Idea

On January 10, 1992, a ship carrying 7,250 bathtub toys lost its cargo during a storm in the northern Pacific Ocean. Knowing where the toys washed ashore helped scientists learn a little more about the path that ocean pollution takes.

A "River" in the Ocean

Ocean pollution is moved around the world by the constant motion of the water. Currents are important water movers.

A **current** is a narrow, fast-moving "river" of water in the ocean.

Currents at the ocean's surface are kept in motion by winds that blow steadily in one direction. When surface currents get close to land, they curve away from it and change direction.

Look at the map of world ocean currents. The **X** shows where the ship lost its cargo. Predict where the bathtub toys washed ashore.

So far, more than 400 bathtub toys have been found along the Alaskan shoreline. Scientists are waiting to see if more toys will wash ashore elsewhere.

The major ocean surface currents ▼

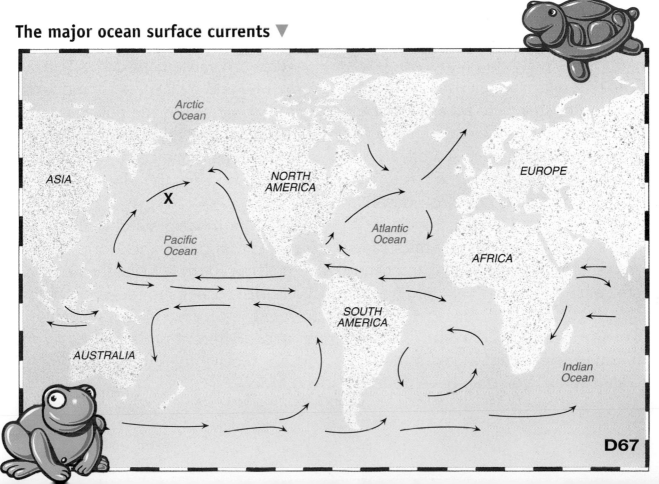

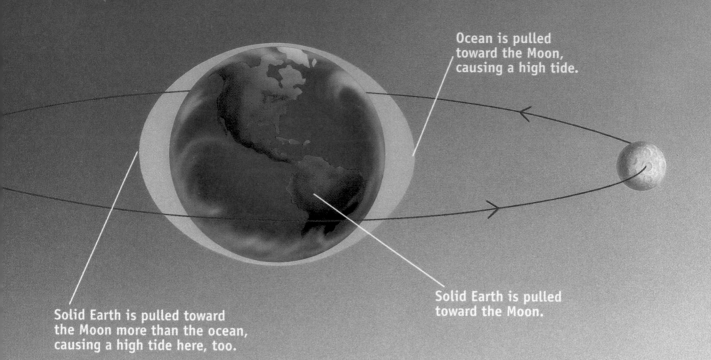

Ocean is pulled toward the Moon, causing a high tide.

Solid Earth is pulled toward the Moon.

Solid Earth is pulled toward the Moon more than the ocean, causing a high tide here, too.

▲ As Earth turns, the tides rise and fall.

These Currents Run Deep

The currents that moved the floating bathtub toys are surface currents. There are also currents deeper in the ocean. Deep ocean currents are caused by differences in water temperature.

In the activity on page D66, you saw that warm water rises and that cold water sinks and takes its place. This is similar to the way deep ocean currents move. Ocean waters are warm near the equator (ē kwāt'ər) and cold near the poles. So ocean waters tend to rise near the equator and sink near the poles. This steady movement of water results in ocean currents.

Ocean Ups and Downs

If you've ever spent a day at the ocean shore, you may have noticed that waves move in closer to shore, and then move back out again. This motion of the water is called tides. **Tides** are the daily rise and fall of ocean water. Tides helped move some of the lost bathtub toys onto shore.

Tides are caused by both gravity (grav'i tē) and by Earth's rotation, or spinning. Gravity is the pull that all things have on one another. Earth's gravity keeps us on Earth. Earth's gravity also keeps the Moon close to Earth.

The Moon has gravity, too. As the Moon circles Earth, the Moon's gravity pulls on Earth. This pull causes the Earth's oceans to move outward toward the Moon. As Earth rotates, or spins, different parts of the oceans receive the greatest pull of the Moon.

High tide (*left*) and low tide (*right*) in Gloucester, Massachusetts

Pollution Goes for a Ride

Tides and currents move polluted ocean water from one place to another. More often than not, pollutants wash back up on the shore near the place they came from. Think back to how oil affected the shoreline you made in the activity on pages D64 and D65. You used cooking oil to pollute the water. The tides you made moved the pollution back up on the shore.

One source of ocean pollution is oil spills. Strong storms at sea can cause oil tankers to break apart. When they do break apart, oil spills out and floats on the ocean's surface. The oil kills animals that live in or near the ocean, and it ruins beaches. You probably wouldn't be too upset to find bathtub toys on a beach. But if you were to find oil covering the sand, it's likely that wouldn't make you very happy.

Although pollution can sometimes be traced to a country or a private company, the oceans belong to the whole world. So the problem of ocean pollution can be solved only when all countries of the world work together. ■

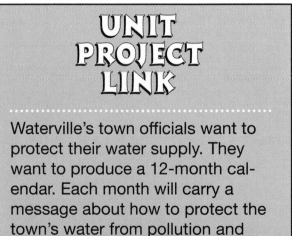

UNIT PROJECT LINK

Waterville's town officials want to protect their water supply. They want to produce a 12-month calendar. Each month will carry a message about how to protect the town's water from pollution and suggest ways to conserve water. Write twelve messages and create a "Conserve and Care" calendar that each school and family in Waterville will want to use.

Mother of Waters

MARYLAND

DELAWARE

VIRGINIA

Chesapeake Bay

Atlantic Ocean

SCIENCE TECHNOLOGY & SOCIETY

Native Americans called it the Mother of Waters. It is 320 km (200 mi) long, it stretches over 12,800 km (8,000 mi) of shoreline, and it has 150 rivers and streams flowing into it. What is it? It's the Chesapeake Bay.

The Chesapeake Bay is the nation's largest estuary (es′tyoo er ē). An estuary is a place where fresh water mixes with salt water. The Chesapeake Bay estuary is home to a great variety of life. It has more than 2,500 different kinds of plants and animals living in its waters and along its shore.

Native Americans also called the bay Great Shellfish Bay because there were so many crabs, clams, and oysters in there.

Many people enjoy eating shellfish, so for years the shellfish industry grew. Then something began to happen. The numbers of shellfish that were caught began to decrease.

There were two reasons for the decrease in shellfish in the estuary: pollution and people. Every stream and river that flowed past farms and factories picked up pollutants and carried them to the Chesapeake Bay. Over the years, 13 million people moved to the land that drains into the bay. These people built towns. They produced sewage and trash. They also overfished the waters. All these things decreased the number of living things in the bay.

Then the federal Environmental Protection Agency (EPA) began a study of the bay. In 1983 they told the states that surround the bay how to save it. The farmers began planting crops in a way that lessened the runoff of fertilizers and chemicals into the bay. Sewage was treated, fishing was limited, and trash was placed in landfills.

Today the water of Chesapeake Bay is improved. In 1989 it was impossible to see down into the water more than 20 cm (8 in.). But today you can see down 46 cm (18 in.). Of course, there is a long way to go. The Native Americans could see to the bottom, 6 m (20 ft) deep!

Lessons learned from the Mother of Waters can be used to control—and prevent—water pollution around the world. ■

Oysters are once again plentiful in the Chesapeake Bay. ▼

═══ **INVESTIGATION 2** ═══

1. Imagine walking on a beach on the east coast of southern Florida. You accidentally drop a ball into the ocean. Where might the ball go?

2. People used to think that the oceans were so big that anything could be dumped into them without harming them. Explain why this isn't so.

INVESTIGATION 3

HOW CAN WE SAVE AND PROTECT WATER?

The amount of water on Earth never changes. Yet the number of people on Earth is growing all the time. How can people protect and save this limited amount of water?

Activity

Down the Drain

How much water does your household use each day? Could you use less? Find out!

- -

Procedure

In your *Science Notebook*, **record** each activity in which you or others in your home use water during one day. Use the table to see how much water each activity uses. Add up the number of gallons of water used for each activity. Then add up the amounts of water used the entire day.

Water-Using Activity	Water (in gallons)
Bath	25
Ten-minute shower	50
Flush of the toilet	5
Faucet running to brush teeth	2
Faucet running to wash dishes	30
Dishwasher load	10
Washing machine load	32

Analyze and Conclude

What surprised you about how your household uses water? How could you use less water?

Activity
Drops Count

Find out just how much water goes down the drain, one drop at a time.

Procedure

1. With a partner, **predict** how much water is wasted in 30 minutes by a dripping faucet. **Record** your prediction in your *Science Notebook*.

2. Use a milk carton as a model of a dripping faucet. Your teacher will make a hole in the bottom of the carton with a pin.

3. Hold your finger over the hole, and have your partner add water to the carton until it is full. Hold the carton above a graduate. Set a timer for one minute.

4. Remove your finger and let water drip from the hole for one minute. Then place the carton in a cup.

5. **Measure** and **record** the amount of water in the graduate.

Step 4

Analyze and Conclude

1. How much water did you collect? **Compute** the amount of water that you could collect in 30 minutes.

2. **Infer** how a dripping faucet can become a big water waster over one year's time.

Isn't Water Free?

STS
SCIENCE
TECHNOLOGY
& SOCIETY

Imagine that you are eating in a restaurant with your family. You ask for a glass of water. When you get the bill for the meal, you see a $5.00 charge added for the water.

Charging this much for a glass of water may seem unfair. Isn't water free, after all, like air? In many areas of the world, water is not free. Many people in the United States already pay a water utility company for the water used in their homes. They're charged for every thousand gallons of water that they use.

A Few Cents a Day

The average cost per thousand gallons of water in the United States is $1.65. This means that in some places, people pay less than $1.65 while in other places they pay more.

A thousand gallons is a lot of water. If you drank eight 8-oz glasses of water a day, a thousand gallons would last for over three and

Most restaurants don't charge for water. ▼

a half years. Getting this much water for $1.65 (or less than a penny per gallon) would amaze people in other countries. People who live on the island of Bermuda pay about $100.00 per thousand gallons of water.

Keeping Track

How do you know when you have used a thousand gallons of water? In places where people pay for water, each building has a water meter. A water meter, shown on the right, is a device that measures the amount of water that comes through a pipe into a home or business. The meter may be in the basement of an apartment building or mounted on the outside of a house.

A meter reader checks how many gallons of water were used. ▼

▲ **How many gallons of water have been used?**

Meter readers are people who work for water companies. They make regular visits to every building that has a water meter. They look at the numbers on the meters to see how much water has been used since the last time the meter was checked. The water company then sends a bill for the amount of water used.

The money that people pay to a water company covers the cost of treating water so that it's safe to drink. It also helps in paying to build and maintain the pipes that bring water into homes.

As the number of people in the world grows, more water will be needed. It may not be long before water supplies are so reduced that everyone will have to pay for water. And in some places, water may become very costly.

A Bargain at Any Price

Water is a bargain in this country. A bargain is an item that is sold at a low price. Maybe that's why some people use a lot of water.

Water Use, Water Waste

In the United States, each person uses an average of 290 L (75 gal) of water a day. A family of four uses about 1,160 L (300 gal) of water a day. Recall the activity that you did on page D72. How many gallons of water does your family use every day?

Because there seems to be plenty of water in many places, most people don't realize how much water they use or how much they waste. How are the people in the drawing below wasting water? Now read the list on the next page to see some ways to conserve, or save, water.

In what ways can you see water being wasted? ▼

How to Save Water

- Instead of running a faucet to get water cold, put a jug of water in the refrigerator.

- Turn off faucets. Get an adult to fix leaky faucets.

- If you do dishes by hand, don't let the water run.

- Don't let the water run while you are brushing your teeth.

- As you wait for running water to get hot, catch the cool water in a bucket or pail and use it for watering plants.

- Take a brief shower (less than five minutes long) instead of a bath. If you take a bath, don't fill the tub all the way.

- Wash a car with a bucket of soapy water first. Then turn on the hose to rinse the car.

- Have an adult help you fill a plastic jug with water and put it into the tank behind your toilet. Every time you flush, you will save the amount of water that's in the jug.

- If you have a dishwasher and washing machine, wash only full loads.

- Water lawns and gardens at dusk or early in the morning to stop too much water from evaporating.

You've seen many ways that people waste water. You're probably most familiar with one way—not repairing leaking faucets. In the activity on page D73, you made a model of a dripping faucet. If the water that leaked filled a coffee cup in ten minutes, then 12,464 L (3,280 gal) would be wasted in a year!

Dumping Down the Drain

Leaks are not the only way that water is wasted. People also waste water when they pollute. The list below shows some ways you and your family can help protect water supplies from pollution. Share with others what you've learned about saving and protecting water.

Keeping Water Safe

- Cleaners such as ammonia go down the drain and can poison the water supply. Vinegar often works just as well as ammonia for cleaning, and it isn't harmful.

- Don't dump the following things down the drain or on the ground: motor oil, medicines, paint thinner, paint, glues, spot removers, furniture polish, and antifreeze.

- Find out where your family can take used motor oil. In some communities, auto parts stores, service stations, or recycling centers will take used motor oil.

- Find out when your community collects harmful wastes.

INVESTIGATION 3

THINK IT WRITE IT

1. Imagine there is a very severe water shortage. You are told you can use only 2 gal of water each day. Write a story about how you would live.

2. Suppose that you were in charge of saving and protecting water in your school. What kinds of things might you tell everybody to do?

REFLECT & EVALUATE

WORD POWER

acid rain
current
polluted
tides

 On Your Own
Review the terms in the list. Then use each term in a different sentence that tells the meaning of the term.

 With a Partner
Write a clue for each term in the list. Then challenge your partner to write the correct term for each clue.

BUILD YOUR PORTFOLIO

Think of things you can do to reduce water pollution. Then make a poster to encourage others to reduce water pollution.

Analyze Information

Study the drawing. Then use the drawing to explain in your own words what will happen the next time it rains.

Assess Performance

Design and carry out an activity to find out how much water you can save by not running the water the entire time you're brushing your teeth. Compare your results with those of others.

Problem Solving

1. You're cleaning out the basement. Explain why you shouldn't pour old paint and paint thinners down the drain. What is the best way to get rid of these materials?

2. Water pollution is not a local problem, it's a global problem. Explain what this means.

3. A water meter doesn't run if water isn't being used. If no one in your home is using water and the water meter is running, what could this mean?

Throughout this unit you've investigated questions related to Earth's water. How will you use what you've learned, and share that information with others? Here are some ideas.

Hold a Big Event
to Share Your Unit Project

Display your model of Waterville. Invite other classes and your family to visit your classroom to see your Waterville model and to learn about where fresh water sources are found, how water is treated and distributed to buildings, and how water can be saved and protected from pollution. Distribute your "Conserve and Care" calendars.

Experiment

Take one of the activities in this unit a bit further. You might make a model of a water cycle by setting up a terrarium in an airtight jar or aquarium. Add soil, some plants, and a little water. Then place the terrarium in the Sun. Observe and record what happens. Or you might experiment with other materials to make a better water filter. Talk with your teacher before you carry out your plan.

Take Action

You've learned ways that people can avoid polluting rivers. You've also learned ways that your family can save and protect water supplies. Use some of these ideas to make posters. Hang your posters in school, at home, or around your neighborhood. The posters should remind people to take care of Earth's water.

UNIT E

ROLES OF LIVING THINGS

Theme: Constancy and Change

GET READY TO

OBSERVE & QUESTION

How are living things adapted for protection?

Plants and animals have lots of interesting ways to protect themselves. In this unit you'll learn some of their secrets!

EXPERIMENT & HYPOTHESIZE

How are living things adapted to their environments?

How do animals stay warm in cold weather? In this unit you'll make models to find out.

INVESTIGATE!

RESEARCH & ANALYZE

As you investigate, find out more from these books.

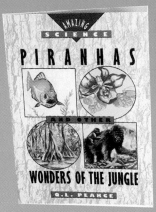

- *Piranhas and Other Wonders of the Jungle* by Q. L. Pearce, illustrated by Mary Ann Fraser (Julian Messner, 1990). Have you ever seen slime molds, vampire bats, or giant water lilies? Read about these and other unusual living things that make their homes in the jungles of the world.

- *One Small Square: African Savanna* by Donald M. Silver, illustrated by Patricia J. Wynne and Dianne Ettl (W. H. Freeman & Co., 1994). Read this book to see how different plants and animals can live together in the African grassland.

WORK TOGETHER & SHARE IDEAS

How are living things adapted to live in tropical rain forests?

Working together, you'll have a chance to apply what you have learned. Find out about the different plants and animals that live in the rain forest. Look for the Unit Project Links for ideas on how you can prepare for a Rain Forest Celebration Day!

CHAPTER 1

RELATIONSHIPS AMONG LIVING THINGS

Can there ever be too much of a good thing? Unfortunately, the answer is *yes*. Take the fertilizer that helps crops grow. As useful as it is, fertilizer can also cause harm by running off into our water supply and damaging it. Relationships, or how one thing affects another, can be tricky!

● ●

Kids Who Adopted a Bay

The Chesapeake Bay Kids don't live in Chesapeake. In fact, they live nearly 160 km (100 mi) from the bay. They are from farmland in the heart of Pennsylvania. But they take care of the bay. Together with their teacher, Shirlee Cavaliere, the Kids collect water from farmland rivers. Then they test the water to find out if it contains fertilizers. The Kids publish the test results and spread this message: Excess fertilizer runs off farms. It goes into streams, then rivers, then the bay. The same fertilizer that made crops grow is making algae grow in the bay. That algae is killing plants. The animals that depend on those plants for food are dying, too. Stop the runoff. Use fertilizers wisely!

As you read Chapter 1, think about the relationships among the living things around you. How can you help protect those relationships?

Coming Up

◀ The Chesapeake Bay Kids at work in the field.

WHAT DO LIVING THINGS NEED?

Imagine that it's a hot day and you're very thirsty. You need to drink a tall glass of water. Water is one of the things you need to live. Other living things need water, too. What else do living things need? In Investigation 1 you'll find out!

Activity

Needs of Seeds

Plants seem to grow almost anywhere. What do they need to live?

MATERIALS

- goggles
- marker
- 3 young plants in paper cups
- water
- metric measuring cup
- *Science Notebook*

SAFETY

Wear goggles during this activity.

Procedure

1. With a marker, write *Soil* on a paper cup containing a young plant growing in soil. Label a second such cup *Soil + Water*. Write *Soil + Water + Sunlight* on a third cup.

Step 1

Soil   Soil + Water   Soil + Water + Sunlight

2. Pour 25 mL of water into the cup labeled *Soil + Water*. Pour another 25 mL of water into the cup labeled *Soil + Water + Sunlight*.

3. Place the cup labeled *Soil* and the cup labeled *Soil + Water* in a place where the plants will get no light. Place the cup labeled *Soil + Water + Sunlight* near a window. **Predict** which conditions will be best for growth. **Record** your prediction in your *Science Notebook*.

Step 4

4. Every day for one week, check to make sure that the soil is moist in the cup labeled *Soil + Water* and in the cup labeled *Soil + Water + Sunlight*. If the soil begins to get dry, add a little water to these cups. Be careful not to overwater the plants.

5. **Make a chart** like the one shown. After one week, **observe** the cups to see what the plants look like. **Record** your observations in your chart.

Conditions	Plants After One Week
Soil	
Soil + Water	
Soil + Water + Sunlight	

Analyze and Conclude

1. Under which conditions did the young plants grow best? What did those plants have that the others did not?

2. How does your prediction compare with your results? How do your results compare with those of your classmates? From the class results, what can you **conclude** about some of the things plants need to live and grow?

Activity

A Pill Bug's Home

A pill bug finds a home that keeps it safe and has the things it needs to live. Find out about two conditions that pill bugs need in this activity.

MATERIALS
- goggles
- rectangular baking pan
- paper towels
- tape
- newspaper
- spoon
- pill bugs in a container with a lid
- flashlight
- small cup of water
- *Science Notebook*

SAFETY

Wear goggles during this activity.

Procedure

1. Cover the bottom of a baking pan with paper towels. Tape the edges of the paper towels to the pan. Also seal with tape any places where paper towels overlap. Place a sheet of newspaper over half of the top of the pan as shown.

2. Use a spoon to carefully take some pill bugs, one by one, from their container and place them in the middle of the pan.

3. **Predict** whether the pill bugs will move toward light or away from light. **Record** your prediction in your *Science Notebook*. Shine a flashlight on the half of the pan not covered by newspaper. **Observe** where the pill bugs move. **Record** your observations.

▼ **Pill bug**

Step 1

E8

4. Remove the sheet of newspaper. **Predict** whether pill bugs will move toward a dry area or a wet area. **Record** your prediction. Sprinkle water on the paper towels in half of the pan to make them moist. Leave the other half of the pan dry.

5. **Observe** where the pill bugs move. **Record** your observations. Carefully put the pill bugs back into their container.

Analyze and Conclude

1. How did your predictions compare with your results? Which do pill bugs prefer—light or darkness? Do they prefer moist, or dry, places?

2. From your results, what two conditions can you **infer** that pill bugs need in their homes?

3. Pill bugs live in the woods. If you went to the woods to look for them, **predict** where you would most likely find them.

INVESTIGATE FURTHER!

EXPERIMENT

Try a similar experiment with earthworms. Work in a small group. Think of two ways you can vary the conditions. Make your plan and show it to your teacher. Then carry out your plan. Share your results with your classmates.

A Perfect Place to Live

What do you really need? Perhaps you need a new soccer ball or a haircut? But you have more basic needs than these. Food, water, and air are some of the things you *really* need. Other living things need food, water, and air, too.

All living things need an environment (en vī'rən mənt) that suits their needs. An **environment** is everything that surrounds and affects a living thing.

Salty or Not, Cold or Hot

Living things often have very different needs. So an environment that is good for one living thing may not be good for another. For example, all water animals need a water environment. But most dolphins need to live in salt water. The ocean is a good environment for most dolphins. Other water animals would die in salt water. They need to live in the fresh water of lakes and streams.

This dolphin lives in the ocean. ▼

A spotted moray eel ▼

Some water animals need to live near the surface of the water. Others need to live near the bottom. If you've ever gone fishing, you may know that bass need the warm water near the surface. But lake trout need the colder waters found at the bottom of a lake.

The spotted moray eel is an ocean animal you won't find at the water's surface. This eel lives at the bottom of the ocean, where it is cold and dark. A reef shark has different needs. This animal lives in the warm, shallow ocean waters of coral reefs.

E11

Turn Off the Lights, Please!

Some living things need a lot of sunlight, and some need total darkness. Plants need sunlight to live. Without sunlight, plants couldn't make food and would die.

Some animals dig down into the soil to live in underground environments. Animals such as earthworms need a dark, moist environment. These animals would dry up in the bright, hot sunlight.

Moles also live underground. A mole has tiny eyes and is almost blind. But a mole doesn't need to see well to dig for the tiny insects and worms that are its food.

▲ A tropical rain forest in Costa Rica.

Moles live underground. ▼

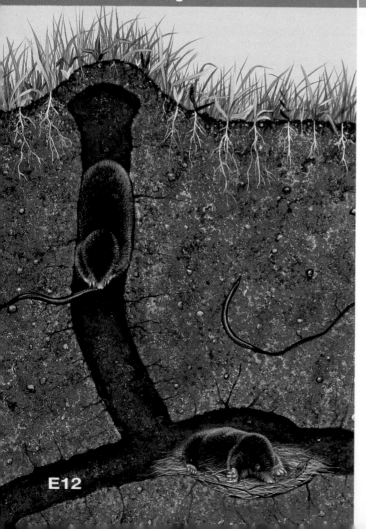

Different kinds of living things need different amounts of sunlight. If you've ever planted flowers, you may have noticed that some need shade and others need a lot of bright sunlight. When you tested pill bugs in the activity on pages E8 and E9, you found out about some of the things pill bugs need. Do pill bugs need a place that is dark, or light?

Very Wet or Very Dry

Some plants need a lot of rain, and others need almost no rain. The plants of the tropical rain forest need to be warm and wet. And they are! It rains almost every day of the year in the rain forest!

▲ Desert plants need very little rain.

Too Tiny to See

All living things need a suitable environment—even living things too small to see with just the eyes. Bacteria (bak tir'ē ə) are living things that can't be seen without a microscope, but they're everywhere. They can be found living in soil, in air, in lakes and ponds, in garbage cans, and even in your stomach! To survive, bacteria need an environment that is warm and wet. Most types of bacteria also need darkness.

From tiny bacteria to the largest whales in the ocean, living things find places that meet their needs. ■

Bacteria need warmth and moisture. ▼

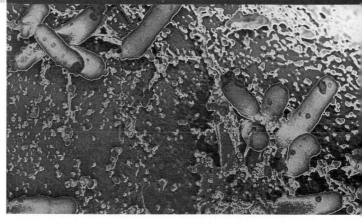

Other plants need a dry place to live. The teddy bear cholla is a cactus that grows in Arizona, in other desert regions of the southwestern United States, and in Mexico. It rains very little in the desert. But that's fine for the cholla and other cactus plants. They don't need a lot of water.

=== INVESTIGATION 1 ===

THINK IT
WRITE IT

1. You put on scuba gear and dive into the ocean. As you explore the underwater world, you see many different kinds of plants and animals. What needs might they have in common?

2. What would happen to a plant or an animal if it didn't get most of the things it needed?

INVESTIGATION 2

HOW DO LIVING THINGS GET THE FOOD THEY NEED?

Think of a time when you were tired and hungry. After a snack you probably felt better and much more awake. What are the different ways living things get food? Find out in Investigation 2!

Activity

MATERIALS

- *Science Notebook*

Meat and Potatoes

Do you eat plants, animals, or both? Find out by doing this activity.

WHAT I EAT	
Food	From Plant or Animal

Procedure

In your *Science Notebook*, **make a chart** like the one shown. **Predict** whether most foods you eat come from plants or animals. For one week, **record** the kinds of foods you eat. List each part of a food and tell where it comes from. At the end of the week, share your observations.

Analyze and Conclude

Do most of the foods you eat come from plants or from animals? How does your prediction compare with your findings?

E14

Activity

A Menu for Molds

Do this activity to find out how living things called molds get food.

Procedure

1. Place one slice of moist bread and one slice of cheese in a sandwich bag. Seal the bag and tape it closed. Put the bag in a warm, dark place for one week. **Predict** what will happen to the foods in the bag. **Record** your prediction in your *Science Notebook*.

2. After one week, use a hand lens to **examine** the foods in the bag. Look for mold. Do not open the bag.

3. **Make drawings** of what you see. **Describe** how the food has changed.

4. Put the bag back in the same warm, dark place for another week. Repeat steps 2 and 3.

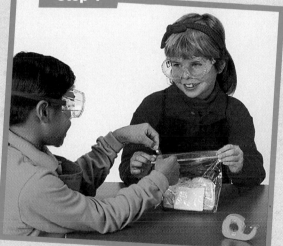

Step 1

Analyze and Conclude

1. What happened to the food in the bag? **Compare** your prediction with your results.

2. From your results, **infer** what molds use for food.

3. **Predict** what would happen to the food if you left it in the bag for several months.

Step 2

What's for Dinner?

Plants make their own food. ▼

Imagine never needing to eat dinner—or breakfast or lunch either! If you were a plant, you would never eat. You would make your own food.

Food Makers

Plants make their own food inside their leaves. The leaves soak up sunlight and use the Sun's energy to make food. This food can be stored in roots, leaves, and other plant parts for use later on. Living things that can make their own food are

called **producers** (pro dōōs′ərz). Plants are producers. Producers make up the basic food supply in the environment. Without them, most other kinds of living things would not be able to exist.

May I See a Menu?

Since you can't produce your own food, as a plant does, you have to get it another way—by eating something else. That means that you are a consumer (kən sōōm′ər). A **consumer** is a living thing that eats plants, animals, or other living things.

What kinds of things are usually on your dinner plate? Crunchy crickets and other insects? You might eat these animals if you were a praying mantis. A praying mantis is an animal eater. Animals that eat only other animals are called **carnivores** (kär′nə vôrz). Spiders, many insects, and some worms are carnivores. Cats, snakes, wolves, owls, and many fish are carnivores, too.

◄ **A praying mantis is a carnivore.**

Wolves are carnivores. ▼

Brown bears sometimes eat plants. ▼

Prairie dogs do not eat other animals. They crawl out of their underground burrows and feed on grass. Marine iguanas (i gwä′nəz) also eat only plants, enjoying a meal of salty seaweed. Animals such as prairie dogs and marine iguanas are herbivores (hʉr′bə vôrz). A **herbivore** is an animal that eats only plants. Caterpillars are herbivores. So are elephants. What other plant-eating animals can you think of?

Many animals are omnivores (äm′ni vôrz). **Omnivores** are animals that eat both plants and animals. Brown bears are omnivores. The bears eat berries and other fruits, but they also eat small animals, like fish.

Raccoons are also omnivores. So are some types of mice, birds, and turtles. In the activity on page E14, you found out whether the food you eat comes from plants, animals, or both. If you eat both plants and animals, you're an omnivore, too!

Breaking It Down

In every environment there is an important group of consumers called decomposers (dē kəm pōz′ərz). **Decomposers** feed on the remains of once-living things and on animal droppings. Bacteria, mushrooms, yeast, and molds are decomposers. Think about the mold activity you did on page E15. What did the molds do to the food in the bag?

Brown bears also eat fish and other animals. ▼

▲ A raccoon is an omnivore.

Decomposers are important to the environment. They break down materials from once-living things into simpler materials. Decomposers release the simpler materials back into water, soil, and air, where they can be used again by other living things. The effects of decomposers can be seen on the forest floor. Rotting logs and leaves are one sign of these living things. ■

Mushrooms are decomposers. ▶

Living Machines

Can a machine be alive? Most machines aren't. But scientists in Massachusetts have invented a machine that is mostly alive. This "living machine" is being used to clean up sewage—the waste water from homes, schools, and businesses.

This living machine is part of a sewage treatment plant in Rhode Island. The machine is made up of rows of round tanks.

A glass greenhouse surrounds the living machine. The glass lets in sunlight and helps keep the temperature steady. The living things were picked for their roles as producers, consumers, and decomposers. Read the captions to see how the "living machine" works.

Waste water flows backwards, forwards, and sideways through the tanks containing plants, animals, and other living things. ▼

Waste water

◄ There are 48 tanks in the living machine. In each tank, floating water plants, such as parrot feathers and duckweed, grow on the surface of the water. Land plants, such as willow trees, lilies, irises, mint, and ginger, grow on rafts in the tanks. There are even banana trees supported by ropes!

E20

Snails eat sludge—a muddy mixture from the sewage that sticks to the sides of the tank. Golden shiner fish feed on rotting plants and bits of solid waste. Clams and mussels eat tiny particles they filter out of the water. ▼

Finally the waste water flows into a small gravel-filled marsh. Reeds, canary grass, cattails, and other marsh plants finish the job of filtering the water. By the time it leaves the living machine, the water is clean. ▼

Clean water

INVESTIGATION 2

THINK IT WRITE IT

1. You're designing a park. You want to make sure the plants and animals in your park will have food. What are the different ways living things get food energy? What living things would you include in your park?

2. Could you and other animals live if there were no plants? Why or why not?

WHAT ARE FOOD CHAINS AND FOOD WEBS?

Slurp! The fast tongue of a frog catches a juicy fly. Gulp! A snake eats the frog. Will the snake become a meal for some other animal? In Investigation 3 you'll explore different eating relationships.

Activity

Making a Food-Chain Mobile

Do you eat hamburgers, fruit, or salad? No matter what you eat, you're part of a food chain. Do this activity to find out more about food chains.

MATERIALS

- books about plants and animals
- old magazines
- scissors
- crayons or colored markers
- tape
- yarn or string
- wire coat hanger
- *Science Notebook*

Procedure

1. In your *Science Notebook*, **make a list** of four living things. First, list one kind of plant. Then, think about the kind of animal that would eat that plant. List that animal. Next, think about an animal that would eat the animal you listed. List the second animal. Now do the same for a third animal. Get ideas by looking through animal books and magazines or from something you have seen.

2. Cut out pictures from old magazines or **draw** pictures of the four living things in your food chain. Then tape your pictures to a piece of yarn, as shown. Put the living things in order of who eats whom. Think back to Investigation 2 to help you decide what should be at the bottom of your food chain. Tape the end of the yarn to a wire hanger. You've made a food-chain mobile.

Analyze and Conclude

1. Which living thing is the producer in your food chain?

2. Which living things are consumers?

3. Look at the food-chain mobiles of your classmates. What can you **infer** about the kind of living thing that is at the bottom of a food chain?

Step 2

Activity

More Links in the Food Chain

Most living things eat more than one kind of food. Because they do, many food chains may be linked together. In this activity you will play a game to see how food chains can link to form food webs.

- -

Procedure

1. Work in a group to **write** the names of the following living things on index cards, one per card: berries, nuts, water plants, mouse, snake, big fish, small fish, crayfish, owl, bear, chipmunk.

2. Place all the cards face up. With your group, **arrange** the cards to show three or four different food chains.

Step 3

3. Place a length of blue yarn so that its ends touch two cards to show that these living things are linked in a food chain. Do this for the living things in each food chain.

4. Now look at the food chains you have made. **Look** for a living thing in one food chain that can eat or be eaten by something in another food chain. Use a length of red yarn to connect these living things that are in different food chains. In this way you will link two or more food chains to form a food web.

Step 5

5. **Find** all the links between food chains that you can. Connect the links with lengths of red yarn. **Make a drawing** of your food web in your *Science Notebook*.

6. Look at the food webs of other groups. **Compare** these webs to the one you made.

7. Think about what would happen if there were no producers. Take away the producer cards. **Infer** what would happen to the living things that eat the producers. **Infer** what would happen to the other members of the food web.

Analyze and Conclude

1. Explain how a food chain is different from a food web.

2. Suppose that most of the plants in a certain place die off. **Hypothesize** about what will happen to the animals that eat those plants.

UNIT PROJECT LINK

You've learned how important producers are to food webs. Research producers that live in tropical rain forests. Find out about the different layers of the rain forest—the canopy, the understory, and the forest floor. What types of plants live in each layer? With your classmates, make a mural showing different rain-forest plants.

Who Eats Whom?

A FOOD CHAIN

Plants

Grasshopper

Lizard

A grasshopper clings to a plant in the bright sunlight and nibbles on a leaf. Suddenly a lizard darts up from behind. It shoots out its tongue and eats the grasshopper. As the lizard slips away through the grass, a snake strikes and swallows the lizard whole. Later, an owl catches the snake and flies off to feed it to her young.

Food Chains

Every living thing needs food. When one animal eats another animal or a plant, they both become part of a food chain. A **food chain** is the path that energy takes as one living thing eats another. In the exam-

ple above, the plant, grasshopper, lizard, snake, and owl are all connected to one another in a food chain. What living things were part of the food-chain mobile you made in the activity on pages E22 and E23?

Some food chains are short, and some are long. But they all begin with a producer.

Links in the Chain

A plant is a producer and can make its own food. To make food,

E26

a plant needs sunlight, water, and air. A producer is the first link in all food chains.

A consumer is the next link in a food chain. Animals are consumers. Some animals, such as grasshoppers, feed on plants. Then other animals, such as lizards, eat the animals that ate the plants. Animals that hunt other animals for food are called **predators** (pred'ə tərz). The animals that are hunted by predators are called **prey**.

An animal can be a predator as well as a prey. For example, a house-fly may be eaten by a frog. In this case the frog is a predator. The fly is its prey. But the frog can become prey if a raccoon makes a meal of the frog. Likewise, the raccoon

▲ **A frog can be a predator and a prey.**

becomes prey if it's eaten by a predator such as a cougar.

If no larger animal eats the cougar, does that mean the cougar is the top consumer in the chain? Not really. When the cougar dies, its body will become food for the last consumers—the decomposers. Bacteria, molds, and other decomposers feed on the remains of animals and break down these remains.

Snake

Owl

A Food Web

Grass is eaten by a rabbit.

A rabbit is eaten by a hawk.

A rabbit is eaten by a snake.

A snake is eaten by a hawk.

Chains Tangle Into Webs

There are some simple food chains in nature. But usually two or more food chains overlap and link, forming a **food web**.

A forest food web might include an oak tree. When the oak tree drops its acorns, hungry squirrels may gnaw at the acorns and collect some for winter. Other animals may feed on the acorns as well. Deer, mice, raccoons, shrews, and bears all eat acorns.

But acorns are not the only food these animals eat. Deer also eat grass, tree leaves, twigs, moss, and

Grass is eaten by a grasshopper.

A grasshopper is eaten by a frog.

A frog is eaten by a bass.

A bass is eaten by a heron.

Small fish are eaten by a bass.

other plant parts. Mice also nibble on grass and eat insects and spiders. Raccoons also eat frogs, fish, fruit, crabs, grasshoppers, and sometimes even bird eggs.

You can see that in a large food web, many animals are connected to one another by the kinds of foods that they eat. Food webs show that every kind of living thing depends on other kinds of living things.

Wherever you look in nature—in forests, lakes, meadows, oceans, or deserts—plants and animals are connected to one another through a web of life. ■

Cane Toads
in Leaping Numbers

Did you ever make a problem worse by trying to fix it? That's what happened in Australia in 1935. At that time, scientists thought they had discovered a way to get rid of insects that were eating crops. The result of their action was a country covered with huge toads, called cane toads. Cane toads may be as much as 23 cm (9 in.) long!

Cane toads live in Hawaii and other parts of the tropics. In 1935, scientists brought a group of cane toads to Australia to eat the beetles that were destroying the sugar cane crops. The scientists' idea might have worked except for one problem. The beetles live inside the sugar cane plants and the toads live on the ground. Their paths never crossed, so the toads never ate the beetles.

A cane toad ▼

Although the cane toads didn't solve the beetle problem, they did make a difference in their new home. The toads changed the natural community (kə myōō'nə tē). A **community** is a group of plants and animals that live in the same area and depend on one another.

The toads became part of the food chains and food webs in their new home. The huge toads gobbled up many of Australia's native lizards, snakes, mice, and birds. Scientists became worried about the possible extinction (ek stiŋk'shən) of these native animals. **Extinction** is the dying out of all living things of a certain kind.

The toad problem quickly multiplied! Cane toads were laying up to 20,000 eggs at a time. And the toads had no natural predators that could eat them and survive. That's because the toads protect themselves from being eaten by giving off poison on their necks. Australian animals that tried to eat cane toads were often poisoned to death!

In spite of the trouble they've caused, cane toads have become part of the culture in Australia. They are thought of by some people as a tourist attraction. One politician suggested putting up a cane toad statue! What do you think? Is Australia's cane toad a pet or a pest? ■

SCIENCE IN LITERATURE

**ONE SMALL SQUARE
AFRICAN SAVANNA**
by Donald M. Silver
Illustrated by
Patricia J. Wynne and Dianne Ettl
W. H. Freeman & Co., 1994

Read about an African savanna, or grassland, in the book *One Small Square: African Savanna* by Donald M. Silver. You'll find pictures, words, and activities that will make you an expert on the living things in this environment.

Read pages 8–23 to find out who eats whom on the African savanna. Draw a savanna food web. Include as many of the creatures shown as you can. Don't forget the little creatures!

Deadly Links

SCIENCE TECHNOLOGY & SOCIETY

Suppose insects were destroying tomato plants you were growing. What would you do? You might spray an insecticide (in sek'tə sīd) on the plants to kill the insects. Insecticides are chemicals used to destroy insects that harm plants or carry diseases.

Killing Pests

Insecticides have been used widely throughout the world. Insecticides can help farmers keep crops growing healthy and strong. But these chemicals may remain in the soil for years. Some insecticides sprayed before you were born may still be in the soil today!

▲ **Insecticides can help crops grow.**

Scientists have learned that insecticides can harm more than the pests they were made to kill. The poisonous chemicals can be carried off by wind and moving water to new places. Once in these new places the chemicals can harm wildlife. This was the case with DDT, an insecticide. DDT can kill many kinds of flies and mosquitoes that carry diseases. Even though DDT was useful for killing pests, it had harmful effects on other animals, such as the bald eagle and the brown pelican.

Follow the path of chemicals through this food chain. ▼

Pelican Problems

In California, DDT came close to killing all of the state's brown pelicans during the 1960s and 1970s. Scientists found that DDT from a factory was carried off in the waste water from the plant. Some of this waste water ended up in ocean waters. There the DDT was taken in by fish. When the brown pelicans ate these fish, the birds took DDT into their own bodies.

As DDT moves along a food chain, it is stored in the bodies of animals for a long time. When it came time for the brown pelicans to lay their eggs, the stored DDT caused most eggs to have very thin shells. Most shells broke before baby pelicans could grow. Because of DDT, there were hardly any new baby brown pelicans during those years. So the number of brown pelicans in California greatly decreased.

Brown pelicans on the East Coast and in Louisiana were also being harmed by DDT. In Louisiana the brown pelican had been named the state bird back when there were close to 100,000 pelicans in the state. Because of DDT, pelicans in Louisiana disappeared completely!

▲ **DDT caused brown pelicans to lay eggs with very thin shells.**

The Start of a Solution

In 1970 the pelican was listed as endangered. Something had to be done, or there would be no brown pelicans left. Luckily, DDT was banned in the United States in 1972. Since then the number of pelicans has been on the rise.

Pelicans were not the only birds that were harmed by DDT. Bald eagles and peregrine falcons also laid eggs with thin shells because of the DDT stored in their bodies.

The law preventing the use of DDT has helped each of these great birds recover from the harmful chemical. But other countries still use DDT. You can imagine what it is doing to the wildlife in those places. In the United States, some kinds of birds and other animals are still in trouble. Even though the use of DDT has been banned, some of the newer chemicals used by people can cause harm to many different kinds of living things. ■

INVESTIGATION 3

1. You visit a forest where many hawks have been dying. You find chemical waste from a nearby factory in the forest soil and stream. How could the chemicals be harming hawks?

2. Think about the different things you eat and where they come from. Draw a diagram that shows you as part of a food web.

REFLECT & EVALUATE

WORD POWER

carnivore
community
consumer
decomposer
environment
extinction
food chain

food web
herbivore
omnivore
predator
prey
producer

On Your Own
Write a definition for each term in the list.

With a Partner
Write each term in the list on one side of an index card and the definition on the other side. Use the cards to quiz your partner.

BUILD YOUR PORTFOLIO

Make a poster that shows an environment with many different plants and animals getting food. Use the words *producer*, *consumer*, *herbivore*, *carnivore*, *predator*, and *prey*.

Analyze Information

Study the drawing. Then explain how the chemicals move through the environment.

Assess Performance

Make a food-chain mobile to show a possible food chain for a city park or a forest. You can do research or base your food chain on your own observations. Include at least four living things on your food-chain mobile.

Problem Solving

1. Some animals are herbivores. Some are carnivores, and others are omnivores. Which are you? How do you know? Use the definitions of all three terms in your answer.

2. A snake can be a predator, but it can also be a prey. Explain how this is possible.

3. Suppose a tree near your home dies. What factors in the environment could cause this?

CHAPTER 2

HOW LIVING THINGS ARE ADAPTED

To survive, or stay alive, plants and animals need to get food. They need to protect themselves from danger, too. How could a good sense of hearing help an animal get food? What part of a plant could stop a hungry animal from eating it?

Since Dinosaur Days

Sharks were around when the terror of the dinosaurs, *Tyrannosaurus rex*, walked on Earth. *Tyrannosaurus* disappeared millions of years ago, but sharks are still with us. That shows that they are well adapted, or well suited, to their watery world.

Here are some facts about sharks.

- A shark can detect the smell of a very small amount of blood from about 2 km (1 mi) away.
- Sharks have excellent eyesight. They can hunt in the dark, and they can sense even the smallest movement of their prey.
- Perhaps most surprising of all, sharks never stop swimming, and they never sleep!

In this chapter you'll read about how many living things survive in their environments.

Coming Up

◀ The word *shark* comes from the German word *schurke*, meaning "villain."

HOW ARE LIVING THINGS ADAPTED FOR GETTING FOOD?

A big eagle swoops down from the sky. It grabs a fish out of the water and flies away. How are eagles adapted to catch, carry, and eat fish? In Investigation 1 you'll explore many adaptations living things have for getting food.

Activity

The Right Beak for the Job

In this activity you'll find out about different kinds of bird beaks. You'll see how their beaks help birds get food.

Procedure

1. Set up a pan with sand, as shown. Add enough water to fill the pan two-thirds full.

2. Bury six to ten raisins in the sand. Sprinkle rice in the shallow water where the sand begins to slope upward.

3. Cut a plastic straw into five pieces. Place the pieces in the water so that they float. Now trade pans with another group.

Step 1

MATERIALS

- goggles
- rectangular pan
- sand
- water
- raisins
- uncooked rice
- plastic straw
- scissors
- toothpick
- plastic fork with tape on tines
- plastic soup spoon
- *Science Notebook*

SAFETY

Do not eat any raisins or rice. Wear goggles during this activity.

4. The raisins represent small animals that live buried deep in the sand or mud. The rice represents small plants and animals that live in shallow waters. The pieces of straw represent fish. A toothpick, plastic fork with taped tines, and plastic soup spoon represent different kinds of bird beaks. In your *Science Notebook,* **predict** which beak is best for getting each kind of food.

Step 5

5. **Make a chart** like the one shown. Use the toothpick to find and pick up raisins in the sand. **Count** the number of raisins you pick up in ten tries. **Record** this number in your chart. Now use the toothpick to pick up rice and then pieces of the straw. **Record** all your results in your chart.

Kind of Beak	Number of Raisins	Number of Rice Grains	Number of Straw Pieces
toothpick			
fork			
spoon			

6. Replace the raisins, rice, and straw pieces. Repeat step 5, using the fork and then the spoon. **Describe** the methods you used with the different beaks and the different kinds of foods.

Analyze and Conclude

1. Which beak was best for collecting which food?

2. Think about the birds that would catch the plants and animals described in step 4. **Hypothesize** what each one's beak would look like.

3. **Infer** what birds with similar kinds of beaks have in common.

INVESTIGATE FURTHER!

RESEARCH

There are over 8,000 different kinds of birds. Do research to find out about several kinds of birds that eat very different kinds of foods. Draw the shape of each bird's beak and label the drawing with the name of the bird and the kind of food that the bird eats.

Catching Lunch

When you say "I'm starved!" does someone make you a sandwich or snack? Animals in nature must work much harder to get a meal. Their task is made a little easier by the adaptations (ad əp tā′shənz) they have. **Adaptations** are behaviors or parts of living things that help them survive in a certain environment. Both plants and animals have adaptations for getting food.

It Makes Good Sense

Many animals have extraordinary vision, a super sense of hearing, or a sharp sense of smell that helps them get food. Hunting birds, such as eagles and hawks, have very good

This snake has poison fangs. ▼

eyes. They can spot prey from over a kilometer (half a mile) away! A dog's keen sense of smell can help uncover a tasty bone buried last year. The dog follows a scent trail that you couldn't smell at all! An owl, hunting at night, is able to swoop down on a mouse it only hears in the dark.

Deadly Weapons

Animals often have parts that can be used as deadly weapons. A praying mantis clamps its front legs shut on butterflies, grasshoppers, and other insects before it eats them. Many snakes have poison fangs that can paralyze and kill their victims. A chameleon (kə mēl′ē ən) has a sticky lump on the end of its tongue that insects get trapped on. A brown bear uses sharp claws and teeth to catch and eat large fish.

A Handy Tool!

In the activity about bird beaks on pages E38 and E39, you discovered that some beaks are better for catching certain kinds of foods. Woodpeckers use their pointed beaks to drill into trees, where they can catch insects.

Hummingbirds have long beaks and tongues that they use for sipping nectar from flowers.

◄ **An owl catches a deer mouse.**

A hummingbird sips nectar from flowers. ▼

The flamingo uses its bill as a strainer to trap tiny plants, shrimp, and snails found in shallow muddy waters. In the tropical rain forest, parrots and cockatoos use their strong beaks to crack nuts and seeds or to tear open fruit.

Mealtime Manners

The behavior (bē hāv′yər) of an animal can also be an adaptation for getting food. **Behavior** is the way an animal typically acts in certain situations.

Electric eels, a kind of fish, have a really shocking way of getting food. They catch fish by stunning them with an electric shock! An archer fish

An archer fish shoots water at an insect. ▼

catches an insect on a nearby water plant by using its long, tubelike mouthparts to fire water drops that knock the insect into the water. Grasshoppers are able to hop more than a meter (3 ft) to get a meal. That's 20 times the length of a grasshopper's body. If you had the muscle power of a grasshopper, you could jump about 24 m (80 ft)!

Some animals use tools from the environment to gather or eat food. While swimming on its back, the sea otter holds a rock on its belly and

A Venus' flytrap catches a cricket for lunch.

◄ A chimpanzee uses a stick to dig for termites.

uses the rock to break open shells. Chimpanzees can eat termites from a stick much the way you eat food from a fork. They peel the bark from a stick and poke it into a termite mound. When they pull out the stick, it is covered with tasty termite treats!

Other animals stalk, or secretly follow, their food. Have you ever watched a neighborhood cat sneak up on a bird? This method is the same one a leopard uses when it leaps on a young gazelle on the African plain.

Plants That Trap Insects

Plants need certain nutrients (nōō′trē əntz) from the soil. **Nutrients** are substances that provide materials needed for growth.

Plants have different adaptations to get these nutrients. The Venus' flytrap and pitcher plants are known for "eating" insects. By trapping and digesting insects, these plants get important nutrients that are missing from the soil in which they grow.

You can see that plants and animals have many adaptations that help them get food. ■

A Quick Tongue

In the trees of a tropical forest, a chameleon walks along the branches in search of prey. The chameleon seems to be moving in slow motion. How can such a slow animal ever catch a fast-moving insect? The chameleon has some unusual adaptations for getting its food. Find out about them on these pages.

ODD EYES The chameleon's eyes look odd because each eye can move separately. With this useful adaptation, the chameleon can keep one eye on its prey while the other eye looks for predators.

WHAT A TAIL! A chameleon moves high up in the trees. If it loses its balance, it can curl its strong tail around a branch to keep from falling.

NEAT FEET The chameleon's foot has three toes joined on one side and two toes joined on the other side. The V-shaped foot is good for grabbing onto branches.

A TALENTED TONGUE The chameleon's tongue is very long—sometimes as long as its entire body. At the end of its tongue is a sticky patch that prey can get stuck on. When inside the chameleon's mouth, the tongue is folded much like an accordion. When prey comes within range, the chameleon shoots out its tongue. Its tongue moves so fast that it would be hard for you to see it move.

Difficult to Spot

The chameleon has a good chance of surprising its prey. That's because of **camouflage** (kam′ə fläzh)—the ability to blend in with the surroundings. Besides helping the chameleon sneak up on its prey, camouflage makes it hard for predators to spot the chameleon. ■

=== **INVESTIGATION 1** ===

THINK IT WRITE IT

1. Think about an animal you often see outside. Write the name of the animal. What kind of food does the animal eat? What behaviors or body parts does the animal have for getting food?

2. List three different animals or plants. For each, list an adaptation and explain how the adaptation is useful for getting food.

HOW ARE LIVING THINGS ADAPTED FOR PROTECTION?

Danger! What do you do? Do you run or hide? Do you stand as still as you can? Living things have different adaptations to protect themselves. Find out about these adaptations in Investigation 2.

Activity

Plant Protection

Unlike animals, plants cannot run from their enemies. Find out about some adaptations that plants have to protect themselves.

MATERIALS
- goggles
- rose cutting with stem and leaves
- holly cutting
- *Science Notebook*

SAFETY
Wear goggles during this activity. Do not touch the rose stem and holly leaves.

Procedure

Observe but do not touch the stem and leaves of a rose. In your *Science Notebook,* **draw** what you see. Label the parts of the drawing you think are adaptations for protection. Next, **observe** but do not touch the holly leaves. **Make a drawing** of a leaf. Label the parts of the leaf that you think are adaptations for protecting the plant.

Analyze and Conclude

Infer how the adaptations of a rose and a holly plant might protect them from being eaten by an animal.

E46

Activity
Pill Bugs' Defense

Find out how these little animals protect themselves from danger.

MATERIALS

- goggles
- pill bugs in a container with a lid
- rectangular pan
- paper towels
- masking tape
- plastic spoon
- pencil with an eraser
- vinegar
- *Science Notebook*

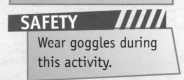

SAFETY

Wear goggles during this activity.

Procedure

1. Work with your group. Place several paper towels in the bottom of a pan. Tape the edges of the paper towels to the pan.

2. Use a spoon to put pill bugs in the middle of the pan. **Observe** them for a few minutes. **Record** what you observe in your *Science Notebook*.

3. **Predict** what a pill bug will do when it is touched. Gently touch several pill bugs with the eraser on the end of a pencil. **Record** what they do.

4. **Predict** how the pill bugs will behave when there are vinegar drops on the paper towels. Put three large drops of vinegar on one side of the pan. Do not put the vinegar on the pill bugs. **Record** what you observe. Return the pill bugs to the container.

Step 1

Step 4

Analyze and Conclude

1. What did the pill bugs do when you touched them? **Compare** their behavior with your prediction. **Infer** how this behavior helps the pill bugs keep from being eaten by a predator.

2. The vinegar represents dangerous materials that may enter a pill bug's environment. **Hypothesize** how the pill bug's behavior may protect it from such a danger.

Activity
Blending In

Frogs, spiders, and birds are just a few of the predators that eat insects. How do insects protect themselves? This activity will help you find out.

Procedure

1. Your job is to **design** and **draw** a new kind of insect—one that could hide from predators in your classroom. Look around your classroom for different colors, shapes, and patterns with which your insect could blend and not be easily seen.

2. To draw your insect, use any or all of the materials listed. Remember that your insect must have camouflage to allow it to blend in and be hard to find.

Step 2

Look for the camouflaged animals in these pictures. ▼

▲ **Crab spider on flower**

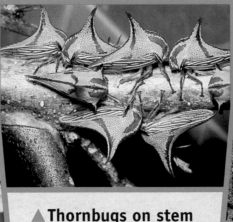

▲ **Thornbugs on stem**

Tulip tree beauty moth on tree ▲

Step 3

3. When you have finished drawing your insect, cut it out. Your teacher will tell you when to "hide" your insect. **Predict** where your insect will be hardest to find. Then put your insect in that place. If your insect hides on the wall, use a very small piece of tape to attach it. See if others can find it.

4. In your *Science Notebook,* **describe** what your insect looks like in its hiding place.

Analyze and Conclude

1. Which insect in your class was the hardest to find? **Hypothesize** why it was hard to find that insect.

2. **Infer** how the color, shape, or size of your insect helped it hide. Explain your answer.

3. **Predict** what would happen to an insect that didn't have any way to hide from predators. How might such an insect be able to survive?

UNIT PROJECT LINK

Many of the animals in the tropical rain forest live in the tops of tall trees, or the canopy layer. Some of these animals *never* come down from their tree top homes! Research how these animals are adapted to this environment. Construct some rain forest animals and attach them to your mural. Make some camouflaged animals and "hide" them among the plants. Also attach predators and their prey to show some feeding relationships.

Hiding Out
and Other Defenses

◀ **The white spots on the fawn help it blend in with the forest floor.**

You Can't See Me

Hide-and-seek is fun. But animals in nature must stay safe from enemies and catch food to eat. How they play the game can be a matter of life or death! For example, camouflage is an important adaptation for defense for many animals. When a young spotted fawn is left alone, it curls up and waits for its mother deer to return. The fawn can keep very still and blend in with the forest floor.

An insect called a katydid has wings that look like the leaves of the trees it lives in. Its wings even have brown spots that look like rotten spots found on real leaves. How did camouflage help your insect hide in the activity on pages E48 and E49?

Don't Come Too Close!

Some plants have sharp thorns or bristles that help protect them from being eaten. An animal that has nibbled on a sweet-smelling rose, for

The thorns on a rose are a sharp defense. ▶

example, and gotten pricked by a thorn is not likely to make that mistake again. Some plants contain poisonous or irritating chemicals that keep many animals away. Have you ever touched poison ivy or poison sumac? If so, you know that weeks of skin sores and itching can result. Because of these effects, many people have learned to stay away from these plants.

Sometimes a plant's defense is its bitter taste. For this reason, some people plant marigold plants around their vegetable gardens. Rabbits are often attracted to the bright orange and yellow colors of the flowers.

A marigold's bitter taste keeps it safe from hungry animals. ▶

◀ **A katydid stays safe because predators mistake it for a leaf.**

But after tasting the marigolds, the rabbits usually go elsewhere in search of more pleasant plants to nibble.

Animals that are covered with spines or prickles usually avoid being eaten. The quills of porcupines and spines of hedgehogs provide such protection. Most of the time a puffer fish does not look prickly. But when it is attacked, or when it fears attack, it can suck in water and blow itself up into a spine-covered ball. Its shape, size, and spines make it impossible for even a large fish to eat the puffer fish!

You're Copying Me!

Some animals are protected from enemies because they look like other, more dangerous animals. Most wasps and hornets have black and yellow stripes. Animals that have been stung by these insects learn to avoid them. Some harmless beetles also have black and yellow stripes. These beetles stay safe because they look like the more dangerous hornets and wasps.

A porcupine's sharp quills keep enemies at a distance. ▼

A relaxed puffer fish ▼

An alarmed puffer fish under attack ▼

Other copycats include the harmless kingsnake, which looks like the poisonous coral snake. Both snakes have red, yellow, and black stripes, but the colors are arranged differently. Although the creature on the right looks like a snake, it's actually a caterpillar from a Costa Rican rain forest. Some butterflies and moths fool predators because of two bright spots on their wings. The spots look like the eyes of large owls.

Tricked You, Didn't I?

The opossum is famous for tricking predators into thinking it's dead. The trick works because the opossum's enemies eat only freshly killed meat. Think back to how the pill bugs protected themselves in the activity on page E47. When you touched the pill bugs, what did they do that might trick a predator?

This caterpillar (*left*) and butterfly (*right*) scare away predators by looking like other animals.

The kingsnake (*right*) is a copycat of the poisonous coral snake (*left*).

E53

▲ **An ostrich protecting its young**

pounces on the tail and eats it while the rest of the lizard escapes!

Many birds pretend to be hurt to protect their chicks. The African ostrich flaps its wings and cries out when a predator heads toward its young. This gets the attention of the predator, which goes after the adult bird instead of the chicks.

Going My Way?

Some animals have behaviors that are adaptations for protection against parasites (par′ə sītz). **Parasites** are creatures that live on or in other living things. Adaptations that protect against parasites have led to some very unusual friendships.

Some lizards have a last-chance defense against predators by losing their tails! The tail continues to twitch after it has dropped off the lizard. This tricks the predator, which

SCIENCE IN LITERATURE

PIRANHAS AND OTHER WONDERS OF THE JUNGLE
by Q. L. Pearce
Illustrated by Mary Ann Fraser
Julian Messner, 1990

What kind of place is a jungle? It's an environment where plants strangle each other and blood-feeding animals lurk. You'll find out about these creatures and more in *Piranhas and Other Wonders of the Jungle*.

How do jungle creatures survive? On pages 34–35 you'll find out how some insects use disguises to protect themselves. Then, on pages 48–49, discover what a matamata is and how it protects itself.

These oxpecker birds eat a meal off the hide of a rhinoceros. ▶

Tickbirds and oxpeckers are small African songbirds. These birds eat ticks and other annoying pests off the tough skin of the rhinoceros, buffalo, and elephant. By allowing the birds to remain on them, these large animals protect themselves from parasites. In exchange, the birds are protected from predators as they dine. Few animals would attack a bird sitting on a fierce rhino.

Another unusual friendship occurs in coral reefs under the sea. A small fish called the cleaner fish removes parasites from the skin, gills, and mouth of many other reef fish. The coral reef fish are protected from parasites, and the cleaner fish has an easily found meal.

As you can see, plants and animals have many defenses. All are a matter of survival. ■

Two cleaner fish eating parasites from a coral reef fish ▼

Medicines From Nature

When you're sick, a family member probably gets you medicine from the drugstore. In some places, though, you might just be told, "Take a hike!"

Hitting the Nature Trail

People all over the world hike along woodland paths to find healing plants. They rely on nature's drugstore for relief. If you lived in the Ozark Mountains of Missouri, your family might brew spicebush tea to bring down your fever. If you lived in the Appalachian Mountains and had a stomachache, someone might serve you a gentle drink of slippery elm bark. This home medicine was used by pioneers over 200 years ago.

Plants produce chemicals that help in their protection and survival. The chemicals are in leaves, bark, roots, blossoms, and seeds. The use of these chemicals as medicine goes back thousands of years.

Cures From Living Things

Many different plant parts and chemicals, as well as animal parts, have been used as medicines. In the 1890s a German chemist discovered

A Cherokee helps heal an early settler with bark and powdered maize. ▶

Aspirin was discovered as a natural chemical in the willow plant. ▶

a natural chemical in the willow plant—aspirin. Aspirin is often taken by adults for the aches of a cold. But some people in the southwestern United States prefer to treat colds and coughs with the spice anise (an'is).

Early settlers in America often relied on medicines used by Native Americans. The Cherokees used bark from the sassafras tree on sores. They then applied a soothing paste of powdered maize, or corn, and soft turkey down feathers!

Navajo (nav'ə hō) healers use the root of the strong-smelling osha plant. Not only does osha root help treat colds, but it also has been found to keep snakes away.

▲ The Ohlone people in California use the roots of the horsetail plant to make a syrup for coughs.

In some places, people use snakes as part of a cure. Some shops in China offer medicines made from snake blood, venom, and skin to improve vision.

Natural First-Aid Kit

Some people keep an aloe plant in the kitchen. Burns from cooking can be soothed by breaking off a fleshy aloe leaf and squeezing its clear liquid onto the burns.

Today, nearly half of all prescribed drugs contain at least one chemical from nature. Scientists have climbed mountains and crossed deserts in their search for plants that can be used to produce new medicines.

Scientists are hopeful that many discoveries will be made in tropical rain forests. Most of the rain forests' plants haven't yet been identified. The search for medicines from nature continues. ■

Plants and animals of the rain forest may hold new cures. ▶

An aloe plant ▼

INVESTIGATION 2

1. Imagine you are walking through a forest to observe the animals that live there. Describe some of the adaptations the animals might have to protect themselves.

2. What are two adaptations that plants may have to protect themselves?

THINK IT
WRITE IT

REFLECT & EVALUATE

WORD POWER

adaptations
behavior
camouflage
nutrients
parasites

On Your Own
Write a definition for each term in the list.

With a Partner
Mix up the letters of each term in the list. Provide a clue for each term and challenge your partner to unscramble the terms.

BUILD YOUR PORTFOLIO

Look through old magazines for pictures of animals that have interesting adaptations. Cut out the pictures and paste them on a large sheet of paper. Next to each picture, write a description of the animal's adaptations. Explain how you think those adaptations help the animal.

Analyze Information

Study the photo of the lobster. What adaptations does the lobster have for catching food or protecting itself?

Assess Performance

Design an animal with adaptations for catching a meal. Also give your animal adaptations that help it protect itself. Draw a picture or use different materials to construct a model of your animal. Write how each adaptation you gave your animal helps it get food or protect itself.

Problem Solving

1. A rabbit hops toward a plant that it wants to eat. But after one bite, the rabbit won't try eating that plant ever again. Explain an adaptation the plant might have that protects it from being eaten by the rabbit.

2. Some animals hunt food only at night. The darkness may protect them from being eaten as they look for food. But how do they find their food in the dark? Explain how certain senses might be adapted to help these animals find food in the dark.

CHAPTER 3

LIVING THINGS IN THE ENVIRONMENT

What living things change the environment the most? If you guessed humans, you're right. And right now people are very quickly changing the country of Brazil. Some of those changes are destroying the environments of plants and animals.

The Very Last Pictures

Luiz Claudio Marigo is a Brazilian wildlife photographer. Many of the animals and plants in his photographs no longer exist. His pictures are all that are left of them. But Luiz Marigo is doing more than recording vanishing animals and their forest homes. He is trying to show Brazilians their country's wonderful wildlife. Marigo wants people to save Brazil's forests. He hopes that if Brazilians see the beauty of their country, they'll stop the destruction.

How did Marigo become a wildlife photographer? His interest in photography began when he was a child. His first trip to a wildlife area changed his life. He knew at once that he would devote himself to capturing nature with his camera.

As you read this chapter, think about the living things that share your environment. How do changes that occur affect the plants, animals, and people around you?

▲ Luiz Claudio Marigo

▲ A photo by Marigo of two Brazilian jaguars

HOW CAN LIVING THINGS CHANGE THE ENVIRONMENT?

Have you ever seen a house being built? Big machines are used to move dirt and cut down trees. In Investigation 1 find out how people and other living things change their environments.

Activity

My Neighborhood Keeps Changing!

Think about an old photograph that shows your home or neighborhood. Then think about your home or neighborhood as it is today. What changes have taken place? People are always making changes to their environments. How do environments change?

Harlem, in New York City, during the late 1920s or early 1930s ▼

Procedure

1. **Observe** the two pictures on page E63. The neighborhood shown has changed in many ways over the years. In your *Science Notebook*, **make a list** of all the changes you can find. **Compare** your list with those of other group members to see if there is anything that you missed.

Step 1

2. Look at your list. **Infer** who made the changes. **Talk with your group** and **hypothesize** how the changes affected living things in the area.

Analyze and Conclude

1. What caused the changes in this neighborhood? **Explain** how these changes affected the environment.

2. Think about the neighborhood that you live in. **Predict** what your neighborhood will look like five years from now. How might people and other living things change your neighborhood?

INVESTIGATE FURTHER!

TAKE ACTION

Make a plan to change the environment around your school in a way that will help living things. You might choose to plant a small garden or make bird feeders. Show your plan to your teacher. If you can, carry it out with your classmates.

E63

Busy Beaver Construction Co.

People build dams to control the flow of water from rivers and streams. The beavers of North America, without any training in construction, or building, do the same thing. These hard-working animals build dams and keep them in repair.

Timber!

Beavers do a lot of work to build a dam. They use their sharp teeth to chew away at the trunks of trees. Beavers can chomp through a tree trunk 1 m (3 ft) thick! The trees come crashing down. Then the beavers cut the trunks and branches into logs, again using their sharp teeth. They float the logs into position in the stream. Then they cement the logs together with mud, stones, and leaves.

A Warm, Dry Lodge

Beavers build dams across the moving waters of streams and rivers because the dams create ponds. Beavers then build their lodges in the still waters of the ponds. A lodge is a small living area made of tree parts and mud. The lodge rises up and out of the pond. The lodge protects a group of beavers from cold weather and from predators.

A Home for Others

The ponds created by dams become homes to other animals, too. Many kinds of fish as well as insects, spiders, frogs, and salamanders live in the quiet ponds. Water birds build nests near the ponds. Many of these animals would not be able to make their homes in undammed streams.

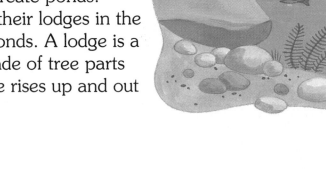

Dam

A Changed Place

Beavers cut down many trees along the shore to build their dams and lodges. When the beavers have cut down most of the trees near the pond, they move. They leave behind the results of their hard work and start all over again.

Over time, the ponds created by beaver dams fill with rich soil. They become beautiful meadows. Plants such as grass and wildflowers grow in the meadows. By cutting down trees, building dams, creating ponds, and making lodges, beavers greatly change the environment. ■

The beavers enter their lodge through an underwater tunnel. ▼

Lodge

People Change the Environment

What would the world look like without the changes people have made? There would be no houses and schools, no stores and factories, no streets and highways. What else would be different?

In the activity on pages E62 and E63, you compared old and new pictures of a neighborhood. How did people change that environment?

Too Wet

Sometimes people change an environment because they want to use the land for farming and building. But the land isn't always suitable for these purposes. For example, the land may be too wet.

That's why some people change wetland environments—swamps, marshes, and bogs. People drain the

SCIENCE IN LITERATURE

PIRANHAS AND OTHER WONDERS OF THE JUNGLE
by Q. L. Pearce
Illustrated by Mary Ann Fraser
Julian Messner, 1990

Piranhas patrol the rivers, hungry to attack even large animals that come their way. Driver ants by the millions march across the jungle, eating any creature in their path. In spite of the dangers, some people make their homes in rain forests.

On page 62 of *Piranhas and Other Wonders of the Jungle*, you can find out how people are changing the rain forests of the world. You'll also learn how the growth of rain forests can cause startling changes. When you read pages 59–61, you'll discover how the jungle has hidden cities where ancient groups of people lived.

water from wetlands to use the land for farming, housing, and industry. Today, only about half the wetlands in the United States remain.

The wetlands are home to many different living things. Birds, insects, fish, frogs, alligators, snakes, turtles, beavers, and a large variety of plants and grasses all live in wetland environments. When people change wetland environments, many living things may lose their homes. The photo below left shows a wetlands environment that was changed.

Making Things Better

People also make changes that improve their environments. Many people are working together to protect the world's wetlands. Some people even fill wetlands with water during long periods of dry weather.

People create new parks in which animals and plants are protected. They plant trees and gardens that become new homes for many different living things. In many ways, people are always changing the natural environment. ■

Giants Stadium, in the background, was built on wetlands in New Jersey. ▼

Students learn about the wetlands at Everglades National Park in Florida. ▼

Bringing Back the Buffaloes

Long ago the Great Plains of the United States and Canada were covered with roaming herds of American bison, also called buffaloes. But the large herds of buffaloes began to disappear. And so did the grasslands, or prairies, they once roamed. People changed much of the prairie land to make it suitable for building and farming.

But today, even without their old prairie land, the buffaloes are back in growing numbers. Take a trip back in time to find out why the buffaloes almost disappeared and how they've come back.

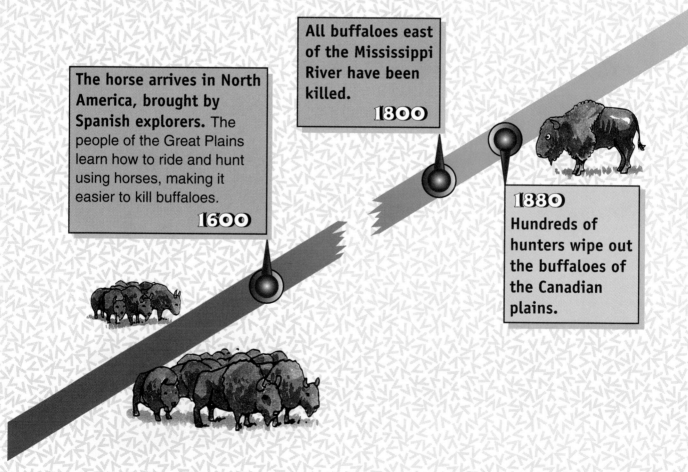

The horse arrives in North America, brought by Spanish explorers. The people of the Great Plains learn how to ride and hunt using horses, making it easier to kill buffaloes.
1600

All buffaloes east of the Mississippi River have been killed.
1800

1880
Hundreds of hunters wipe out the buffaloes of the Canadian plains.

Several thousand buffaloes are moved to Wood Buffalo Park in Alberta, Canada.
1920

2000

1990s
Because they are protected, buffaloes are no longer in danger of becoming extinct.

Yellowstone National Park

1894
The buffalo is nearly extinct. Theodore Roosevelt, who would later become President of the United States, wants to protect the buffalo. Congress passes a law against killing buffaloes. The herds slowly begin to grow again.

Over 20,000 buffaloes live in the United States, and more than 15,000 live in Canada's Wood Buffalo Park. The number of buffaloes continues to grow because hunting buffaloes is still against the law.

Today, most buffaloes are in parks because the prairie land they once roamed has been changed. Farmland, factories, towns, and roads have replaced much of the old prairies. ■

INVESTIGATION 1

1. You are a scientist exploring a tropical rain forest. You observe that a large part of the forest has been cut down. How might such a change affect the living things in that area? Explain your answer.

2. Explain three ways living things change the environment. Your examples can include changes made by people, other animals, or plants.

How Are Living Things Adapted to Their Environments?

Why do you sweat when your environment is hot and shiver when it's cold? These are examples of adaptations. In Investigation 2 discover other ways living things are adapted to their environments.

Activity

Keeping Heat In

Adaptations help living things survive. In this activity find out how some animals are adapted to cold weather.

MATERIALS
- 2 large plastic jars
- 2 small plastic jars
- down feathers
- hot tap water
- 2 thermometers
- timer
- *Science Notebook*

SAFETY ///////
Clean up any spills immediately.
Be careful when handling glass thermometers.

Procedure

1. In this activity, you'll **make models** of two animals. One has feathers. The other one does not. **Talk with your group** and **predict** which animal model will lose more heat in 30 minutes. **Record** your prediction in your *Science Notebook*.

2. **Make a chart** like the one shown.

Time (in min)	Temperature (°C) Model With Feathers	Temperature (°C) Model Without Feathers
0		
15		
30		

3. To make your models, place a small jar in a larger jar. Place down feathers around the small jar. Cover the sides of the small jar completely with feathers but don't pack the feathers tightly.

4. Place another small jar in a different larger jar. Don't put anything around this small jar.

5. Fill each small jar halfway with hot tap water. Take care not to wet the feathers. Put a thermometer in each small jar. **Measure the temperature** of the water in each jar. **Record** your readings under the correct heading on the first line in your chart.

Step 5

6. After 15 minutes, **record** the temperature of the water in each jar. Wait another 15 minutes. Then **record** both temperatures again.

Analyze and Conclude

1. By how many degrees did the temperature in each jar change?

2. Which animal model lost more heat? How does this result compare with your prediction?

3. Study your models. **Hypothesize** about how down feathers help a bird stay warm.

Beating the Heat

Both animals and plants have adaptations that protect them from extreme heat. On a blazing hot day in summer, what do you do to stay cool? To protect your skin from burning in the Sun and your body from overheating, you'd likely head for a shady spot.

Your body has a built-in way of cooling down. In hot weather your skin becomes covered with tiny droplets of perspiration, or sweat. Sweating is an adaptation to prevent overheating. When sweat dries up, the drying process cools your skin.

Although perspiring is an important adaptation to humans, few other animals perspire. In a desert, if an animal perspires, it will quickly become dried out. There is little water available in the desert to replace the body's lost moisture.

Life in the Desert

How does a desert animal, which lives where the Sun scorches the sand all day, survive? There are no tall leafy trees for shade. In some deserts, daytime temperatures reach 65°C (150°F). Rain is scarce, and there are few water holes to drink from. Deserts may seem to be impossible places to live. But, amazingly, the world's deserts are home to thousands of kinds of plants and animals. All have adaptations to "beat the heat."

The Namib Desert in Namibia, Africa ▼

E72

Insects Keep Cool

Some desert insects have body designs that keep them cool. One little beetle that lives in the Namib Desert of southwestern Africa survives by keeping its body away from the hot sand. How does it do this?

Nicknamed the stilt beetle, this insect tiptoes across sun-baked sand dunes on long stiltlike legs.

The black color of some beetles can be a problem in the desert. This is because dark colors heat faster than light ones. Many desert beetles have white or yellow wax covering their dark bodies. The light-colored wax reflects the sun, keeping the insect's body cool. Because wax is waterproof, the waxy covering also helps hold in moisture, keeping the beetle from drying out.

How is the stilt beetle adapted to its desert environment? ▼

Never Thirsty

The behaviors of desert animals are also adaptations to the hot, dry environment. Kangaroo rats have some unusual adaptations for conserving water and staying cool in the desert. A kangaroo rat may go its entire life without ever taking a drink of water! Kangaroo rats get moisture from the food they eat—seeds, juicy grasses, and pulp of cactus plants. These animals don't sweat and they seldom urinate. Kangaroo rats are active only at night.

▲ **A kangaroo rat burrows in the sand to stay cool during the day.**

The saguaro cactus grows in deserts of the southwestern U.S. and northern Mexico. ▼

During the day, kangaroo rats sleep sealed inside their "cool" burrows. Their burrows are about 0.3 m (1 ft) below the desert sand. Since the Sun doesn't heat this sand directly, the temperature in the burrow is a cool 30°C (86°F).

Hidden Water

Plants also have adaptations to the hot, dry desert environment. Cactus plants hold a lot of water inside. They have thick stems and slender, spiny leaves that keep in moisture. Cactus roots are widespread just beneath the desert's surface. These shallow roots can rapidly take in water from a rare desert rainfall before the hot Sun causes the water to dry up. The water then is stored for weeks inside the cactus.

The largest kind of cactus is the saguaro (sə gwär′ō). After years of growing slowly, a saguaro can reach 15 m (50 ft) in height and can store hundreds of liters of water. ■

A flowering saguaro cactus ▼

UNIT PROJECT LINK

Another environment that you have read about in this unit is the tropical rain forest. Tropical rain forests have many important resources that can't be found anywhere else in the world. Find out what these resources are and how the rain forest is helpful to people. Also find out why tropical rain forests are disappearing. Make a poster that lists things you and your friends can do to help save the rain forests.

When the Going Gets Tough...

Maple trees drop their leaves, blue jays fly south, and black bears curl up in dens and go into a deep sleep. These things all happen as the cold of winter approaches. Why?

In nature there are many cycles—summer and winter, rainy season and dry season, and others. These natural cycles happen in different places around the world. Sometimes a cycle creates big changes in the environment. Then plants and animals have to change in some way, too, in order to survive.

▲ **Lesser golden plover**

Winter Travel

How can an animal survive through a cold, snowy winter if it can't find enough food to eat? One way is for the animal to **migrate** (mī′grāt), or travel to a warmer place where it can find food.

Many kinds of birds migrate. It's not the cold weather that makes them leave. As you saw in the activity on pages E70 and E71, down feathers can help birds stay warm. Some birds can survive cold

weather as long as they can find enough food. Some seed-eating birds don't migrate.

But insect-eating birds and birds whose food is often covered by snow or ice usually migrate before winter comes. Some fly long distances. The lesser golden plover migrates over 3,200 km (2,000 mi)—from Alaska to Hawaii. And the Arctic tern migrates 20,000 km (12,000 mi)—from the Arctic in the north to the Antarctic in the south!

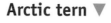
Arctic tern ▼

Winter Sleep

How else do animals survive a cold winter without food? Some animals go into a deep sleep, called **hibernation** (hī bər nā′shən). Bears, ground squirrels, woodchucks, snakes, and bats all may hibernate during winter.

While an animal is in this deep sleep, its heart beats slower, it breathes less, and its body temperature usually drops. All these changes mean that an animal uses up less energy. Therefore, it can survive a long time without eating.

When warmer weather returns, the animal begins to warm up, too. Its heart starts beating faster, and soon it wakes up—to spring and a new supply of food!

A chipmunk sleeps through most of the winter but may wake up on warmer days to eat. ▼

▲ **The lesser golden plover and the Arctic tern are two kinds of birds that migrate.**

Plants in Winter

Plants are rooted to one spot, so they can't migrate. But their activities can slow, as if they were going into a deep sleep.

As winter approaches, many trees—such as maples, oaks, poplars, elms, and chestnuts—lose their leaves. Without leaves, a tree can't make food. So it must live off food that is stored elsewhere in the plant—for example, in the roots.

Some plants, such as ferns, die above ground. But their roots survive underground through winter. When the weather warms up, the plants begin to grow again. ■

▲ Each autumn, trees like this maple lose their leaves.

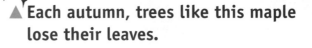

INVESTIGATION 2

1. There is snow on the ground and on tree branches and bushes. You see only one or two kinds of birds. What adaptation do the birds have for keeping warm? Why did other kinds of birds leave?

2. What adaptation do you have to beat the heat? Do most desert animals have the same adaptation? Explain your answer.

WORD POWER

hibernation
migrate

 On Your Own
Write a definition for each term in the list.

 With a Partner
Write both terms on a sheet of paper. With your partner, draw pictures that show the meanings of the words. Use as many animal examples as you can in your drawings.

BUILD YOUR PORTFOLIO

Write a paragraph explaining some of the different ways in which living things are adapted to their environments. Be sure to use the words from the list in your paragraph.

Analyze Information

Study the drawing. Explain how the beavers change their environment.

Assess Performance

Look for ways people are changing the environment near your home or school. Write about any changes you see. Describe how these changes affect other living things.

Problem Solving

1. A family on vacation decides to go scuba diving. The group leader tells the family not to take any of the plants and animals from their underwater environment. Why is it important for the divers not to change the underwater environment?

2. What kinds of adaptations must living things have to survive in the desert? Give a few examples of adaptations of animals and plants that live in the desert.

Throughout this unit you've investigated questions related to the roles of living things. How will you use what you've learned and share that information with others? Here are some ideas.

Hold a Big Event
to Share Your Unit Project

Have a Rain Forest Celebration Day! Display the mural you created of rain forest plants and animals. Invite your parents and other classes to visit your classroom and learn about the rain forests. Give "jungle talks" and explain how the different living things in the rain forest live together. Explain why people should care about saving the rain forest and what they can do to help.

Experiment

Plan a long-term project based on an activity in this unit. You might study what materials decompose and what materials don't. Bury materials such as a slice of bread, an apple, a piece of newspaper, and a piece of plastic. Dig up and observe the materials one month later. What happened to each item?

Research

Learn more about an animal adaptation, such as camouflage, or a plant adaptation, such as thorns. A good place to look is in *Ranger Rick* magazine or in other nature magazines.

Take Action

Planting trees and bushes is a great way to help the environment. Write a plan describing how your class could do this. How can the class raise money to buy plants? Where should they be planted? If possible, carry out your plan.

WHAT'S FOR LUNCH?

Theme: Systems

GET READY TO

OBSERVE & QUESTION

What happens to food after it's swallowed?

What's it like to eat a meal in space? Without gravity, does food go "down" to the stomach? How different is eating in space from eating on Earth?

Find out what happens to food after it's swallowed. Discover the ways food changes and how it moves through the body.

EXPERIMENT & HYPOTHESIZE

Why does your body need food?

Foods contain various kinds of materials, called nutrients, that are needed by your body. Investigate which foods have which nutrients. Do hands-on activities to test some common foods for nutrients. Find out what's healthful and what's not in the foods you eat.

INVESTIGATE!

RESEARCH & ANALYZE

As you investigate, find out more from these books.

- ***Outside and Inside You*** by Sandra Markle (Bradbury Press, 1991). Look in a mirror and stick out your tongue. That's one way to get a look at taste buds. An even better way is to look in this book. You'll find lots of amazing photographs showing the inside of the human body.

- ***How My Parents Learned to Eat*** by Ina R. Friedman (Houghton Mifflin, 1994). Many families have their own special ways of preparing and eating foods. Find out about two ways that people eat in this charming book.

WORK TOGETHER & SHARE IDEAS

How can you build a food pyramid supermarket?

Working together, you'll have a chance to collect food packages and set up a food-pyramid supermarket in your classroom. Then you and your classmates can plan healthful menus. Look for the Unit Project Links for help with practicing food shopping and learning to make wise food purchases.

CHAPTER 1

THE FOODS WE EAT

High fat. Too much sugar. Not enough fiber. Too much salt. You hear a lot of talk about diet on radio and TV. You read about diet in newspapers and magazines. Do you find it confusing? In this chapter you'll find out why you need a healthful diet. You'll also learn *what* a healthful diet is.

Someone's in the Kitchen

What's for dinner? Do you ever wonder how the person who cooks at your home thinks up different meals to prepare? Maybe you've seen that person looking through a newspaper or magazine for some new ideas.

The person who decides what goes into the food section of a newspaper or magazine is called a food editor. Jonell Nash is the food editor of *Essence*, a monthly magazine with more than a million readers.

Jonell Nash's articles provide recipes and include tempting pictures of the food. Dishes often include vegetables and fruits that are in season. Each recipe ends with important health information about that food. Nash makes sure that all recipes are tested. Then she knows that the foods will taste as good as they look.

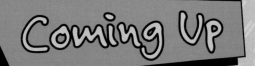

Coming Up

▶ Jonell Nash researches recipes from around the world as food editor of *Essence* magazine.

INVESTIGATION 1

WHY DOES YOUR BODY NEED FOOD?

Do you ever eat a food just because you know it's good for you? Food gives you fuel for energy and materials for growth. In Investigation 1 you'll find out how the foods you eat keep your body going.

Activity

Put It to the Test

You know that foods give you fuel for energy. Foods that contain starch are a good source of that fuel. You can test foods to find out which have starch in them.

Procedure

1. **Make a chart** in your *Science Notebook* like the one shown.

TEST FOR STARCH			
Kind of Food	**Prediction**	**Color of Iodine Spot**	**Does It Contain Starch?**

2. When iodine touches a food that has starch in it, the iodine turns black. Work with your group. Examine the foods you will test for starch. Together **predict** which foods will turn iodine black. **Record** the name of each food and your predictions in your chart.

3. Put a potato slice in a pie pan. Your teacher will place one drop of iodine on the potato. **Observe** the potato. In your chart **record** your observations and whether the potato contains starch.

Step 3

4. Repeat step 3, using other foods. **Record** your observations in your chart. Also **record** whether the foods contain starch. **Compare** your results with those of other groups.

Analyze and Conclude

1. Which foods contain starch? Which foods don't contain starch? **Compare** your predictions with your test results.

2. If you wanted to plan a dinner with lots of starch, what foods would you include?

3. Starch is a nutrient (noo'trē ənt). A **nutrient** is something in food that your body needs for energy, growth, and repair. Why is it important to know which foods give you nutrients?

Activity

Finding Fat

Fat is needed in your diet for your body to work properly. What fat is in your diet? Test some foods to find out.

MATERIALS
- foods to test
- brown bag paper
- water
- vegetable oil
- 2 droppers
- *Science Notebook*

SAFETY
Do not eat any materials used in this activity.

Procedure

1. **Make a chart** in your *Science Notebook* like the one shown. Work with your group. Examine the foods you'll test for fat. Together **predict** which foods will have fat in them. **Record** the name of each food and your predictions in your chart.

TEST FOR FAT			
Kind of Food	Prediction	Grease Spot?	Does It Contain Fat?

2. Fold a square of brown bag paper into eight equal sections. Unfold the paper.

3. On one section of the paper, put a few drops of water. On a second section, put a few drops of vegetable oil. Label each section with the name of the material you put on it.

4. Test each kind of food by rubbing it gently back and forth in a different section of the paper. Label each section. Put your paper in a warm place to dry.

5. After the spots dry, hold the paper up to bright light. Look at the sections labeled *water* and *vegetable oil*. Vegetable oil is a fat, water is not.

6. Compare the spot left by each food with the spots left by vegetable oil and by water. **Record** whether each food left a grease spot. A grease spot means the food contains fat.

Analyze and Conclude

1. Which foods contain fat? How could you tell?

2. Compare the test results for the potato slice and the potato chip. **Hypothesize** why they differ.

3. Hypothesize why it is important to know which foods contain the nutrient fat.

INVESTIGATE FURTHER!

EXPERIMENT

Try testing some of your favorite snack foods for fat. Which ones contain fat? If you were trying to cut down on fat, which foods would you avoid?

Where Nutrients Come From

You probably know that your body needs food for energy. But did you know that your body also uses food for growth and to heal wounds? In fact, food supplies everything your body needs to work. The parts of food that your body uses for energy, growth, and repair are called **nutrients**. It's the amount of nutrients in a food that makes a food healthful or not. Nutrients in foods can be classified into six groups, as shown in the table below. How is each nutrient used by the body?

NUTRIENTS

Sources	Types	What They're Used For	
	Carbohydrates	• Energy	
	Fats	• Energy • Keep body warm	• Help body use vitamins • Cushion joints
	Proteins	• Build body parts for growth • Control body functions	• Fight disease • Repair injured body parts
	Water	• Makes up over half of your body • Remove waste	• Required in all body processes • Control body temperature
	Vitamins	• Trigger body functions • Help blood clot	• Help release energy from other nutrients
	Minerals	• Make up bones and teeth • Trigger body functions	• Control the amount of body fluids

F10

Fuel Foods

Nutrients that your body uses for energy are called **carbohydrates** (kär bō hī´-drāts). Sugars and starches are the two main kinds of carbohydrates. When you tested the foods in the activity on pages F6 and F7, you learned that potatoes, bread, and cooked noodles are good sources of starch. Look at the photo at the right to find some sources of starch and some sources of sugar.

Sugars and starches are carbohydrates. ▼

▲ **Cheese, butter, and certain cuts of meat are high in fat.**

A Little Goes a Long Way

Fats are the nutrients that have the greatest amounts of energy. In fact, a portion of fat has over twice as much energy as the same amount of sugar or starch. The nutrient table lists ways your body uses fats. Which foods in the activity on pages F8 and F9 contain fat?

Many snack foods are very high in fat. Fat becomes a health problem when a person eats too many fatty foods. Then the body stores the extra fat it can't use right away.

Building Blocks for Growth

Proteins (prō′tēnz) are nutrients that give your body the building blocks for growth. Much of your body is made up of proteins. Your skin, muscles, hair, lungs, and eyes are all made of proteins.

Proteins help your body work. For example, the protein in blood carries oxygen. Other proteins control how fast you grow. If you don't get enough protein in your diet, your body can't grow, repair itself, or work properly. What foods give you protein?

Proteins are the building blocks for growth. ▼

Staying Afloat

Water is a very important nutrient for your body. The nutrient table on page F10 lists some of the ways your body uses water. Without water you could live for only a few days. You can live for weeks without food.

Your body loses water every time you breathe, perspire, or get rid of body wastes. To make up for this loss, you need to take in 2 L to 3 L (2 qt to 3 qt) of water every day. That's a lot of water to drink. Fortunately you also get water from the foods you eat.

▲ **Most foods contain water.**

Helper Nutrients

Vitamins (vīt'ə minz) and **minerals** (min'ər əlz) are nutrients that help your body work. Unlike carbohydrates, proteins, and fats, they do not supply energy or materials for growth. If you eat a healthful diet, you'll get all the vitamins and minerals you need.

Without vitamins and minerals, you wouldn't have strong bones or teeth. You couldn't use the energy from food, either. Use the nutrient table on page F10 to find out what else vitamins and minerals do.

Vitamins help release energy from other nutrients. ▼

◀ Vitamins and minerals are found in many foods.

INVESTIGATE FURTHER!

EXPERIMENT

Record all the foods you eat in one day. Then use the nutrient table on page F10 to help you identify the nutrients in each food.

F13

RESOURCE

Boosting Nutrients

SCIENCE TECHNOLOGY & SOCIETY

Do you ever read the cereal box while you're eating a bowl of cereal? Maybe you've noticed that many things are added to cereal. Anything added to a food before it is packaged is called a food additive. Food companies use food additives to keep foods fresh, to make foods look better, to make foods feel better in your mouth, and to add nutrients to foods. On these pages you'll find out about food additives that are nutrients.

A Nutrient Punch

Food companies add nutrients to foods for two reasons. One reason is to supply nutrients that might be missing from people's diets. The second reason is to replace nutrients, mainly vitamins and minerals, that are lost when foods are prepared.

Vitamin and mineral additives help prevent some diseases. For example, if people don't get enough vitamin D in their diets, they can get rickets, a disease that causes the bones to be weak. Since food companies started adding vitamins and minerals to

▲ **Why is vitamin D added to milk?**

foods, diseases such as rickets have become rare in the United States.

Nutrients—Lost and Found

How can foods lose nutrients? When foods are washed, shredded, ground, or cooked, some vitamins and minerals are destroyed. Take wheat, for example. When it's ground into white flour, more than four fifths of its vitamin B_6 is lost in processing. Other vitamins and minerals are also lost. So food companies add back some of these lost nutrients.

F14

Fortified Foods

You can tell which foods have added nutrients by reading food labels. If you see the word *fortified* or *enriched*, you can be sure that nutrients have been added. Foods that often contain added nutrients include bread, cereal, flour, pasta, milk, and salt.

You may think that any food with added nutrients is healthful. But you must consider more. Look at the kinds and amounts of nutrients a food contains. If a cereal is high in fat and sugar, it really isn't healthful. You'll learn to read food labels in Investigation 3. Then it will be easy to choose healthful foods. ■

▲ **Food additives make some foods more healthful.**

═══════════════ INVESTIGATION 1 ═══════════════

1. Some people take vitamins every day, though many doctors say this isn't necessary. Based on what you've learned, who should take vitamins and who probably doesn't need to?

2. List the six nutrients found in food. Tell why your body needs each one.

HOW DOES YOUR DIET STACK UP?

Now that you've learned about nutrients, you can begin to identify which foods are healthful and which are not very healthful. In Investigation 2 you'll decide how your diet stacks up.

Activity

MATERIALS
• *Science Notebook*

Rate Your Diet

Think about the foods you eat. Is your diet healthful? Find out!

- -

Procedure

1. A healthful diet is made up of foods high in nutrients. **Predict** how healthful your diet is. Choose from the list below. **Record** your prediction in your *Science Notebook*.

    A. very healthful   **C.** unhealthful

    B. healthful   **D.** very unhealthful

2. **Make a chart** like the one shown, but make it larger so you'll have room to write in all the foods you eat.

Meal	Day 1	Day 2	Day 3
Breakfast			
Lunch			
Dinner			
Snacks			

3. For each of the next three days, **record** everything that you eat. It's best to list the foods in a meal right after you eat.

4. When your chart is complete, **analyze** it. First read the column for Day 1. Then think about what nutrients are in each food. You may wish to refer to the table on page F10. Are the foods you eat providing you with all the nutrients you need? **Record** your thoughts.

5. Repeat step 4 for Day 2 and Day 3.

Analyze and Conclude

1. On which day did your diet give you the most nutrients? How do you know?

2. On which day do you think your diet contained the fewest nutrients? Which of the foods that you ate were lowest in nutrients?

3. Now **rate** your diet, using the terms listed in step 1. **Compare** how healthful your diet is with your prediction.

4. Even diets high in nutrients can be improved. **Write** a paragraph in your *Science Notebook* telling how you could improve your diet.

Start at the Bottom

What did you find out about your diet from the activity on pages F16 and F17? Is it as healthful as you predicted? Now find out more about how to have a healthful diet.

Remember that your body needs a variety of nutrients for energy, growth, repair, and other activities. You get the nutrients from the foods you eat. Look at the graph. It shows the amounts of fats, proteins, and carbohydrates you should have in your diet. When you eat a healthful diet, you'll also get vitamins, minerals, and water.

NUTRIENTS NEEDED FOR A HEALTHFUL DIET

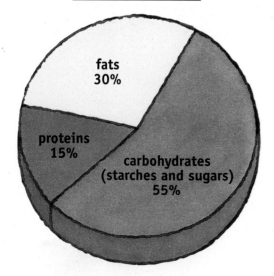

fats
30%

proteins
15%

carbohydrates
(starches and sugars)
55%

The Food Pyramid

Making healthful food choices can be hard to do. Luckily the United States Department of Agriculture (USDA) gives people advice about healthful foods. The USDA has developed the Food Guide Pyramid (pir'ə mid) to make it easier to choose healthful foods.

The food pyramid is a guide for planning a healthful diet. A **healthful diet** is made up of a variety of foods that supply all the nutrients needed by the body. In a healthful diet, you get the right amounts of carbohydrates, proteins, and fats. And you also get all the vitamins, minerals, and water that your body needs.

Look at the six food groups in the food pyramid on the next page. Each group is made up of foods that have the same kinds of nutrients. Compare the food groups in the pyramid with the groups of foods in the nutrient table on page F10. What similarities do you see?

Find the bread, cereal, rice, and pasta group at the bottom of the food pyramid. Foods from this group are good sources of carbohydrates.

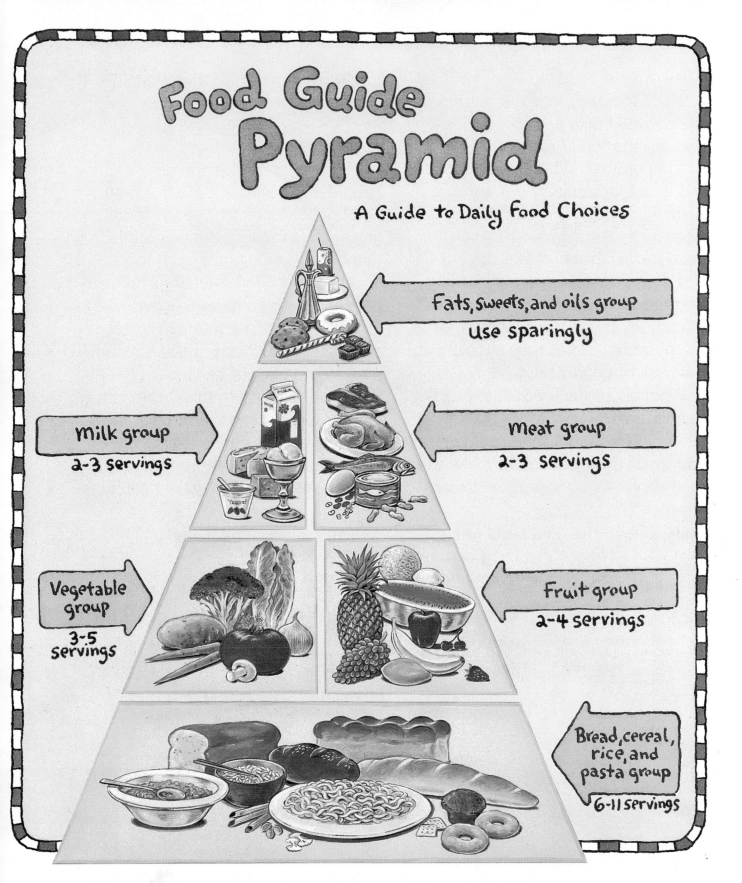

Food Guide Pyramid

A Guide to Daily Food Choices

Fats, sweets, and oils group
Use sparingly

Milk group
2-3 servings

Meat group
2-3 servings

Vegetable group
3-5 servings

Fruit group
2-4 servings

Bread, cereal, rice, and pasta group
6-11 servings

The vegetable and fruit groups are also good sources of starch as well as natural sugars. The meat and milk groups, near the top of the pyramid, are foods that give you the proteins, minerals, and fats you need.

Amounts Count

The food groups at the bottom of the pyramid take up more space than do the food groups at the top of the pyramid. Why do you think this is so? Compare the graph on page F18 with the food pyramid on page F19. You can see that you need more carbohydrates in your diet than you do any other nutrient. So the foods that are good sources of carbohydrates form the base of the pyramid, just as they should form the base of your diet.

What about the foods at the top of the pyramid? These foods have more fat and added sugar than foods at the bottom of the pyramid. To make wise food choices, you should eat fewer foods from the top of the pyramid than from the bottom.

A Good Plan

The next step in planning a healthful diet is to choose the right amounts of foods from each food group. The food pyramid gives the number of servings for each food group. You'll need the larger number of servings if you're very active.

You can see that the fats, sweets, and oils group doesn't have a recommended number of servings. That's because the foods in this group don't have many nutrients. If you eat too many foods from this group, your body might not get the right amounts of nutrients it needs to stay healthy.

Bread, cereal, rice, and pasta group ▼

Food	Serving Size
Bread	1 slice
Cereal	30 g (1 oz)
Cooked cereal, rice, or pasta	125 mL ($\frac{1}{2}$ c)

Fruit and vegetable groups ▼

Food	Serving Size
Raw leafy vegetables	250 mL (1 c)
Cooked vegetables	125 mL ($\frac{1}{2}$ c)
Vegetable juice	375 mL ($\frac{3}{4}$ c)

How Much Is Enough?

You're now well on your way to planning a healthful diet. Planning is easy if you follow the guidelines in the food pyramid. "But wait a minute," you say. "How many vegetables make one serving? How much milk should I drink?" Don't worry. The USDA has thought of that, too. Look at the tables below and on page F20 to see some serving sizes for each food group.

Another thing to think about when planning a healthful diet is variety. Be sure to eat different foods from each food group every day. ■

How many servings from each food group are in this meal? ▼

Milk group ▼

Food	Serving Size
Milk or yogurt	250 mL (1 c)
Natural cheese	45 g (1½ oz)
Processed cheese	60 g (2 oz)

Meat group ▼

Food	Serving Size
Meat, poultry, fish	60 g–90 g (2 oz–3 oz)
Cooked, dry beans	125 mL (1½ c)
Peanut butter	30 mL (2 tbsp)
Eggs	1

Pyramid Bases

Have you ever seen pictures of the Great Pyramid in Egypt? A pyramid is made up of four triangles. They come together and form a point at the top. The base is wider, so it will support the rest of the pyramid.

You can think of the food pyramid in this same way. The bread, cereal, rice, and pasta group is the base of the food pyramid. These foods are good sources of starch, a carbohydrate. Remember that carbohydrates should form over half of your diet. So, you might say that starch is a base that supports the rest of a healthful diet.

Starch Bases Around the World

In the United States, people get most of their starch base by eating foods such as cereal, bread, bagels, tortillas (tôr tē′əz), rice, pasta, and potatoes. But people in different parts of the world eat different foods.

rice

kasha

breads and cereals

pita

corn

▲ Starch-based foods from around the world

tortillas

potatoes

pasta

cassava

falafel in pita

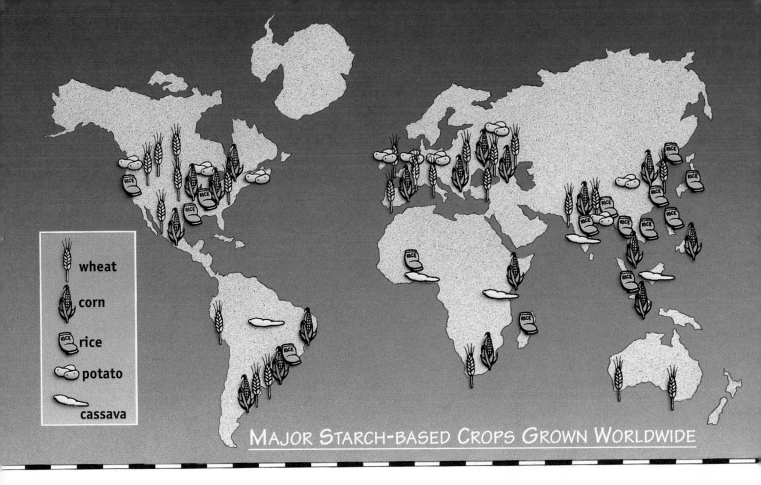

wheat
corn
rice
potato
cassava

MAJOR STARCH-BASED CROPS GROWN WORLDWIDE

If you had lunch in Brazil, you might eat boiled rice and mashed black beans along with chicken, tomatoes, and fruit. In the former Soviet Union, almost everyone eats kasha (kä'shə), or cooked wheat, to which vegetables and lamb pieces are sometimes added. In Egypt you could have falafel (fə läf'əl)—mashed garbanzo beans, garlic, and green onions fried like a hamburger. This tasty mixture is served in a pita (pē'tə), or pocket bread. Japanese children might eat boiled rice, fish, vegetables, fruit, and tofu (tō'fo͞o).

Which foods in each meal described are the starch bases? Starch forms the base of people's diets around the world. Look at the map above to see where starch bases are grown worldwide. ■

INVESTIGATION 2

1. Use the Food Guide Pyramid on page F19 to plan a menu for one day. Your menu should include the recommended number of servings of all five food groups.

2. List your five favorite snacks. Which ones are healthful? Think of a healthful snack to replace each snack from the fats, sweets, and oils group.

How Can You Make the Right Food Choices?

Grocery stores are filled with thousands of foods. In this investigation you'll learn how to read food labels and use the information on them to make good food choices.

Activity

How Sweet It Is!

How much sugar is in your breakfast cereal? Use information on the package to find out.

- -

Procedure

1. Line up six cereal boxes. With your group, **predict** how much sugar is in a serving of each cereal. Reorder the boxes, from the cereal with the most sugar to the one with the least sugar, based on your prediction.

2. In your *Science Notebook*, **make a chart** like the one shown. List the cereals in your chart, using the order you decided on in step 1.

INGREDIENTS: CORN, BLUEBERRIES (BLUEBERRIES, HIGH FRUCTOSE CORN SYRUP, PARTIALLY HYDROGENATED VEGETABLE OIL (COTTONSEED OR SOYBEAN OIL), MALIC ACID, TARTARIC ACID, NATURAL FLAVOR), RICE, SUGAR, WHEAT, OATS, ALMONDS, BROWN SUGAR, PARTIALLY HYDROGENATED SUNFLOWER OIL, MALTED CORN AND BARLEY SYRUP, SALT, CORN SYRUP, WHEY, NATURAL AND ARTIFICIAL FLAVOR. BHT ADDED TO PACKAGING MATERIAL TO PRESERVE PRODUCT FRESHNESS.
VITAMINS AND MINERALS: NIACINAMIDE, VITAMIN A PALMITATE, REDUCED IRON, ZINC OXIDE (SOURCE OF ZINC), VITAMIN B6, RIBOFLAVIN (VITAMIN B2), THIAMIN MONONITRATE (VITAMIN B1), VITAMIN B12, FOLIC ACID, VITAMIN D.

CEREAL DATA		
Cereal	Does It Contain Sugar? What Kinds?	Where Is Sugar on the Ingredients List?

3. Turn the boxes so that you can see the list of ingredients (in grē′dē ənts) on each box. Ingredients are the materials that make up a mixture. Read the ingredients on the box you listed first in your chart. Look for sugar. There are different kinds of sugars, as you can see from the table below. **Record** in your chart the kinds of sugars in the cereal.

Step 3

4. Ingredients are always listed in order of amount, from greatest to least. Count where on the ingredients list each different kind of sugar is found. **Record** your findings in your chart.

5. Repeat steps 3 and 4 for all of the cereals. **Compare** your findings with those of other groups.

Analyze and Conclude

KINDS OF SUGAR	
Sucrose	Lactose
Dextrose	Glucose
Honey	Molasses
Fructose	Corn syrup
Maltose	Corn sweetener

1. Which cereal has the most sugar? How does this compare with your prediction?

2. Which cereal has the most kinds of sugars? Which cereals have no sugar?

3. How will reading lists of ingredients help you choose a healthful cereal?

Activity
Check the Label

MATERIALS
• food packages
• *Science Notebook*

In addition to an ingredients list, most food items have a Nutrition Facts label. Learn how to read and compare these labels to help you choose a healthful diet.

- -

Procedure

1. Find the Nutrition Facts label on several food packages. Line up the packages so that the labels face you.

Step 1

2. In your *Science Notebook*, **make a chart** like the one shown. Look closely at the Nutrition Facts labels to find the number of Calories (kal'ə rēz) for one serving of each food. A Calorie is a unit used to measure the amount of energy in a food. **Record** the number of Calories in one serving of each food.

NUTRITION FACTS				
Food	Calories in One Serving	Amount of Fat and Saturated Fat	Amount of Cholesterol	Amount of Salt (sodium)

3. Fat is an important nutrient. But eating too much fat, especially saturated (sach'ə rāt id) fat, is not healthful. Eating too much cholesterol (kə les'tər ôl), a fatty material, can also be unhealthful. Find the amounts of fat listed on each food label. Find the amounts of cholesterol listed. **Record** this information in your chart.

4. Salt is another important nutrient. Salt is also called sodium (sō'dē əm). People need only a small amount of sodium in their daily diets. Some foods contain a lot of sodium. **Analyze** each label to find out how much sodium is in a food. **Record** this information in your chart.

Analyze and Conclude

1. Which food has the most fat and saturated fat? Which has the least? Which has the most cholesterol? Which has the least? Which has the most sodium? Which has the least?

2. Foods with a lot of Calories can cause people to gain weight. Which food has the most Calories? Which has the fewest Calories? Look at the labels. What is the relationship between the amount of fat and the number of Calories?

3. **Compare** the foods in your chart and **rate** them this way: Highly Recommended, Recommended in Small Amounts, and Not Recommended. Explain your ratings.

INVESTIGATE FURTHER!

EXPERIMENT

Look at the Nutrition Facts label on a box of cereal. How much cereal is in one serving? Measure this amount into a bowl. How does it compare to the amount of cereal you usually eat? How would the listed amounts of fat, cholesterol, and sodium change for the amount of cereal you usually eat?

What's in a Label?

When you've gone to the grocery, have you ever seen people stop to read a food label? Many people want to know what amounts of fat, vitamins, minerals, and Calories are in the foods they eat. The nutrition information on food labels helps them make wise choices.

You found out about Nutrition Facts on food labels in the activity on pages F26 and F27. You can learn more now by reading this label.

SERVING SIZE Serving size is the amount of food recommended that you eat at one time. The nutrient values on the label are based on this amount of food.

CALORIES The number of Calories in a food is the amount of energy your body could get from that food. Someone your age needs 1,600 to 1,800 Calories each day.

CALORIES FROM FAT Both fats and carbohydrates give your body energy. You should choose foods with a small number of Calories from fat.

TOTAL FAT AND SATURATED FAT This is the amount of fat in each serving. Saturated fat is part of the total fat in food. Saturated fat can increase the risk of heart disease.

CHOLESTEROL Cholesterol is a fatty material that can lead to heart disease. You should limit the amount of cholesterol in your diet.

SODIUM Sodium is another word for salt. Too much salt can lead to high blood pressure. Choose foods low in salt.

Nutrition Facts

Serving Size $\frac{1}{2}$ cup (114 g)

Servings Per Container 4

Amount Per Serving

Calories 90	Calories from Fat 30

	% Daily Value
Total Fat 3 g	5%
Saturated Fat 0 g	0%
Cholesterol 0 mg	0%
Sodium 300 mg	13%

TOTAL CARBOHYDRATE This is the amount of sugars and starches in each serving. Carbohydrates are good energy sources.

DIETARY FIBER Fiber is part of the total carbohydrates in food. Fiber helps you digest food, and it can help reduce the risk of heart disease and cancer.

SUGARS Sugars are also part of the total carbohydrates in each serving. Why should you avoid foods in which the amount of sugar is close to the amount of total carbohydrates?

PROTEIN This is the amount of protein in each serving. Protein from meats and dairy products also has saturated fat and cholesterol.

VITAMINS AND MINERALS These numbers tell you what fractional part of your total vitamin and mineral needs are in each serving. Get the vitamins and minerals you need each day by eating a variety of foods.

Total Carbohydrate 13 g		**4%**
Dietary Fiber 3 g		**12%**
Sugars 3 g		
Protein 3 g		

Vitamin A	80%	*	Vitamin C	60%
Calcium	4%	*	Iron	4%

Percent Daily Values are based on a 2,000 Calorie diet. Your daily values may be higher or lower depending on your calorie needs:

Calories		2,000	2,500
Total Fat	Less than	65 g	80 g
Sat. Fat	Less than	20 g	25 g
Cholesterol	Less than	300 mg	25 g
Sodium	Less than	2,400 mg	300 mg
Total Carbohydrate		300 g	2,400 mg
Fiber		25 g	375 g
			30 g

Calories per gram:
Fat 9 • Carbohydrate 4 • Protein 4

PERCENT DAILY VALUE This section is a guide to help adults see how many grams of fats, sodium, and carbohydrates they should have each day.

UNIT PROJECT LINK

With your group, discuss healthful foods that you can eat for breakfast, lunch, dinner, and snacks. List the foods you all agree are healthful. Then make up menus for five days. Consider what you've learned about nutrients and food groups. Make the menu for each day different. Work on your menus as you complete Chapter 1.

What Are You Eating?

When was the last time you ate at a fast-food restaurant? Did you eat a healthful meal? You can eat healthful fast foods if you choose carefully.

Junk-Food Facts

Many young people eat foods that have a lot of added fat, sugar, and salt. Such foods are often called **junk foods** because they have a lot of Calories but not many nutrients.

People eat junk foods because they are easy to get. Junk foods also taste good due to all the sugar, fat, and salt in them. Many young people get used to eating junk foods. They may choose fried or fatty foods at fast-food restaurants. Or their schools might serve foods like potato chips and French fries.

Now many schools and fast-food restaurants are changing their menus. They are serving foods low in fat and sodium. They are also offering more fresh fruits, vegetables, and whole grains.

Ad Power

It's hard for healthful food to compete with junk food. Fast-food restaurants may offer special prizes. Many have playgrounds and games. Lots of young people want to eat where they can have fun.

You can choose healthful foods when you eat out. ▼

Food companies also make junk food look good by putting it in bright packages. Remember the cereals in the activity on pages F24 and F25? Which boxes were most appealing to you and your classmates?

Too Much Junk Food

What's wrong with eating junk food? First, junk foods don't count for any servings from the food pyramid. Junk foods fill people up. Then people are too full to eat healthful foods. If young people don't get the nutrients they need, they won't grow as they should. Eating junk foods now can lead to a lifetime of poor eating habits and to various health problems, such as weight gain or tooth decay.

You don't have to completely avoid candy, salty snacks, or fast foods to stay healthy, though. Just be aware of what you're eating. If you eat a hamburger and French fries, be sure to eat fresh fruit, vegetables, milk, and bread or pasta at the next

▲ **You can eat a meal like this occasionally but not every day.**

meal. Then you can be sure that you're getting the nutrients your body needs for growth and energy. ■

INVESTIGATION 3

1. Write down your favorite fast-food meal. What servings from the food pyramid would it count for? What would you have to eat the rest of the day to get all the servings that you need?

2. Explain how food labels can help you make wise food choices. What kinds of foods should you avoid?

INVESTIGATION 4

HOW CLEAN IS CLEAN ENOUGH?

How often have you heard, "Wash your hands before dinner"? Have you ever wondered why you have to wash your hands even when they look clean? In this investigation you'll find out why looking clean may not be clean enough.

Activity

Tater Trouble

They can't be seen, but they're there. They are sometimes called germs, and they are everywhere. This activity will show you some of the places where germs might be hiding.

Procedure

1. Rub your hands all over a slice of raw potato. Put the potato slice into a plastic bag. Seal the bag and label it *A*.

2. Wash and dry your hands. Put on plastic gloves. Place a second slice of raw potato in another plastic bag. Seal the bag and label it *B*.

MATERIALS

- 3 slices of raw potato
- 3 small sealable plastic bags
- grease pencil
- plastic gloves
- *Science Notebook*

SAFETY

Do not eat any material used in this activity. Do not open the bags at the end of the activity.

Step 2

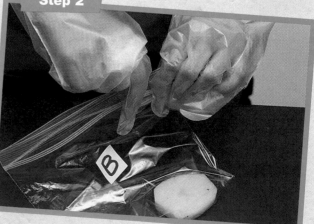

Step 3

3. While still wearing the gloves, rub a third slice of potato on the floor. Seal this slice in another plastic bag and label it *C*.

4. Store the bags in a warm place. With your group **predict** how each potato slice will look after one week. **Record** your predictions in your *Science Notebook*.

5. After one week, observe the potato slices in the sealed bags. Do not open the bags. **Compare** your predictions with your observations. **Describe** how each slice looks. **Record** your descriptions.

Analyze and Conclude

1. **Hypothesize** about what caused the differences in the way the slices look.

2. **Examine** the potato slice in the bag labeled *A*. From your observations, **infer** why it is important to wash your hands when preparing or eating food.

Keeping Foods Fresh

Have you ever thrown away food because it was moldy, sour, or stale? Food spoils because bacteria (bak tir'ē ə) are growing in it. Bacteria are tiny living things that can cause illness.

To keep foods fresh, bacteria on the foods must be killed or at least have their growth slowed down. As you can see in the time line, people have been finding different ways to keep foods fresh or preserved since early times.

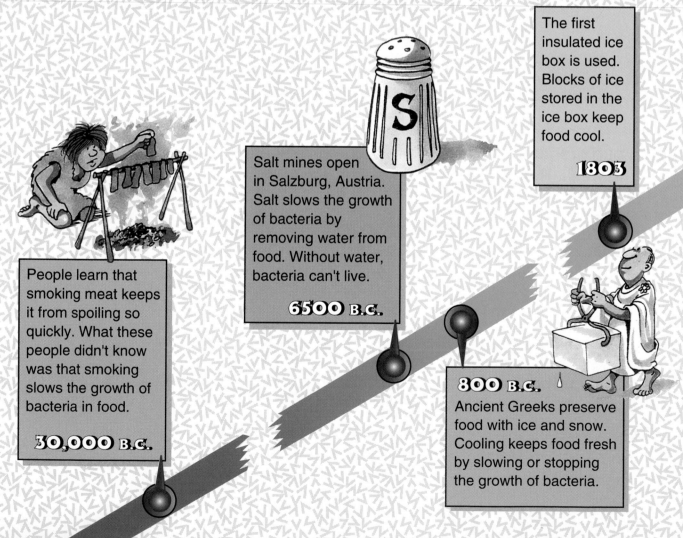

The first insulated ice box is used. Blocks of ice stored in the ice box keep food cool.

1803

Salt mines open in Salzburg, Austria. Salt slows the growth of bacteria by removing water from food. Without water, bacteria can't live.

6500 B.C.

People learn that smoking meat keeps it from spoiling so quickly. What these people didn't know was that smoking slows the growth of bacteria in food.

30,000 B.C.

800 B.C.
Ancient Greeks preserve food with ice and snow. Cooling keeps food fresh by slowing or stopping the growth of bacteria.

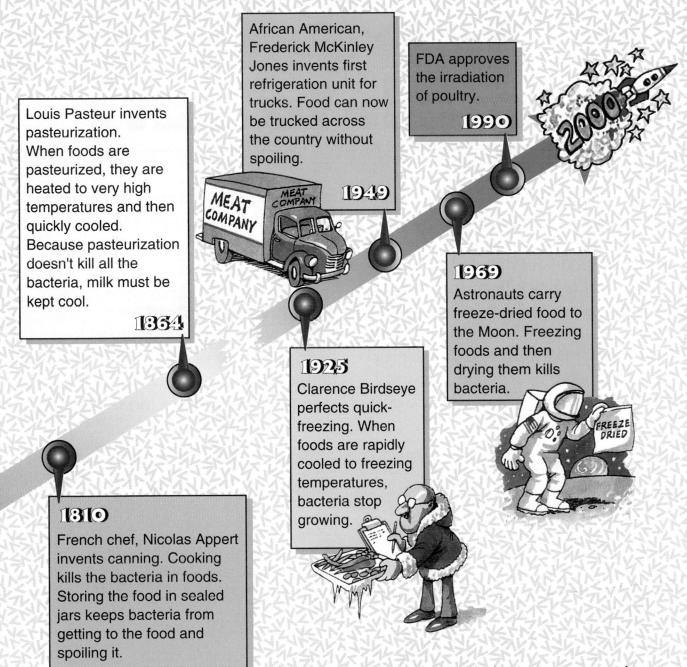

Louis Pasteur invents pasteurization. When foods are pasteurized, they are heated to very high temperatures and then quickly cooled. Because pasteurization doesn't kill all the bacteria, milk must be kept cool.

1864

African American, Frederick McKinley Jones invents first refrigeration unit for trucks. Food can now be trucked across the country without spoiling.

1949

FDA approves the irradiation of poultry.

1990

1969

Astronauts carry freeze-dried food to the Moon. Freezing foods and then drying them kills bacteria.

1925

Clarence Birdseye perfects quick-freezing. When foods are rapidly cooled to freezing temperatures, bacteria stop growing.

1810

French chef, Nicolas Appert invents canning. Cooking kills the bacteria in foods. Storing the food in sealed jars keeps bacteria from getting to the food and spoiling it.

Some people have concerns about how foods are preserved. Salted foods can add too much salt to the diet. Freezing destroys some vitamins. It's hard to imagine, though, not having ways to keep foods fresh. There will certainly be new ways to preserve foods in the years to come. Stay tuned! ■

Is It Safe Enough to Eat?

Keeping clean around food is a good habit to have. Do you remember the activity on pages F32 and F33? If food isn't handled properly, you could get sick from eating it. **Bacteria** are tiny living things that can cause illness. Bacteria growing on food or poisons produced by bacteria are what cause people to get sick. Luckily, bacteria can grow only at certain temperatures. Controlling temperature and keeping food clean are two important ways to keep food safe to eat.

Too Hot or Too Cold?

The best place to store food is in the refrigerator or the freezer. Cool temperatures slow down or even stop the growth of bacteria. Foods

SCIENCE IN LITERATURE

Ina R. Friedman

How My Parents Learned to Eat

A READING RAINBOW SELECTION

Illustrated by Allen Say

HOW MY PARENTS LEARNED TO EAT
by Ina R. Friedman
Houghton Mifflin, 1994

Do your relatives prepare certain foods whenever you have family get-togethers? Do you have special ways to eat these foods? Many families do.

In *How My Parents Learned to Eat* by Ina R. Friedman, an American sailor wants to marry a young Japanese woman. But he is afraid to eat with her because he cannot use chopsticks. She is afraid that she cannot use knives and forks. Find out if they can overcome their fears and learn to eat together.

▲ **Keep hot foods hot and cold foods cold to prevent bacteria from growing.**

stored in the refrigerator should be used within one to five days, depending on the food. Foods can be safely stored in the freezer from three months to a year.

Cooking at high temperatures kills the bacteria in foods. Raw meat and eggs often carry bacteria that can cause illness. So eat only fully cooked meat and eggs.

Once foods are cooked, they must be served hot. Bacteria will start growing rapidly in warm food left on a counter to cool. Leftovers should be stored in cool, clean containers and refrigerated right away. When you're ready to eat leftovers, be sure they're hot all the way through.

Is It Clean Enough?

Everything that touches food must be clean. Most bacteria are killed by washing the surfaces that touch food with soap and hot water. The soap breaks apart bacteria and the hot temperature kills them. You can help keep bacteria off food by following the safety rules listed in the table below.

KEEPING FOOD CLEAN
Wash hands with hot, soapy water before and after preparing food.
Clean up the kitchen often, especially after preparing raw meat, poultry, fish, and eggs.
Use clean dishcloths — not sponges.
Wash can lids before opening; wash the can opener after each use.
Use different spoons to stir raw and cooked foods.
Never cough or sneeze over food.

Why Do I Feel So Sick?

If you eat food that isn't handled or stored properly, you could get an illness called food poisoning. Signs of food poisoning are nausea, diarrhea, cramps, fever, and vomiting. People with food poisoning usually get sick within a few hours of eating spoiled food. But it may take three days before you have any symptoms.

One kind of food poisoning is caused by eating meat, poultry, fish, or eggs that aren't fully cooked or haven't been handled properly. A second type of food poisoning comes from bacteria found on the skin and hair, in the nose and throat, and in wounds. A third kind of food poisoning is most often found in undercooked hamburger patties and in unpasteurized milk.

Whom to Call?

You should call the local health authorities if you get food poisoning from eating at a restaurant or other public place or from eating packaged food. The health officials will notify other people who might have eaten the spoiled food. For the most part you can avoid food poisoning by following the guidelines for cooking, storing, and handling food that you've just read about. ■

◀ **Never eat food from a bulging can like this. It could cause food poisoning.**

INVESTIGATION 4

1. Imagine that you open a can of soup and notice that the soup doesn't look or smell right. Describe what you would do.

2. Explain why it's important to keep everything that touches food clean when handling food. What are some rules you should follow to keep foods safe to eat?

REFLECT & EVALUATE

WORD POWER

bacteria
carbohydrate
fat
healthful diet
junk food
mineral
nutrient
protein
vitamin
water

On Your Own
Review the terms in the list. Then identify the terms that name the six groups of nutrients.

With a Partner
Make up a quiz, using all the terms in the list. Challenge your partner to complete the quiz.

PORTFOLIO

Draw a diagram of the food pyramid. Draw or cut out pictures of your favorite foods to use on your food pyramid.

Analyze Information

Study the graph. Then tell how this graph can help you have a healthful diet.

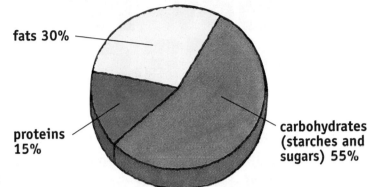

fats 30%

proteins 15%

carbohydrates (starches and sugars) 55%

Assess Performance

Compare the Nutrition Facts labels on at least three different packages of similar kinds of foods, such as three kinds of crackers. Decide which of the foods is the most healthful to eat and which is the least healthful to eat. Explain why.

Problem Solving

1. Suppose you go to a fast-food restaurant with a friend. You want to eat healthfully. What would you order? Explain your choice.

2. Why isn't it healthful to get your carbohydrates from candies, cookies, and cakes?

3. Your favorite breakfast cereal has food additives. Tell how the food additives could be healthful or unhealthful.

4. Imagine you're planning a camping trip. What kinds of foods could you take to have both a healthful and a safe diet?

CHAPTER 2

HOW THE BODY USES FOOD

To get all the nutrients that your body needs, you must eat a healthful diet. But the food you eat is not in a form your body can use immediately. It must first be broken down, or digested, into the basic nutrients. Your teeth help to get this process started.

Enjoy Yourself!

Twenty years ago, nearly all American children had some tooth decay. But things have improved. Today, half the children in the United States have never had a single cavity. Part of this improvement comes from children making regular dental visits.

Dentists today try hard to make children feel comfortable in their offices. Dr. Heber Simmons, Jr., is a children's dentist in Jackson, Mississippi. He has an office that overlooks a lake. Often the children visiting him get a good view of muskrats and beavers at play. Sometimes they can even see an alligator that is nearly 3 m (10 ft) long.

Dr. Simmons wants children to enjoy dental visits. Dr. Simmons and other dental health workers have helped many children form good dental habits. In this chapter you'll find out how your teeth help you break down food. Then you'll see why good dental habits are important.

Coming Up

◀ Children look forward to dental checkups with Dr. Simmons.

WHERE DOES DIGESTION BEGIN?

Make your own mouth water! Imagine that you are about to eat something delicious. Think about how it smells. Your mouth is probably full of saliva by now. How does saliva help you to digest food? In Investigation 1 you'll find out.

Activity

A Matter of Taste

How would you describe the taste of an apple? Find out about taste in this activity.

Procedure

1. In your *Science Notebook*, **make a chart** like the one shown.

Salty	Sweet	Sour	Bitter

2. Your tongue is covered with taste buds. Along with your nose, taste buds help you to taste food. Your taste buds can identify four tastes—salty, sweet, sour, and bitter.

3. Close your eyes. Have a partner choose one food, from a closed container, for you to taste. Keep your eyes closed and hold the food on your tongue.

Step 3

MATERIALS
- 4 different foods in closed containers
- grated apple, grated pear, grated potato on paper plates
- plastic spoons
- cup of water
- *Science Notebook*

SAFETY
Eat foods only with your teacher's permission.

4. Remove the food and take a sip of water. Then **describe** how it tasted. Open your eyes and have your partner tell you which food you tasted. **Record** the name of the food under the heading in your chart where you think it belongs.

5. Repeat steps 3 and 4 for each of the other foods in the closed containers.

6. Now close your eyes and hold your nose. Have your partner give you a little bit of one of the grated foods to taste. Try to **identify** the food. Repeat with the other grated foods. Your partner will **record** your responses and whether or not you correctly identified each grated food.

Step 6

Analyze and Conclude

1. Review your chart. What are the different tastes that your tongue can sense? What foods did you put in each category?

2. In step 6, were you able to identify the grated foods? Why or why not?

3. How do foods taste when you have a cold? **Infer** what condition might affect your sense of taste when you have a cold. **Explain** your inference.

Where It All Begins

Do you ever wonder what happens to food after you eat it? It goes to your body's cells. A **cell** is a basic unit that makes up all living things. Each cell of your body uses energy from food to carry out its job.

Before your body's cells can use the energy in food, the food must first be broken down. The process of breaking down food into a form that your body can use is called **digestion** (di jes′chən). Food is broken down by being ground up and churned. This is physical diges-tion. It's also broken down by chemicals during chemical digestion.

After food is completely digested, it enters your bloodstream. Then it travels to all of your body's cells. There it's used for energy, to build new cells, and to repair worn cells.

Chew on This

There's a good reason to chew your food carefully. The first part of digestion takes place in your mouth. Look at the drawing on page F45 as you learn about digestion.

Digestion breaks down a sandwich into forms your body can use. ▼

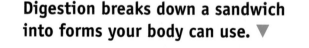

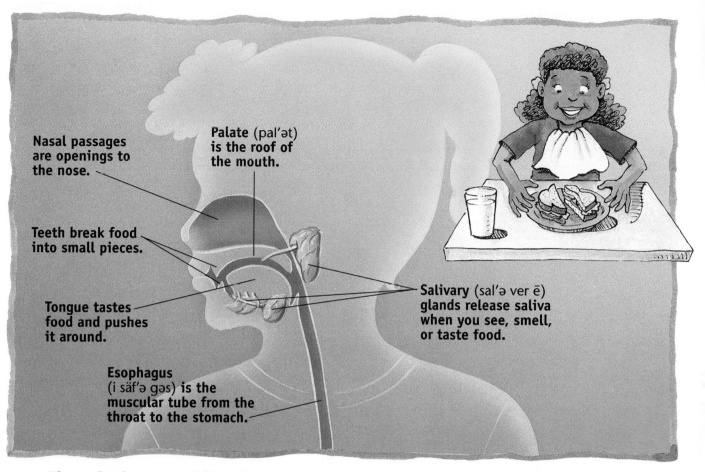

Nasal passages are openings to the nose.

Palate (pal'ət) **is the roof of the mouth.**

Teeth break food into small pieces.

Tongue tastes food and pushes it around.

Salivary (sal'ə ver ē) **glands release saliva when you see, smell, or taste food.**

Esophagus (i säf'ə gəs) is the muscular tube from the throat to the stomach.

▲ **These body parts aid in digestion in the mouth.**

Think of eating a sandwich. First, your front teeth cut off a piece of sandwich small enough to fit inside your mouth. Then your lips close around your teeth and seal the food inside. Now digestion can begin! Your teeth grind the bite of sandwich. The cutting, tearing, and grinding action of your teeth physically breaks the food into smaller pieces.

Flexing Your Tongue

Now think about how you use your tongue as you eat. When you did the activity on pages F42 and F43, you concluded that the tongue is used for tasting. But what else does it do?

Move your tongue around inside your mouth. See if you can make it reach all around your teeth. Your teeth would not be much help in digestion without your tongue. After your front teeth cut off a piece of sandwich, your tongue takes over. It moves the food to the grinding surfaces of the back teeth.

Press your tongue hard against the roof of your mouth. Your tongue is very strong. It mashes the wet food against the top part of your mouth, called the **palate**.

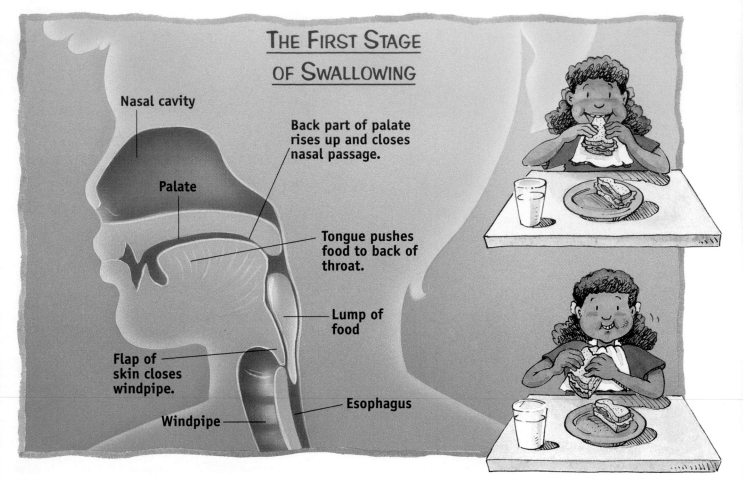

THE FIRST STAGE OF SWALLOWING

Nasal cavity

Back part of palate rises up and closes nasal passage.

Palate

Tongue pushes food to back of throat.

Lump of food

Flap of skin closes windpipe.

Esophagus

Windpipe

Digestion Before Eating!

What happens when you smell dinner cooking? If it's food that you like, your mouth probably starts to water. This can even happen when you're just thinking about food. The watery liquid that rushes into your mouth is called **saliva** (sə lī′və).

Where does saliva come from, and what does it do? Saliva is made in the **salivary glands**, which are found under your jaw, under your tongue, and near your ears. Your saliva contains chemicals that break down starches to sugar. Saliva begins the chemical digestion of food. It also moistens food so that it slides down your throat. This role of saliva is part of physical digestion.

Down the Hatch

You have thoroughly chewed the bite of sandwich, and your tongue has mixed it with saliva. It has turned into a soggy lump. Now it's ready to be swallowed. There are two parts to swallowing. You can control the first part of swallowing. But you probably do it without thinking about it.

In the first part of swallowing, the lump of food is far back in your throat. Food in that part of your throat causes your body to respond automatically. A small flap of skin covers the windpipe, the tube leading to your lungs. Then food can't go down the "wrong" way. At the same time, the back part of the palate rises up and closes off the

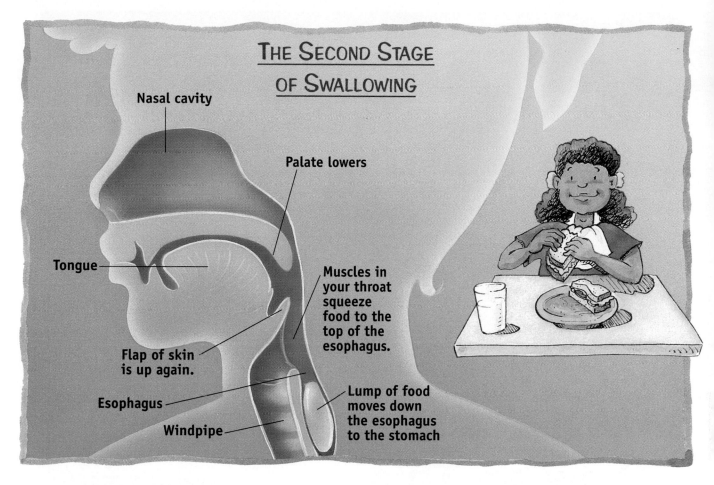

THE SECOND STAGE OF SWALLOWING

Nasal cavity

Palate lowers

Tongue

Muscles in your throat squeeze food to the top of the esophagus.

Flap of skin is up again.

Esophagus

Windpipe

Lump of food moves down the esophagus to the stomach

nasal passage, the opening to your nose. This is why you can't swallow and breathe at the same time. But if you laugh or talk while you eat, you might choke.

In the second part of swallowing, the muscles in your throat squeeze the lump of food into the top of your esophagus. The **esophagus** is the muscular tube that connects the mouth to the stomach. The palate lowers and the flap of skin moves up and uncovers the windpipe. These events complete the second stage of swallowing. From the top of the esophagus, the food travels to the stomach. From the stomach it moves through the rest of the digestive system. ■

=== INVESTIGATION 1 ===

THINK IT WRITE IT

1. How does chewing makes it easier for saliva to begin breaking down food with chemicals?

2. What is digestion? List the steps of digestion that take place in the mouth. Then briefly describe what happens to food in the first and second stages of swallowing.

INVESTIGATION 2

HOW CAN YOU KEEP YOUR TEETH HEALTHY?

You are probably losing some of your baby teeth. At the same time, permanent teeth are coming in. These are the last natural teeth you'll get. You'll learn how to take good care of your teeth in Investigation 2.

Activity

Chew on This

Think about the shapes of your teeth. How does each kind of tooth help you to eat?

MATERIALS
- mirror
- celery stick
- *Science Notebook*

SAFETY
During this activity, eat foods only with your teacher's permission.

Procedure

Use a mirror to examine your teeth. How many kinds of teeth do you see? **Draw** their shapes in your *Science Notebook*. **Talk with your group** and **infer** how each kind of tooth works when you eat. **Record** your inferences. Then eat a celery stick while you look into the mirror. **Observe** how the different kinds of teeth work. **Record** these observations.

Analyze and Conclude

1. Describe how each kind of tooth works when you eat.

2. What would it be like to eat without any teeth?

Activity
A Toothy Problem

Do you clean your teeth after you eat? Try this activity to find out the best ways to do it.

MATERIALS
- goggles
- newspaper
- plastic knife
- peanut butter
- comb
- cup of water
- baking pan
- toothbrush
- dental floss
- paper towels
- *Science Notebook*

SAFETY

Wear goggles. Do not taste any materials. Wipe up spills immediately.

Procedure

1. Cover your work area with newspaper. Then use a plastic knife to spread peanut butter over a comb. Be sure to get the peanut butter between all the teeth of the comb.

2. **Talk with your group** and together **predict** how easy or hard it will be to get all the peanut butter off. **Record** your prediction in your *Science Notebook*.

Step 1

3. Rinse the peanut-butter-covered comb in a cup of water over a baking pan. Try to get off as much peanut butter as you can. **Record** your results.

4. Use a toothbrush and water to brush the peanut butter from between the teeth. Brush the fronts and the backs of the teeth. **Record** your results.

5. Use dental floss to get rid of any peanut butter that is left. **Record** your results.

Analyze and Conclude

1. Was it easy, or hard, to get all the peanut butter off the comb? **Compare** your prediction with your results.

2. Which got the most peanut butter off the comb—rinsing, brushing, or flossing?

3. Imagine that you have just eaten a peanut-butter sandwich. **Hypothesize** about the best way to clean your teeth.

Take Care of Your
Teeth and Gums!

When you were about six months old, your very first tooth appeared. In time, you had 20 baby teeth or first teeth. Do you remember losing your first tooth? Soon after, a larger tooth grew in. Most people have all 32 of their permanent teeth, or second teeth, by the time they're about 20 years old.

Different Shapes and Jobs

Your teeth are designed to cut, tear, crush, and grind food. They play an important role in physical digestion of food. When you did the activity on page F48, you saw the different kinds of teeth you have and inferred what they do. Now look at the drawing and check your ideas.

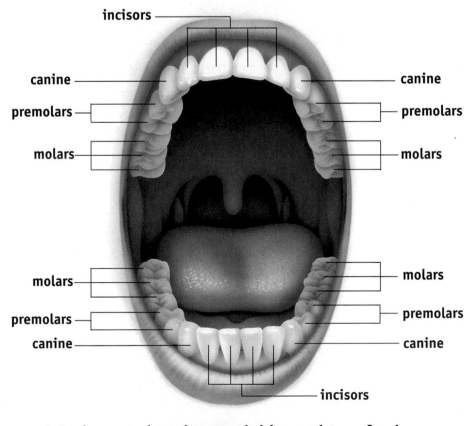

incisors · canine · premolars · molars · canine · premolars · molars · molars · premolars · canine · molars · premolars · canine · incisors

▲ Incisors and canine teeth bite and tear food. Premolars and molars grind and crush food.

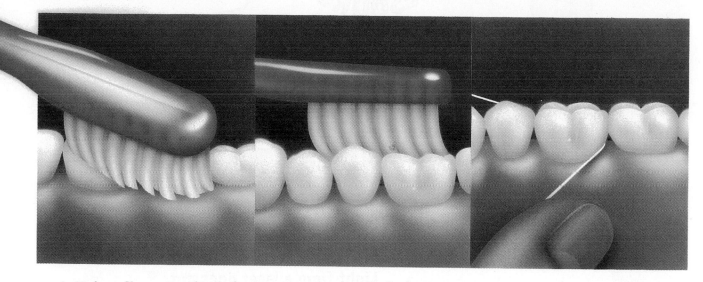

▲ **Using floss to clean between your teeth is just as important as brushing your teeth.**

How Clean Is Clean?

Because your teeth have such an important job to do, it's necessary to keep them clean and healthy. If teeth are not clean, then tiny living things called bacteria (bak tir′ē ə) will multiply in your mouth. Bacteria can make a coating that sticks to teeth like glue. The coating is **plaque** (plak). After you eat, it's important to brush your teeth so that plaque doesn't have a chance to form.

Remember how hard it was to get the peanut butter off the comb used in the activity on page F49? It also takes time to do a good job of cleaning your teeth. First, brush your teeth thoroughly. Then use dental floss to clean the places you can't reach with a toothbrush. Study the drawing above. Is this the way you clean your teeth? It should be!

If you don't clean your teeth properly, bacteria can grow and make an acid that can eat through the outer layer of teeth! Bacteria cause tooth decay, called caries, when the acid makes a hole in a tooth. The decay can spread inside a tooth, causing a painful toothache. If it's not removed, plaque can also lead to gum disease.

A Trip to the Dentist

Besides brushing and flossing your teeth, you should visit a dentist at least twice a year. At the dentist's office, the dental hygienist (hī jēn′-ist) cleans your teeth. Then the dentist may take X-rays to look for decay. If you have caries, the dentist numbs your teeth. Then the dentist uses a drill to remove the decay and fills the hole.

Is all of this work to have clean, healthy teeth worth it? Think how long you will need your teeth. Then answer the question. ■

The Dentist's Toolbox

Have you ever looked closely at the kinds of tools your dentist uses? Your dentist probably uses some tools that have been around for a long time. These include a long-handled mirror, a high-speed drill, and a hose to suck saliva out of your mouth. There are probably some other interesting devices you'd never find in a hardware store.

In recent years there have been many advances in tooth care. High-speed drills that turn 500,000 times per minute are now in use. Faster turning means that the dentist can fix your teeth faster. Some drills also have fiber-optic lights—ones that can bend—to help the dentist see better.

Using Sound and Light

Some of the newest dental tools are ultrasonic (ul trə sän'ik). This means the tools use sound waves. Ultrasonic tools are used to scrape plaque off teeth and to remove parts of diseased gums.

Light from the flashlight spreads out. Light from a laser does not. ▼

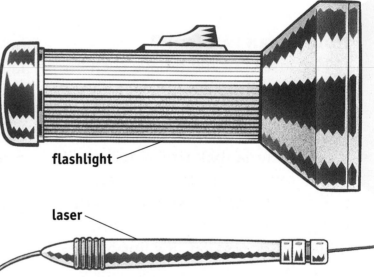

flashlight

laser

The laser (lā'zər) is another new tool in dentistry. A laser makes a narrow beam of light that's strong enough to burn through things. Some lasers can even burn holes in diamonds! The light from a laser is different from sunlight or the light from a bulb. Laser light travels in only one direction instead of spreading out in all directions. Compare the two beams of light in the drawing.

The laser is very useful in dentistry. It's now used for treating diseased gums, killing bacteria between the teeth and gums, and removing plaque. The laser can destroy diseased areas without harming the healthy areas nearby. This is because diseased areas are darker than healthy ones. The darker areas absorb, or take in, the laser beam faster than the lighter, healthy areas do.

Research is also going on to design a laser that will replace the dental drill. Dental lasers are quiet and painless. They remove the decay quickly. The dentist's toolbox of the future will contain many new and wonderful tools. ■

INVESTIGATE FURTHER!

RESEARCH

Ask your dentist how lasers are used. Maybe your dentist is using these new tools. Discuss what you find out with your classmates.

INVESTIGATION 2

1. What can happen to teeth if too many bacteria grow in your mouth?

2. List the steps for having healthy teeth. Explain why healthy teeth are important.

WHAT HAPPENS TO FOOD AFTER IT'S SWALLOWED?

You probably know that after food is swallowed it goes to the stomach. But what happens then? In Investigation 3 you'll find out.

Activity
The Big Breakdown

Enzymes are chemicals that help break down food to a form that can be used by the body. In this activity you'll see how one kind of enzyme does its work.

Procedure

1. You will use a glucose test strip to find out if glucose, a kind of sugar, is present in different foods. A glucose test strip changes from light green to dark green or brown when it comes in contact with glucose.

MATERIALS
- goggles
- glucose test strips
- apple juice
- orange juice
- cranberry juice
- milk
- lactase drops
- spoon
- *Science Notebook*

SAFETY
Wear goggles during this activity.
Do not taste any materials. Wipe up any spills immediately.

Step 1

2. In your *Science Notebook*, **make a chart** like the one shown. **Talk with your group** and **predict** what will happen to a glucose test strip when you dip it into apple juice. **Record** your prediction in your chart.

GLUCOSE PRESENT?		
Food	**Prediction**	**Result**

3. Dip the strip into apple juice. Decide whether there is glucose in apple juice. **Record** your findings in your chart. **Compare** your prediction with your findings.

Step 3

4. Repeat steps 2 and 3 with orange juice, with cranberry juice, and with milk.

5. Now put one drop of lactase into the milk. Stir it with a spoon. Dip a glucose test strip into the milk. **Record** your observations.

Analyze and Conclude

1. What happened to the glucose test strip in the apple juice, orange juice, and cranberry juice? Which contained glucose? How do you know?

2. **Compare** the glucose test strips you used before and after you added lactase to the milk. How were they alike or different? **Make an inference** about what could cause a difference.

3. Lactase is an enzyme made by the body. Lactase breaks down milk sugar to glucose. Some people do not make enough lactase. If such people drink milk, they can become ill. **Hypothesize** how these people might be able to drink milk without becoming ill.

INVESTIGATE FURTHER!

EXPERIMENT

How do you think lactase drops might affect milk products? Work with your group. Make a list of milk products that you can test. Perform the tests. Agree on a way to keep track of your data. Report your findings to your classmates.

Activity
Fiber Findings

MATERIALS
• *Science Notebook*

Diets high in fiber are healthful. Fiber is a material the body can't digest, but it helps the body digest food. Everyone should eat foods that have a lot of fiber. In this activity you'll find out which foods those are.

Procedure

1. Scientists say that people should eat between 20 g and 35 g of fiber a day. Without looking at the tables, **predict** which foods that you eat are high in fiber. **Discuss** your predictions with other group members. **Record** your predictions in your *Science Notebook*.

2. The tables show how much fiber is in one serving of some foods. Choose from the tables foods that would provide all the fiber you need in a day. Choose different kinds of foods to help you have a healthful diet.

Fiber Figures

These tables list the grams of fiber in one serving of food.

Breads and Cereals

Oatmeal bread	2 g
Whole-wheat tortilla	2 g
White bread	1 g
White flour tortilla	1 g
Bran cereal	22 g
Shredded wheat cereal	6 g

3. **Record** the foods you choose for a day's worth of fiber. Next to each choice, write the amount of fiber in one serving. Add up the number of grams of fiber.

Beans, Grains, and Pastas

Split pea soup	5 g
Navy, pinto, or kidney beans	6 g
Lentil soup	5 g
Cooked barley	4 g
Brown rice	3 g
Spaghetti (plain)	2 g

Analyze and Conclude

1. What is the total amount of fiber (in grams) in the foods you chose? How does the amount compare with the amount in your own diet?

2. Foods that are good sources of fiber have 2–3 g of fiber per serving. Foods that are high in fiber have 4 g or more per serving. Make two lists. First, list your favorite good sources of fiber. Then list your favorite foods that are high in fiber.

3. What do you notice about the foods in the tables that are very low in fiber? What do you notice about the foods that are very high in fiber? How can you use this information to make choices for a healthful diet?

UNIT PROJECT LINK

Review the menus your group made for the Chapter 1 Unit Project Link. Now collect empty packages of foods or make models of food packages. Label the food group to which each package belongs. Continue collecting food packages or making food package models as you study Chapter 2.

Fruits

Apple	3 g
Pear	4 g
Dried apricots or figs	2 g
Banana	3 g
Orange	6 g
Strawberries	3 g
Grapes	2 g
Cantaloupe	1 g
Watermelon	1 g

Vegetables

Green peas	4 g
Baked potato with skin	6 g
Carrots	3 g
Broccoli	2 g
Spinach	2 g
Corn	2 g
Green beans	1 g
Lettuce	1 g
Tomato	1 g

Snacks

Fruit bars	3 g
Wheat-bran crackers	2 g
Granola bars	1 g
Wheat crackers	1 g
Oatmeal cookies	1 g

After You Swallow

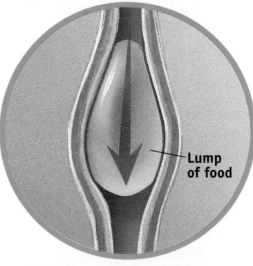

▲ These astronauts are eating in space. How does food go to the stomach when there is little gravity?

You've just taken a bite of dinner and swallowed it. What happens next? After you swallow, food enters the esophagus, the tube that goes from the throat to the stomach. The inside of the esophagus is coated with a slippery material that makes it easier for food to move.

Muscles (mus′əlz) can move by tightening and relaxing. Muscles in the walls of the esophagus push the food along in a way similar to the way you squeeze toothpaste from a

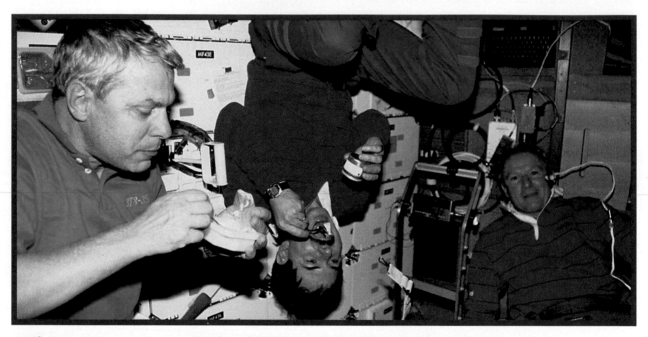

Lump of food

▲ It's the muscles of the esophagus that squeeze food toward the stomach.

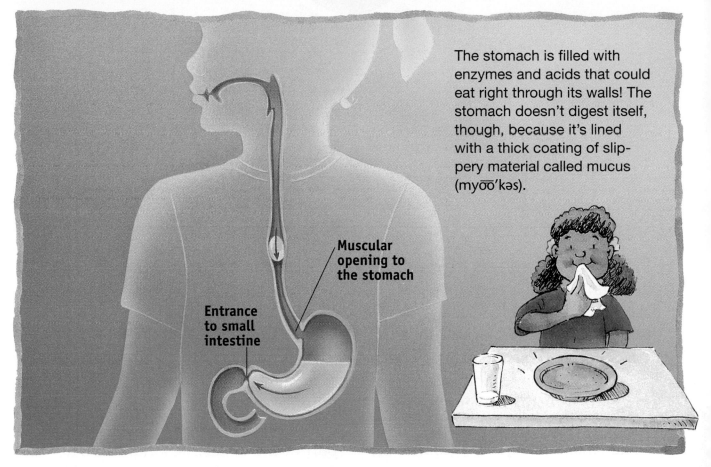

The stomach is filled with enzymes and acids that could eat right through its walls! The stomach doesn't digest itself, though, because it's lined with a thick coating of slippery material called mucus (my$\overline{oo}$'kəs).

Muscular opening to the stomach

Entrance to small intestine

▲ **Food becomes a liquid, called chyme, in the stomach.**

tube. Seconds after being swallowed, food reaches the stomach. The entrance to the stomach is also muscle. This muscle opens to let food in and closes to keep food from moving back up the esophagus.

The Storage Tank

Your **stomach** is a muscular sac that has two main jobs—to store food and to help with digestion. In the activity on pages F54 and F55, you learned about chemicals called **enzymes** that help break down food. There are enzymes in saliva that digest starch and stomach enzymes that digest proteins.

The stomach also contains a strong acid and other chemicals. Stomach

acid helps the enzymes work, breaks down food, and kills bacteria. The other chemicals control the release of enzymes and signal the stomach to make more acid. The enzymes, acid, and chemicals in the stomach are often called digestive juices.

Churn Over

Muscles in the stomach wall mash and churn food, mixing it with digestive juices. Soon the food turns into a thick liquid called **chyme** (kīm). It takes about three to four hours for chyme to leave your stomach. Carbohydrates pass through quickly, but proteins and fats take longer to move into the small intestine, where digestion continues. ∎

The Final Stretch

The small intestine is where digestion is finished and nutrients are absorbed into the bloodstream. It's the final stretch. The **small intestine** is a long, coiled digestive organ. The only thing small about it, though, is its width. In length, it's about 6 m (20 ft).

The small intestine makes its own digestive juices. It also gets enzymes and other chemicals from the liver, gallbladder, and pancreas (pan'krē-əs). Muscles in the wall of the small intestine squeeze and push the chyme along. As they do, digestive juices mix in.

Nutrients Exit to Bloodstream

Nutrients are absorbed in the last part of the small intestine. Look at the drawing below to see the inside of the small intestine. It has many

Major parts of the digestion system ▼

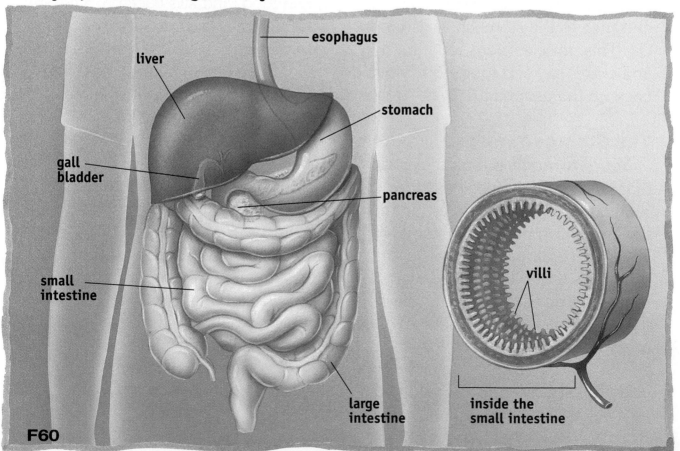

esophagus

liver

stomach

gall bladder

pancreas

small intestine

villi

large intestine

inside the small intestine

tiny finger-shaped parts, called villi (vil'ī). The villi become coated with nutrients. The nutrients pass through the villi into tiny blood vessels. From the blood vessels the nutrients are carried by the blood throughout the body to all the cells.

Waste Disposal

Some parts of foods can't be digested. For example, many foods from plants contain **fiber,** a material that the body can't digest. Think back to the activity on pages F56 and F57. From the tables, what foods did you learn are high in fiber? What foods contain little fiber?

Why is it important to eat a lot of fiber if your body can't digest it? Many kinds of fiber absorb water and hold onto it in the intestine. Fiber adds bulk to the waste and keeps the waste soft, making it easier for the waste to pass from the body. The fiber also helps muscles in the intestines to move, which aids digestion.

All the undigested material, or waste, passes from the small intestine into the large intestine. The **large intestine** stores waste and absorbs water from it. About 24 to 48 hours after a meal is eaten, the large intestine moves the waste out of the body.

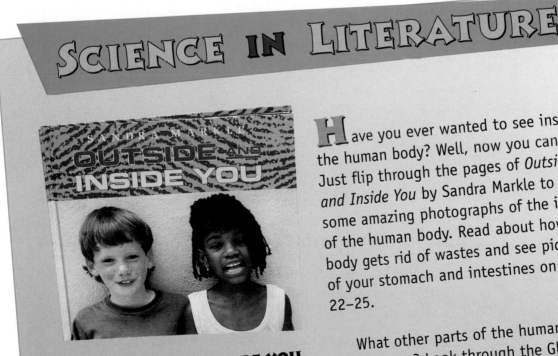

SCIENCE IN LITERATURE

OUTSIDE AND INSIDE YOU
by Sandra Markle
Bradbury Press, 1991

Have you ever wanted to see inside the human body? Well, now you can! Just flip through the pages of *Outside and Inside You* by Sandra Markle to see some amazing photographs of the inside of the human body. Read about how your body gets rid of wastes and see pictures of your stomach and intestines on pages 22–25.

What other parts of the human body interest you? Look through the Glossary on pages 35–38. Find the pages for those parts and check them out.

Why All the Growling?

Does your stomach ever growl or gurgle after a meal? It can be a surprise—an embarrassing surprise—if you're with others in a quiet room! What's going on inside your body? Look at the drawing below and you'll find out. ■

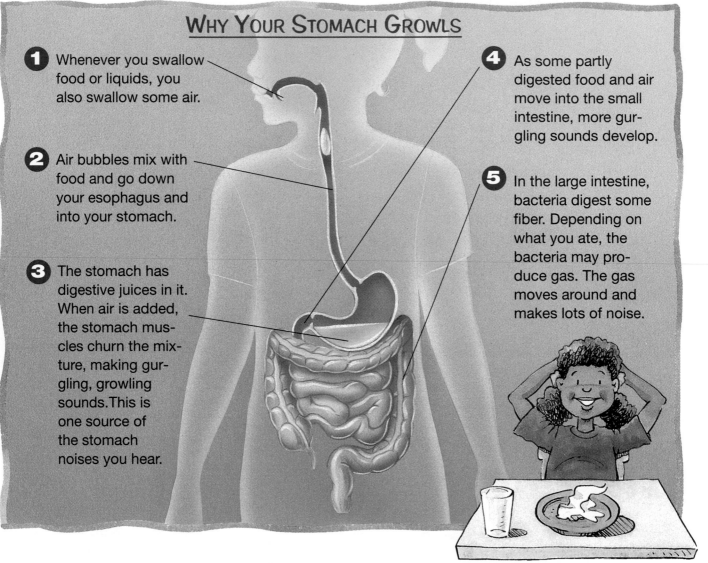

WHY YOUR STOMACH GROWLS

1 Whenever you swallow food or liquids, you also swallow some air.

2 Air bubbles mix with food and go down your esophagus and into your stomach.

3 The stomach has digestive juices in it. When air is added, the stomach muscles churn the mixture, making gurgling, growling sounds. This is one source of the stomach noises you hear.

4 As some partly digested food and air move into the small intestine, more gurgling sounds develop.

5 In the large intestine, bacteria digest some fiber. Depending on what you ate, the bacteria may produce gas. The gas moves around and makes lots of noise.

INVESTIGATION 3

1. What could a person do if he or she lacked the enzyme lactase, which breaks down milk sugar to glucose?

2. Describe the stages of digestion that food goes through after it is swallowed. Where are nutrients from digested food absorbed into the blood?

REFLECT & EVALUATE

WORD POWER

cell	palate
chyme	plaque
digestion	saliva
enzymes	salivary glands
esophagus	small intestine
fiber	stomach
large intestine	

 On Your Own
Review the terms in the list. Then use as many terms as you can in a labeled diagram to show the parts of the digestive system.

With a Partner
Write each term in the list on one side of an index card and the definition on the other side. Use the cards to quiz your partner.

BUILD YOUR PORTFOLIO

Write a paragraph explaining what happens after you take a bite of a sandwich. Include how your body gets nutrients from the sandwich.

Analyze Information

Study the drawing. Then explain how the digestion of food begins in the mouth. Include what happens when you think of food and smell food.

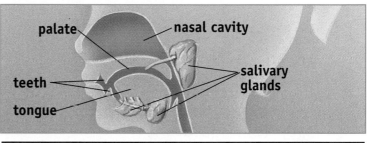

Assess Performance

Your tongue is covered with taste buds that can tell salty, sweet, sour, or bitter tastes. Plan an experiment to find out if taste buds are grouped together on your tongue. After your teacher has reviewed your plan, carry out the experiment with a partner. Compare your results with those of other groups.

Problem Solving

1. Imagine that you have no teeth. How would this affect the digestion of your food? What special foods would you have to eat?

2. You learned that the small intestine is lined with villi. How do villi help the small intestine do its job better than if they weren't there?

3. Sometimes after eating a meal with a lot of meat, people complain of feeling full for a long time. Based on what you know about the digestion of food, why do you think this is so?

INVESTIGATE FURTHER!

Throughout this unit you've investigated questions related to nutrition and digestion. How will you use what you've learned and share that information with others? Here are some ideas.

Hold a Big Event
to Share Your Unit Project

In this unit, you've studied nutrients, healthful diets, handling food safely, and digestion. You'll also found out how to keep your teeth and your digestive system healthy. To show what you've learned, create and display a food pyramid supermarket. Invite other classes and your family to see your pyramid and what you've learned about planning healthful menus. Be sure your menus include what you know about food groups, serving sizes, nutrients, fiber, and ingredients.

Research

Look back through this unit. Do you see a topic or book on nutrition or digestion that interests you? Perhaps you want to know about what acids are in your stomach, or how freeze-dried foods are made for astronauts. Go to the library to learn more about it.

Take Action

Talk to your family about healthful diets. Show them the Food Guide Pyramid on page F19. Together plan some menus based on the food pyramid and recommended serving sizes. Then help shop for foods and prepare a healthful meal for your family.

SCIENCE Handbook

THINK LIKE A SCIENTIST

> You don't have to be a professional scientist to act and think like one. Thinking like a scientist mostly means using common sense. It also means learning how to test your ideas in a careful way.

> In other words, *you* can think like a scientist.

Make a Hypothesis

Plan and Do a Test

Make Observations

To think like a scientist, you should learn as much as you can by observing things around you. Everything you hear and see is a clue about how the world works.

Ask a Question

Look for patterns. You'll get ideas and ask questions like these.

- Does a dripping faucet waste a lot of water?

- How does the time that the Sun sets change from day to day?

Make a Guess Called a Hypothesis

If you have an idea about why something happens, make an educated guess, or hypothesis, that you can test. For example, let's suppose that your hypothesis about sunset time is that it changes by one minute each day.

Plan and Do a Test

Plan how to test your hypothesis. Your plan would need to consider some of these problems.

- How will you measure the time that the Sun sets?

- Will you measure the time every day?

- For how many days or weeks do you need to measure?

Record and Analyze What Happens

When you test your idea, you need to observe carefully and write down, or record, everything that

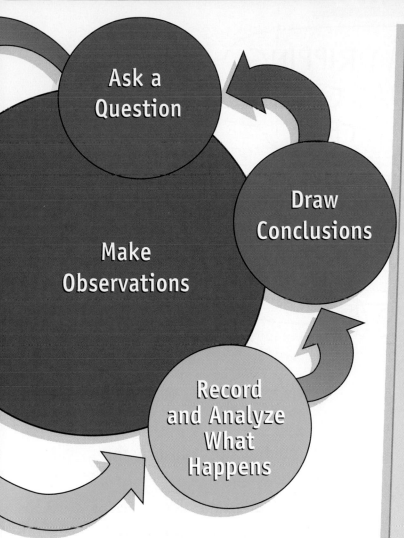

Ask a Question

Draw Conclusions

Make Observations

Record and Analyze What Happens

happens. When you finish collecting data, you may need to do some calculations with it. For example, you might calculate how much the sunset time changes in a week.

Draw Conclusions

Whatever happens in a test, think about all the reasons for your results. Sometimes this thinking leads to a new hypothesis.

If the time of the sunset changes by one minute each day, think about what else the data shows you. Can you predict the time that the Sun will set one month from now?

PRACTICE SCIENTIFIC REASONING SKILLS

To think like a scientist, you need to practice certain ways of thinking.

Always check for yourself.
Ask, "How do I know it's true?" Be willing to find out for yourself.

Be honest and careful about what you observe.
It's easy to only look for the results you expect. It's harder to see the unexpected. But unexpected results lead scientists to ask more questions. They also provide information on how things work.

Don't be afraid to be wrong.
Based on their observations, scientists make many hypotheses. Not all of these hypotheses turn out to be correct. But scientists can learn from wrong "guesses," because even wrong guesses result in information that leads to knowledge.

Keep an open mind about possible explanations.
Make sure to think about all the reasons why something might have happened. Consider all the explanations that you can think of.

DOES A DRIPPING FAUCET WASTE A LOT OF WATER?

Here's an example of an everyday problem and how thinking like a scientist can help you explore it.

Nan's class is learning about saving water. Nan knows saving water is important, so she's surprised when she sees a dripping faucet. Nan showed the dripping faucet to her friend Carlos. He thinks such a little drip won't waste much water. "But it drips all the time," thinks Nan. "All the little drips may add up to a lot of water."

Make Observations → Ask a Question

Nan and Carlos wanted to find out more about the dripping faucet. They brainstormed questions that they wanted to answer.

- Does the dripping faucet waste water?

- How much water is lost by the dripping faucet?

Nan and Carlos decided to focus on the second question since they knew they could measure how much water was dripping. They were not sure what the answer would be. But they thought it was a good question to answer.

> **Scientific investigations often begin by thinking about what you already know. This can lead you to discover some ideas that you're not sure about and it can help you ask a question you want to answer.**

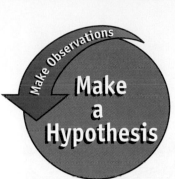

Make a Hypothesis

Nan and Carlos watched the dripping faucet. They started counting the number of drips that fell in one minute. But they couldn't decide what was a little or what was a lot of water based on drips.

Nan suggested they measure how much water dripped out of the faucet in six hours. She also thought they should decide how much "a lot" was. They agreed to test the statement that the faucet drips 250 mL (1 c) of water in 6 hours. They decided that more than 250 mL would be "a lot." This statement was their hypothesis. A hypothesis is a possible answer to a question.

When you use what you've observed to suggest a possible answer to your question, you are making a hypothesis. If you can't think of an experiment or make a model to test your hypothesis, try changing it to something simpler and easier to test.

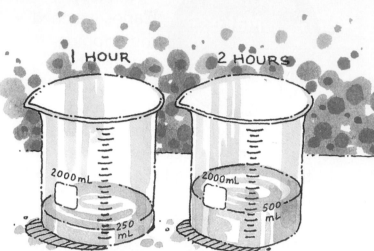

Plan and Do a Test

Make Observations

Carlos and Nan worked together and planned a way to test their hypothesis. They would need a container to catch all of the dripping water from the faucet. So Carlos asked Ms. Webb, their teacher, for a beaker that would hold at least 1,000 mL of water. The beaker that Mrs. Webb gave them had lines drawn on it. The lines showed, in milliliters, how much material the beaker could hold.

At 9:00 A.M., Carlos and Nan put the beaker under the dripping faucet. They made sure the water dripped directly into the beaker.

One way to try out your hypothesis is to use a test called an experiment. When you plan an experiment, make sure that it helps you to answer your question. Try to imagine what might happen when you do your experiment. Sometimes things happen that make the experiment not work properly. If the experiment doesn't work, you can change the plan for your experiment and try again.

Record and Analyze What Happened

Make Observations

Nan and Carlos checked the beaker every hour. Each hour, they recorded the time and the amount of water in the beaker. By 3:00 P.M., Nan and Carlos were very surprised by their findings. After 6 hours, the beaker had 1,500 mL of water in it!

They made a pictograph, like the one above, of what they observed.

When you do an experiment, you need to write down, or record, your observations and data. Then you need to organize your data in a way that helps you understand it. Then you analyze the data to learn what it tells you about your hypothesis.

MEASURING DRIPS

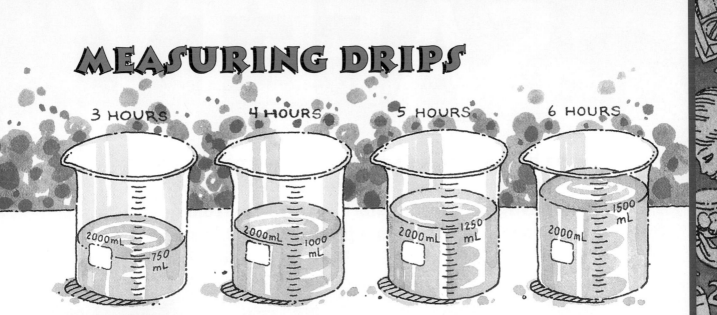

3 HOURS 4 HOURS 5 HOURS 6 HOURS

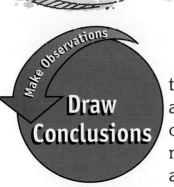

Make Observations

Draw Conclusions

Nan and Carlos told their class about the results of their experiment. Everyone agreed that dripping faucets waste a lot of water. But they still had questions.

Do all dripping faucets waste this much water?

Do only faucets drip, or do water pipes drip, too?

If a little drip adds up to so much water, how much water do we use in everyday activities?

The students decided to plan experiments to find out the answers to their questions. Carlos and Nan decided to carry their experiment further. They decided to find out how much water the dripping faucet wastes in 24 hours.

After you have analyzed your data, you should use what you have learned to draw a conclusion. A conclusion is a statement that sums up what you have learned. Think about whether or not the information you have gathered supports your hypothesis. If it does, figure out how to explore your idea more thoroughly. But always think about the new questions you can ask from what you've discovered.

SAFETY

The best way to be safe in the classroom is to use common sense. Prepare yourself for each activity before you start it. Get help from your teacher when there is a problem. Most important of all, pay attention. Here are some other ways that you can stay safe.

Stay Safe From Stains

- Wear protective clothing or an old shirt when you work with messy materials.

- If anything spills, wipe it up or ask your teacher to help you clean it up.

Stay Safe From Flames

- Keep your clothes away from open flames. If you have long or baggy sleeves, roll them up.

- Don't let your hair get close to a flame. If you have long hair, tie it back.

Stay Safe From Injuries

- Protect your eyes by wearing safety goggles when you are told that you need them.
- Keep your hands dry around electricity. Water is a good conductor of electricity, so you can get a shock more easily if your hands are wet.
- Be careful with sharp objects. If you have to press on them, keep the sharp side away from you.
- Cover any cuts you have that are exposed. If you spill something on a cut, be sure to wash it off immediately.
- Don't eat or drink anything unless your teacher tells you that it's okay.

Stay Safe During Cleanup

- Wash up after you finish working.
- Dispose of things in the way that your teacher tells you to.

MOST IMPORTANTLY

If you ever hurt yourself or one of your group members gets hurt, tell your teacher right away.

HAIR Keep it out of the way of a flame.

DON'T MAKE A MESS If you spill something, clean it up right away. When finished with an activity, clean up your work area. Dispose of things in the way your teacher tells you to.

EYES Wear safety goggles when you are told to.

MOUTH Don't eat or drink ANYTHING unless your teacher tells you it's okay.

CLOTHES Keep long sleeves rolled up. Protect yourself from stains. Stay away from open flames.

HANDS Keep your hands dry around electricity. Cover any cuts. Wear gloves when told to. Wash up after you finish.

Using a Hand Lens

A hand lens is a tool that magnifies objects, or makes objects appear larger. This makes it possible for you to see details of an object that would be hard to see without the hand lens.

Look at a Coin or a Stamp

1. Place an object such as a coin or a stamp on a table or other flat surface.

2. Hold the hand lens just above the object. As you look through the lens, slowly move the lens away from the object. Notice that the object appears to get larger.

3. Keep moving the lens until the object begins to look a little blurry. Then move the hand lens a little closer to the object until the object is once again in sharp focus.

▲ Place the lens above the object.

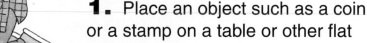

▲ Move the lens slowly toward you.

If the object becomes blurry, you need to move the lens toward the object. ▶

Using a
Calculator

After you've made measurements, a calculator can help you analyze your data. Some calculators have a memory key that allows you to save the result of one calculation while you do another.

Find an Average

The table shows the amount of rain that fell each month of one year. Use a calculator to find the average monthly rainfall.

1. To add the numbers, enter a number and then press the plus sign (+). Repeat until you enter the last number. Then press the equal sign (=).

2. If you make a mistake, push the clear entry key (CE). Enter the number again, and then continue adding.

3. Your total should be 1,131. You can use the total to find the average. Just press divide (÷) and enter 12, the number of months in a year.

4. Your answer should be 94.25.

Rainfall	
Month	Rain (mm)
Jan.	214
Feb.	138
Mar.	98
Apr.	157
May	84
June	41
July	5
Aug.	23
Sept.	48
Oct.	75
Nov.	140
Dec.	108

clear entry

divide

equal

plus

Using a Balance

A balance is used to measure mass. Mass is the amount of matter in an object. Place the object to be massed in the left pan of the balance. Place standard masses in the right pan.

Measure the Mass of an Orange

1. Check that the empty pans are balanced, or level with each other. When balanced, the pointer on the base should be at the middle mark. If it needs to be adjusted, move the slider on the back of the balance a little to the left or right.

2. Place an orange on the left pan. Then add standard masses, one at a time, to the right pan. When the pointer is at the middle mark again, each pan holds the same amount of matter and has the same mass.

3. Add the numbers marked on the masses in the pan. The total is the mass in grams of the orange.

Using a Tape Measure or Ruler

Tape measures and rulers are tools for measuring the length of objects and distances. Scientists most often use units such as meters, centimeters, and millimeters when making length measurements.

Use a Tape Measure

1. Wrap the tape around the jar.

2. Find the line where the tape begins to wrap over itself.

3. Record the distance around the jar in centimeters.

Use a Metric Ruler

1. Place the ruler or the meter-stick on the floor. Line up the end of the ruler with the heel of your shoe.

2. Notice where the other end of your shoe lines up with the ruler.

3. Look at the scale. Record the length of your shoe in centimeters and in millimeters.

Using a Thermometer

A thermometer is used to measure temperature. When the liquid in the tube of a thermometer gets warmer, it expands and moves farther up the tube. Different scales can be used to measure temperature, but scientists usually use the Celsius scale.

Measure the Temperature of a Cold Liquid

1. Take a chilled liquid out of the refrigerator. Half-fill a cup with the liquid.

2. Hold the thermometer so that the bulb is in the center of the liquid. Be sure that there are no bright lights or direct sunlight shining on the bulb.

3. Wait a couple of minutes until you see the liquid in the tube stop moving. Read the scale line that is closest to the top of the liquid in the tube. The thermometer shown reads 4°C (40°F).

Measuring

Volume

A graduated cylinder, a measuring cup, and a beaker are used to measure volume. Volume is the amount of space something takes up. Most of the containers that scientists use to measure volume have a scale marked in milliliters (mL).

Measure the Volume of Juice

1. Pour the juice into a measuring container.

2. Move your head so that your eyes are level with the top of the juice. Read the scale line that is closest to the surface of the juice. If the surface of the juice is curved up on the sides, look at the lowest point of the curve.

3. Read the measurement on the scale. You can estimate the value between two lines on the scale.

▲ **The bottom of the curve is at 35 mL.**

◀ **This graduated cylinder has marks for every 5 mL.**

This beaker has marks for each 25 mL. ▼

▼ **This measuring cup has marks for each 25 mL.**

MEASUR

Area
A basketball court covers about 4,700 ft². It covers about 435 m².

Volume
1 L of sports drink is a little more than 1 qt.

Temperature
The temperature at an indoor basketball game might be 25°C, which is 77°F.

SI Measures

Temperature
Ice melts at 0 degrees Celsius (°C)

Water freezes at 0°C

Water boils at 100°C

Length and Distance
1,000 meters (m) = 1 kilometer (km)

100 centimeters (cm) = 1 m

10 millimeters (mm) = 1 cm

Force
1 newton (N) =
1 kilogram x meter/second/second
(kg x m/s²)

Volume
1 cubic meter (m³) = 1 m x 1 m x 1 m

1 cubic centimeter (cm³) =
1 cm x 1 cm x 1 cm

1 liter (L) = 1,000 milliliters (mL)

1 cm³ = 1 mL

Area
1 square kilometer (km²) = 1 km x 1 km

1 hectare = 10,000 m²

Mass
1,000 grams (g) = 1 kilogram (kg)

1,000 milligrams (mg) = 1 g

EMENTS

Mass and Weight
A basketball has a mass of about 650 g. It weighs about $1\frac{1}{2}$ lb.

Length/Distance
A basketball rim is about 10 ft high, or a little more than 3 m from the floor.

Rates (SI and English)
km/h = kilometers per hour

m/s = meters per second

mph = miles per hour

English Measures

Volume of Fluids
8 fluid ounces (fl oz) = 1 cup (c)

2 c = 1 pint (pt)

2 pt = 1 quart (qt)

4 qt = 1 gallon (gal)

Temperature
Ice melts at 32 degrees Fahrenheit (°F)

Water freezes at 32°F

Water boils at 212°F

Length and Distance
12 inches (in.) = 1 foot (ft)

3 ft = 1 yard (yd)

5,280 ft = 1 mile (mi)

Weight
16 ounces (oz) = 1 pound (lb)   2,000 pounds = 1 ton (T)

GLOSSARY

Pronunciation Key

Symbol	Key Words	Symbol	Key Words
a	c**a**t	g	**g**et
ā	**a**pe	h	**h**elp
ä	c**o**t, c**a**r	j	**j**ump
		k	**k**iss, call
e	t**e**n, b**e**rry	l	**l**eg
ē	m**e**	m	**m**eat
		n	**n**ose
i	f**i**t, h**e**re	p	**p**ut
ī	**i**ce, f**i**re	r	**r**ed
		s	**s**ee
ō	g**o**	t	**t**op
ô	f**a**ll, f**o**r	v	**v**at
oi	**oi**l	w	**w**ish
͞oo	l**oo**k, p**u**ll	y	**y**ard
͞o͞o	t**oo**l, r**u**le	z	**z**ebra
ou	**ou**t, cr**ow**d		
		ch	**ch**in, ar**ch**
u	**u**p	ŋ	ri**ng**, dri**n**k
ʉ	f**u**r, sh**i**rt	sh	**sh**e, pu**sh**
		th	**th**in, tru**th**
ə	**a** in **a**go	*th*	**th**en, fa**th**er
	e in ag**e**nt	zh	mea**s**ure
	i in penc**i**l		
	o in at**o**m	
	u in circ**u**s	A heavy stress mark ' is
		placed after a syllable that
b	**b**ed	gets a heavy, or primary,
d	**d**og	stress, as in **picture**
f	**f**all	(pik'chər).

H18

A

acid rain (as′id rān) Rain, containing a large amount of acids, that results from the burning of fossil fuels. (D56) *Acid rain* can harm living things.

adaptation (ad əp tā′shən) Behavior or part of a living thing that helps it survive in a certain environment. (E40) A rose's thorns and a camel's hump are *adaptations*.

air pollution (er pə lōō′shən) Any harmful or unclean materials in the air. (C50) Burning fuels can cause *air pollution*.

aquifer (ak′wə fər) Underground layers of soil, sand, or gravel that store ground water. (D27) The water in a well usually comes from an *aquifer*.

astronomer (ə strän′ə mər) A scientist who studies the origin, features, and motion of objects in space. (B14) *Astronomers* use telescopes, cameras, and space probes to study the stars.

atmosphere (at′məs fir) The layer of gases surrounding Earth or another planet. (B12) Earth's *atmosphere* is made up of gases such as oxygen.

axis (ak′sis) The imaginary line on which an object rotates. (B38) Earth's *axis* runs between the North Pole and the South Pole.

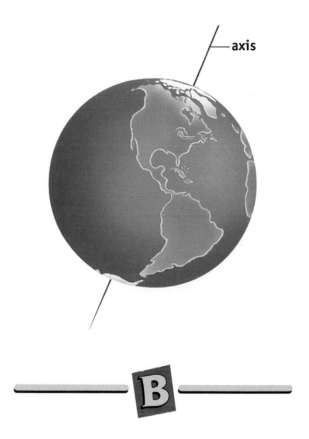

axis

B

bacteria (bak tir′ē ə) Tiny living things that can cause illness. (F36) Some *bacteria* cause diseases, such as tetanus and strep, but others are helpful to the body.

behavior (bē hāv′yər) The way an animal usually acts in a certain situation. (E42) One *behavior* of pill bugs is to move toward moist, dark places.

camouflage (kam′ə fläzh) The ability to blend in with the surroundings. (E45) An animal's fur or skin can be *camouflage*, helping the animal hunt or avoid hunters.

carbohydrates (kär bō hī′drāts) Food sugars and starches that are used by the body for energy. (F11) Potatoes, noodles, apples, and cereals all contain *carbohydrates*.

carnivore (kär′nə vôr) An animal that eats only other animals. (E17) Wolves, cougars, lions, hawks, and owls are *carnivores*.

cell (sel) The tiny unit that makes up all living things. (F44) Each *cell* can grow, respond, reproduce, and use energy, yet all your cells work together to keep you alive.

chyme (kīm) A thick, souplike mixture of food and digestive juices. (F59) *Chyme* forms as the stomach digests food.

community (kə myoo′nə tē) A group of plants and animals that live in a certain area. (E31) A pond's plants and animals form a *community*.

complete metamorphosis (kəm plēt′ met ə môr′fə sis) The four-stage life cycle of some insects. (A25) A life cycle that goes from egg to larva to pupa to adult is described as a *complete metamorphosis*.

condense (kən dens′) To change form from a gas to a liquid. (C43, D16) When water vapor in the air cools, it *condenses* into tiny droplets of liquid water.

conduction (kən duk′shən) The transfer of heat through direct contact between particles of matter. (C35) Heat moves by *conduction* from warmer matter with faster-moving particles to cooler matter with slower-moving particles.

conductor (kən duk′tər) A type of material that transfers heat or electricity. (C36) Metals are good *conductors* of heat.

cone (kōn) The part of a conifer that produces pollen or seeds. (A52) Each *cone* is a woody stalk covered with stiff scales.

constellation (kän stə lā'shən) A group of stars that form a pattern that looks like a person, animal, or object. (B47) Different *constellations* are visible from Earth at different times of year.

consumer (kən sōōm'ər) A living thing that eats other living things to survive. (E16) Animals are *consumers*.

convection (kən vek'shən) The circulation of heat through a liquid or gas (fluid). (C36) *Convection* takes place in a room with a heater: As hot air rises from the heater, cool air flows down to take its place.

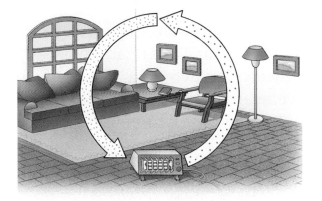

crater (krāt'ər) A bowl-shaped pit. (B11) *Craters* on the Moon and on Earth were formed by meteorites striking the surface.

current (kʉr'ənt) A stream of water or air. (D67) The hot-air balloon rode a *current* of air as it moved toward the mountains.

decomposer (dē kəm pōz'ər) A living thing that breaks down and feeds on the remains of once-living things. (E18) *Decomposers* such as mushrooms recycle the remains of once-living things.

digestion (di jes'chən) The process of breaking down food into a form that can be used by the body's cells. (F44) The body breaks down food by physical and chemical *digestion*.

dissolve (di zälv′) To mix or cause to mix one material, usually a solid, in another material, often a liquid, so that both materials separate into tiny particles that can't be seen. (D44) Sugar *dissolves* rapidly in hot water.

distilled water (di stild′ wôt′ər) Water that does not contain minerals, chemicals, or air. (D44) *Distilled water* is pure water.

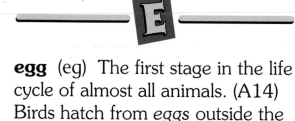

egg (eg) The first stage in the life cycle of almost all animals. (A14) Birds hatch from *eggs* outside the mother bird's body.

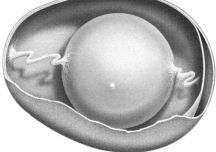

embryo (em′brē ō) An animal or plant in the earliest stages of its development. (A15, A41) A plant *embryo* is the tiny plant that is found inside a seed.

energy (en′ər jē) The ability to move something or cause a change in matter. (C11) A car uses *energy* from gasoline to run.

energy of motion (en′ər jē uv mō′shən) The energy that moving matter has. (C11) Sliding downhill on a sled, tossing a basketball into the air, and flying a kite in the wind are examples of *energy of motion*.

environment (en vī′rən mənt) All the surrounding living and non-living things that affect a living thing. (E10) A drop of water, a rotting log, a desert, the ocean, and a rain forest are examples of different *environments*.

enzymes (en′zīmz) Chemicals in the body, some of which help speed up the process of digestion. (F59) Digestive *enzymes* in the stomach help the breakdown of food in the body.

equator (ē kwā′tər) An imaginary line that circles Earth halfway between the two poles. (B64) If you live near the *equator,* you live in a hot climate because your region receives direct sunlight year-round.

esophagus (i säf'ə gəs) The muscular tube that connects the mouth to the stomach. (F47) After you swallow food, it travels through the *esophagus* to the stomach.

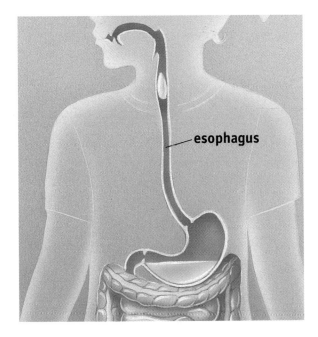

esophagus

evaporate (ē vap'ə rāt) To change form from a liquid to a gas. (C42, D15) On a warm dry day, water puddles on the sidewalk *evaporate* quickly.

extinction (ek stiŋk'shən) The permanent disappearance of all living things of a certain kind. (E31) The dinosaurs' *extinction* is a mystery that many scientists are working to solve.

fats (fats) High-energy nutrients that are oily or greasy. (F11) Cheeses, meats, nuts, and butter are foods that are usually high in *fats*.

fiber (fī'bər) Strands of plant material that are indigestible. (F61) Although *fiber* can't be digested, it aids in the process of digestion.

flare (fler) A bright area on the surface of the Sun caused by a solar storm. (B27) A solar *flare* is hotter than surrounding areas of the Sun and so is brighter.

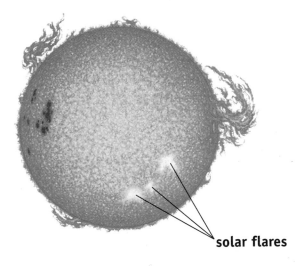

solar flares

food chain (fo͞od chān) The path that energy takes through a community as one living thing eats another. (E26) The first link in a *food chain* is usually a plant.

food web (fo͞od web) Two or more overlapping food chains. (E28) A *food web* connects animals through the plants and animals that they eat.

fossil fuel (fäs′əl fyo͞o′əl) A fuel formed over time from the remains of plants or animals. (C50) *Fossil fuels* such as oil, coal, and natural gas are found underground.

freeze (frēz) To change form from a liquid to a solid. (C43) The loss of heat causes a liquid to *freeze*.

friction (frik′shən) A force that keeps two objects from moving past one another easily. (C29) *Friction* causes your hands to get warm when you rub them together.

fruit (fro͞ot) The part of a flower that forms around a seed. (A47) Cucumbers, tomatoes, oranges, peaches, and pears are *fruits*.

fuel (fyo͞o′əl) A material that can be used for energy. (C50) Wood is a *fuel* used in many countries.

gas (gas) A state of matter that has no definite shape and does not take up a definite amount of space. (D14) A *gas* spreads out evenly to fill whatever space it is in.

germ (jʉrm) A tiny organism that can cause disease. (D49) Chlorine kills some of the *germs* in water.

germinate (jʉr′mə nāt) To sprout and begin to develop into a seedling. (A42) Most kinds of seeds need moisture, air, and warmth to *germinate*.

gravity (grav′i tē) A force that pulls two or more objects toward each other. (B22, D36) To fly into space, a rocket must overcome Earth's *gravity*.

ground water (ground wôt′ər) The water found beneath Earth's surface. (D27) In some areas, *ground water* fills the small spaces that are between underground rocks, soil, and sand.

hard water (härd wôt′ər) Water in which large amounts of minerals are dissolved. (D44) The minerals in *hard water* can stain clothing and give water an unpleasant taste.

healthful diet (helth′fəl dī′ət) A diet made up of a variety of foods that supply all necessary nutrients. (F18) A *healthful diet* is one that is high in fruits, vegetables, and cereals and low in fats and sweets.

heat (hēt) The energy of moving particles of matter. (C12) Adding *heat* to matter causes its particles to move faster.

herbivore (hʉr′bə vôr) An animal that eats only plants. (E18) Cows, butterflies, mice, and rabbits are *herbivores*.

hibernation (hī bər nā′shən) A deep sleep that helps some animals survive the winter. (E77) An animal that is in *hibernation* breathes more slowly, has a slower heartbeat, and has a lower body temperature.

incomplete metamorphosis (in kəm plēt′ met ə môr′fə sis) The three-stage life cycle of some insects. (A26) A life cycle that goes from egg to nymph to adult is described as an *incomplete metamorphosis*.

insulator (in′sə lā tər) A poor conductor of heat or electricity. (C36) Air that is trapped in the small spaces between fibers of clothing acts as an *insulator*.

junk food (juŋk fōōd) A food low in nutrients and high in fat, sugar, or salt. (F30) Candy, potato chips, and soda are *junk foods*.

large intestine (lärj in tes′tən) The digestive organ that stores waste and absorbs water from it. (F61) The major job of the *large intestine* is to absorb water from wastes and return it to the blood-stream.

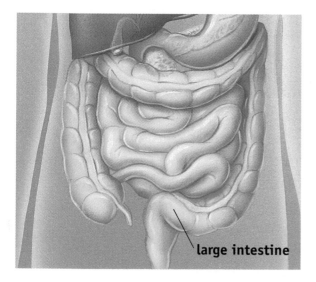

large intestine

larva (lär′və) The second stage in the life cycle of an insect that undergoes complete metamorpho-sis. (A25) A butterfly *larva* is called a caterpillar.

life cycle (līf sī′kəl) The series of changes that occur during the lifetime of a living thing. (A9) An insect goes through three or four stages in its *life cycle*.

liquid (lik′wid) A state of matter that has no definite shape but takes up a definite amount of space. (D14) At room temperature, water is a *liquid*.

lunar eclipse (lōō′nər i klips′) The darkening of the Moon when it moves into Earth's shadow. (B78) During a *lunar eclipse*, Earth blocks the Sun's light from reach-ing the Moon directly.

matter (mat′ər) Anything that has mass and takes up space. (C11) Every living and nonliving thing around you is made of *matter*.

melt (melt) To change form from a solid to a liquid. (C42) Ice *melts* at 0°C (32°F) or warmer.

meteorite (mēt′ē ər īt) A chunk of rock or metal that has fallen from space. (B11) A *meteorite* may be as small as a grain of sand or as large as a house.

migrate (mī′grāt) To move to another region as the seasons change. (E76) Many northern birds and butterflies *migrate* south during the winter.

minerals (min′ər əlz) Chemicals that can be important nutrients. (F13) Calcium is a *mineral* found in milk and cheese.

natural resource (nach′ər əl rē′sôrs) A material found in or on Earth that people use. (D10) *Natural resources* include water, minerals, oil, plants, and animals.

nutrient (nōō′trē ənt) Any substance used by living things for energy, growth, repair, or other life processes. (E43, F10) Proteins, carbohydrates, and fats are *nutrients* found in food.

nymph (nimf) The second stage in the life cycle of an insect undergoing incomplete metamorphosis. (A26) A grasshopper *nymph* looks similar to a small adult.

omnivore (äm′ni vôr) An animal that eats both plants and animals. (E18) Because bears will eat both berries and fish, bears are classified as *omnivores*.

orbit (ôr′bit) The path a planet, moon, or other object takes around another. (B47) The Moon is seen in different phases as it moves through its *orbit* around Earth.

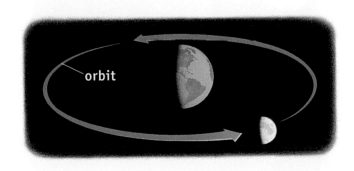

orbit

palate (pal′ət) The roof of the mouth. (F45) During the first part of digestion, the tongue mashes food against the *palate*.

parasite (par′ə sīt) A living thing that, at some point in its life, lives on or in another living thing. (E54) Fleas and lice are *parasites*.

petal (pet′′l) The brightly colored part of a flower that helps attract birds, bees, and other insects to the flower. (A46) A *petal* is one of the three main parts of a flower.

phase (fāz) Any stage in the series of changes in the apparent shape of the Moon. (B53) The Moon's shape appears to change with each *phase*.

pistil (pis′til) The central part in a flower that produces the seed. (A45) For seeds to form in a plant, the pollen must travel to the *pistil*.

planet (plan′it) Any large body that orbits a star and does not produce light of its own. (B47) Earth is a *planet*.

plaque (plak) The coating produced by bacteria on uncleaned teeth. (F51) *Plaque* is caused by bacteria in the mouth.

pollen (päl′ən) The powdery grains in a flower; they must be carried from a stamen to a pistil in order for seeds to form. (A46) Bees move *pollen* from one flower to another.

pollination (päl ə nā′shən) The process by which pollen reaches a pistil. (A46) After *pollination*, a flower can produce seeds.

polluted (pə lo͞ot′əd) Containing unwanted or harmful material. (D58) Breathing *polluted* air can be harmful to your lungs.

precipitation (prē sip ə tā′shən) The liquid or solid forms of water that fall to Earth. (D16) Rain, sleet, hail, and snow are different kinds of *precipitation*.

predator (pred′ə tər) An animal that hunts other animals for food. (E27) Hawks, cougars, and sharks are *predators*.

prey (prā) An animal hunted for food by another animal. (E27) Rabbits, mice, small fish, and insects are often *prey* for other, larger animals.

producer (prō do͞os'ər) A living thing that can make its own food. (E16) Plants, such as trees and grass, are *producers*.

prominence (präm'ə nəns) A huge loop of gas that appears on the edge of the Sun. (B27) *Prominences* are caused by magnetic storms on the Sun.

proteins (prō'tēnz) Nutrients used by the body for growth and repair. (F12) *Proteins* are found in foods such as meats, beans, nuts, and dairy products.

pupa (py͞oo'pə) The third stage in the life cycle of an insect undergoing complete metamorphosis. (A25) As a *pupa*, an insect is enclosed in a cocoon, or case.

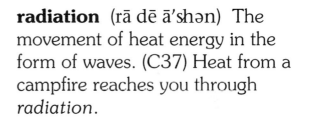

R

radiation (rā dē ā'shən) The movement of heat energy in the form of waves. (C37) Heat from a campfire reaches you through *radiation*.

reservoir (rez'ər vwär) The body of water that is stored behind a dam. (D27) A *reservoir* stores fresh water for a town or city.

revolve (ri välv') To move in a circle or orbit. (B47) Earth *revolves* around the Sun.

rotation (rō tā'shən) Turning around an axis. (B38) Earth takes 24 hours to complete one *rotation*.

saliva (sə lī′və) The watery liquid, secreted into the mouth, that aids in chewing, swallowing, and digesting. (F46) *Saliva* moistens food, making it easier to swallow the food.

salivary glands (sal′ə ver ē glandz) Small organs that make saliva. (F46) The *salivary glands* are found under the jaw, under the tongue, and next to the ears.

scale (skāl) A cone's woody part on which seeds grow. (A51, A53) A pine cone's *scales* protect its seeds.

season (sē′zən) Any of the four parts of the year. (B65) The four *seasons* are spring, summer, fall, and winter.

seed coat (sēd kōt) The part of a seed that protects the plant embryo. (A41) The *seed coat* of a coconut is hard, thick, and brown.

seedling (sēd′liŋ) The new plant that develops from an embryo and has roots, a stem, and leaves. (A43) A tomato *seedling* can be started indoors in early spring and planted outside in May.

small intestine (smôl in tes′tən) The long, coiled organ in which most digestion takes place. (F60) Nutrients in food are absorbed into the bloodstream from the *small intestine.*

soft water (sôft wôt′ər) Water in which few minerals are dissolved. (D44) Minerals can be removed from water to make *soft water.*

solar eclipse (sō′lər i klips′) The blocking of light from the Sun when the Moon moves between it and Earth. (B77) During a *solar eclipse*, the Sun's light is blocked by the Moon.

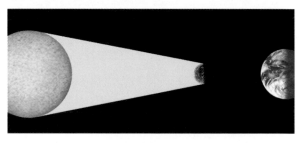

solar energy (sō′lər en′ər jē) Energy produced by the Sun. (C20) *Solar energy* can be used to produce electricity.

solar system (sō′lər sis′təm) The Sun and all the planets and other objects that orbit it. (B47) Earth is one of nine planets in the *solar system.*

solid (säl'id) A state of matter that has a definite shape and takes up a definite amount of space. (D14) A rock, a piece of ice, and a chair are all examples of *solids*.

species (spē'shēz) A group of living things that can produce young by mating with one another. (A10) The lion *species* cannot produce young of the gorilla *species*.

stamen (stā'mən) The part of a flower that produces pollen, which is needed to form seeds. (A45) *Stamens* are often long and have a fuzzy end.

star (stär) A ball of very hot gases that gives off light and other kinds of energy. (B27) The Sun is a *star*.

stomach (stum'ək) A muscular sac that stores food and helps in digestion. (F59) The *stomach* squeezes and churns food into a souplike mixture.

stored energy (stôrd en'ər jē) Energy that can cause matter to move or change. (C11) Fuels have *stored energy* from the Sun.

sunspot (sun'spöt) A dark area on the surface of the Sun, caused by a solar storm. (B27) A *sunspot* appears darker because it is cooler than surrounding areas of the Sun.

surface water (sur'fis wôt'ər) Fresh water in lakes, streams, and rivers. (D26) People often pipe *surface water* to nearby cities and towns.

telescope (tel'ə skōp) An instrument that makes distant objects appear nearer and larger. (B14) A *telescope* is used to study stars and other planets.

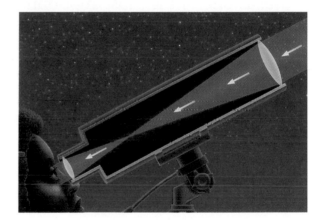

temperature (tem'pər ə chər) How hot or cold something is. (C28) *Temperature* is measured with a thermometer.

tide (tīd) The rise and fall of the ocean surface, mostly caused by the pull of the Moon's gravity. (D68) Along coasts, there are two high *tides* and two low *tides* during each day.

vitamins (vīt′ə minz) Chemicals, found in foods, that are important nutrients. (F13) *Vitamins* do not supply energy, but they are important to many body processes.

water (wôt′ər) A chemical, formed from hydrogen and oxygen, that is essential to life. (F12) *Water* is one of the most important nutrients.

water cycle (wôt′ər sī′kəl) The path that water follows from Earth to air and back again. (D16) In the *water cycle*, water evaporates from lakes and oceans into the air, and then condenses and falls back to Earth as rain or snow.

water pressure (wôt′ər presh′ər) The pushing of water on a surface. (D36) The deeper the water, the greater the *water pressure* becomes.

water vapor (wôt′ər vā′pər) Water that is a gas. (D15) Steam, which is invisible, is a form of *water vapor*.

INDEX

* Activity

CREDITS

Front Cover: *Design, Art Direction, and Production:* Design Five, NYC; *Photography:* Jade Albert; *Photography Production:* Picture It Corporation; *Illustration:* Burton Morris. **TOC:** Lori Anzalone; Terry Boles; Bob Brugger; Liz Conrad; A. J. Miller; Verlin Miller; Andrew Shiff; Peter Stallard; Jerry Zimmerman.

ILLUSTRATORS

UNIT 3A Chapter A1: Doreen Gay-Kassel: 24; Adam Mathews: 30, 31; Steve McInturff: 10, 11; A. J. Miller: 14, 15; Kathy Rusynyk: 8, 9. **Chapter A2:** Lori Anzalone: 46, 47, 63; Skip Baker: 53; Paul Blakey: 41, 42, 43, 56; Ka Botzis: 41; Julie Carpenter: 60; Eldon Doty: 40; Dan McGowan: 49, 52, 53, 54.

UNIT 3B Chapter B1: David Barber: 28; Jenny Campbell: 20, 22, 23; Richard Courtney: 7, 12, 13, 27, 29, 30, 31; Randy Hamblin: 10; A. J. Miller: 21; Robert Roper: 22; Stephen Wagner: 15. **Chapter B2:** Skip Baker: 42, 43; Tim Blough: 51, 52, 54; Michael Carroll: 38, 39, 52, 53, 54; Dennis Davidson: 46, 47; Eldon Doty: 48, 49; Verlin Miller: 39; Tom Powers: 37, 40, 45, 57; Susan Simon: 55, 56. **Chapter B3:** Liz Conrad: 64, 65, 66; Dennis Davidson: 77, 78; Eureka Cartography: 70; Traci Harmon: 70, 71; Uldis Klavins: 64, 65, 66; Jean and Mou–Sien Tseng: 68, 69, 76, 77, 78.

UNIT 3C Chapter C1: Larry Jost: 10, 11, 12, 13; Scott Luke: 8; Dave Winter: 21; Leslie Wolf: 20. **Chapter C2:** Terry Boles: 35; Randy Hamblin: 38, 39; Akio Matsuyoshi: 27, 28, 29, 45; Susan Melrath: 34; A. J. Miller: 35; Robert Roper: 37; Jim Turgeon: 42, 43, 44. **Chapter C3:** Ken Condon: 58, 62; Richard Courtney: 50, 51; Carlyn Iverson: 59; Nina Laden: 51, 52, 53; Joseph Scrofani: 54, 55, 60, 61, 63.

UNIT 3D Chapter D1: Bob Brugger: 9, 10, 11; Dan Clyne: 26, 27, 28; Glasgow & Assoc.: 11; Mike Meaker: 14, 15; Sergio Roffo: 24, 25; Robert Roper: 18, 19; Stephen Wagoner: 16, 17, 29. **Chapter D2:** Joe Boddy: 36; Larry Jost: 50, 51, 53; Robert Roper: 38, 39; Andrew Shiff: 43. **Chapter D3:** Terry Boles: 64, 65; Eldon Doty: 62, 63; Patrick Gnan: 68; Susan Johnston Carlson: 67, 70; Lazslo Kubini: 70; Bob Ostrum: 63; Tom Pansini: 58, 59, 76, 77, 78, 79; Robert Schuster: 61; Peter Stallard: 74, 75, 77, 78; Jerry Zimmerman: 67.

UNIT 3E Chapter E1: Higgins Bond: 11, 12; Jenny Campbell: 26, 27, 28, 29; Sarah Jane English: 30; Jackie Geyer: 27; Verlin Miller: 20, 21; Jim Owens: 16, 17, 18, 19; Jim Salvati: 32, 33, 35. **Chapter E2:** Jenny Campbell: 50, 51, 52, 53, 54, 55; Sarah Jane English: 56, 57, 59; Doreen Gay-Kassel: 49; Susan Melrath: 57; Phil Wilson: 44, 45. **Chapter E3:** Eldon Doty: 68, 69; Tina Fong: 72, 73; Jackie Geyer: 63, 66; Deborah Pinkney: 64, 65, 79; Robert Schuster: 76, 77.

UNIT 3F Chapter F1: Stephan Bauer: 23; Dan Brawner: 18, 19, 39; Eldon Doty: 34, 35; Sarah Jane English: 18, 19, 22; Joseph Scrofani: 10; Michael Sloan: 30, 31; Stephen Wagner: 17; Gary Yealdall: 14, 15. **Chapter F2:** Dan Clyne: 52, 53; Robert Margulies: 45, 46, 47, 58, 59, 60, 62, 63; Leonard Morgan: 50, 51; Julie Noonan: 56, 57; Andrew Shiff: 45, 46, 47, 59, 60, 62.

Glossary: Richard Courtney, A. J. Miller, Robert Margulies, Andy Meyer, Robert Roper, Stephen Wagner

Handbook: Laurie Hamilton, Catherine Leary.

PHOTOGRAPHS
All photographs by Silver Burdett Ginn (SBG) unless otherwise noted.

Unit A Opener 1–3: *border* G. I. Bernard/Animals Animals. 2: Grant Huntington for SBG; *l.* © M. Reardon/Photo Researchers, Inc. **Chapter 1** 4: *bkgd.* Fred Hirschmann; *inset* Erik Hill/Anchorage Daily News. 8: Dwight R. Kuhn. 14: E. R. Degginger/Color-Pics, Inc. 16: *t.* E. R. Degginger/Color-Pics, Inc.; *b.* Frans Lanting/Minden Pictures. 17: *l.* Chick Maste;r *r.* Gil Taylor/Chick Master 18: *t.* Hans & Judy Beste/Animals Animals; *b.r.* © M. Reardon/Photo Researchers, Inc. 19: *t.* Miriam Austerman/Animals Animals; *m.* Michio Hoshino/Minden Pictures; *b.* Frans Lanting/Minden Pictures. 23: *b.l.* J. H. Robinson/Animals Animals; *b.r.* R. Mendez/Animals Animals. 24: Courtesy Evelyn O'Shea. 25: *t.l.* E. R. Degginger/Animals Animals; *t.r.* Patti Murray/Animal Animals; *b.l., b.r.* Patti Murray/Animals Animals. 27: *t.l.* Raymond A. Mendez/Animals Animals; *t.r.* John Pontier/Animals Animals; *b.* © David & Hayes Norris/Photo Researchers, Inc. 30: Anne Heimann. 31: *t.* Dwight R. Kuhn; *b.l.* Anne Heimann; *b.r.* Trevor Barrett/Animals Animals. 32: Flip Nicklin/Minden Pictures. 33: Jeff Foott/DRK Photo. 34: Michio Hoshino/Minden Pictures. **Chapter 2** 36: *bkgd.* Antonio M. Rosario/The Image Bank; *inset* Jill Krementz. 38–39: Grant Huntington for SBG. 42: *t.* S. Nielsen/Imagery; *m.* Runk/Schoenberger/Grant Heilman Photography; *b.* E. R. Degginger/Color-Pics, Inc. 43: Dwight R. Kuhn. 44–45: Grant Huntington for SBG. 48: *l.* Jim Strauser/Grant Heilman Photography; *r.* Jim Strawser/Grant Heilman Photography. 50: Grant Huntington for SBG; 51: *t.l.* Grant

Huntington for SBG; *t.r.* E. R. Degginger/Color-Pics, Inc.; *m.r.* E. R. Degginger/Color-Pics, Inc.; *b.l.* Grant Huntington for SBG; *b.r.* E. R. Degginger/Color-Pics, Inc. 55: *t.l.* David Austen/Tony Stone Images; *t.r.* Mark Stouffer/Earth Scenes; *b.* Don Pitcher/Stock Boston. 57–59: Grant Huntington for SBG. 60: Barry L. Runk/Grant Heilman Photography. 61: *l.* Runk/Schoenberger/Grant Heilman Photography. 62: *l.* Runk/Schoenberger/Grant Heilman Photography; *r.* Jim Strauser/Grant Heilman Photography.

Unit B Opener 1–3: *border* Frank P. Rossotto. 2: *t.* George Post. **Chapter 1** 4–5: *bkgd.* Lick Observatory; *inset* Victor Aleman/2 Mun-Dos Communications. 6: Grant Huntington for SBG. 11: *t.* NASA; *b.* H. R. Bramaz/Peter Arnold. 12: NASA/The Stock Market. 13: NASA. 14: Roger Ressmeyer/Starlight. 16: Photri. 17: NASA. 18–19: Grant Huntington for SBG. 23: *l.* NASA/Starlight (Photo by Neil Armstrong); *r.* © NASA/Science Source/Photo Researchers, Inc. 24–26: Grant Huntington for SBG. 29: *t.* Photri; *b.* © Pekka Parviainen/Science Photo Library/Photo Researchers, Inc. 30: *t.* National Solar Observatory/Sacramento Peak; *b.* NASA/F. Rossotto/StockTrek. **Chapter 2** 32–33: *bkgd.* E. R. Degginger/Color-Pics, Inc. 34: Grant Huntington for SBG. 35: *t.* Grant Huntington for SBG; *b.* E. R. Degginger/Color-Pics, Inc. 37: *l.* Grant Huntington for SBG; *m.* Grant Huntington for SBG; *r.* Grant Huntington for SBG. 38: © Sylvain Grandadam/Photo Researchers, Inc. 40: Dennis Cox/ChinaStock. 40–41: *bkgd.* Robert Holmes; *inset* Oddo & Sinibaldi/The Stock Market. 41: *t.l.* Robert Holmes; *t.m.* D & J McClurg/Bruce Coleman; *t.r.* Norman Owen Tomalin/Bruce Coleman; *b.* © Dale E. Boyer/Photo Researchers, Inc. 46: Thomas Hooper/© National Geographic Society. 50: Grant Huntington for SBG. 52: NASA. **Chapter 3** 58–59: *bkgd.* John Gerlach/Tom Stack & Associates; *inset* Doranne Jacobson. 60: Ken Karp for SBG. 61: Ken Karp for SBG. 62: Ken Karp for SBG. 63: Ken Karp for SBG. 67: *bkgd.* Tibor Bognar/The Stock Market; *inset* Robert Frerck/Odyssey Productions; *inset* D. Donne Bryant. 68: Superstock. 69: Courtesy, National Maritime Museum. 71: *t.* Superstock; *b.* Brian Stablyk/Tony Stone Images. 73: *t.* George Post; *b.* S. Nielsen/Imagery. 74: Ken Karp for SBG. 75: Ken Karp for SBG. 76: Ken Sakamoto/Black Star. 79: Ken Karp for SBG.

Unit C Opener 1–3: *border* David Barnes/The Stock Market. 2: Grant Huntington for SBG. **Chapter 1** 4–5: *bkgd.* Camerique/H. Armstrong Roberts; *inset* Ruth Tenzer Feldman. 6–10: Grant Huntington for SBG. 11: Alan Oddie/PhotoEdit. 12–16: Grant Huntington for SBG; 17: David Phillips for SBG. 18: *t.l.* Joe Cornish/Tony Stone Images; *t.r* Superstock; *b.l.* David Phillips for SBG; *b.r.* Phil Degginger/Color-Pics, Inc. 19: *l.* The Image Bank; *r.* Bob Krist/Tony Stone Images. **Chapter 2** 23–24: *bkgd.* Renato Rotolo/Liaison International; *inset* ©Bob Halinen/Anchorage Daily News/Liaison International. 36: *l.* Richard Hutchings for SBG; *r.* Isaac Geib/Grant Heilman Photography. 38: *l.* Barry L. Runk/Grant Heilman Photography. 38–39: *bkgd.* John Shaw/Tom Stack & Associates. 39: *b.* Climb High/Signs and Symbols. 42: *t.* Richard Hutchings for SBG. 43: *t.* Arthur D'Arazien/The Image Bank. 44: *t.* David R. Frazier ; *b.m., b.r.* Grant Huntington for SBG. **Chapter 3** 46–47: *bkgd.* Comstock. 52: *t.* Comstock; *b.* Thomas Braise/The Stock Market. 53: *t.* John Edwards/Tony Stone Images; *b.* Zefa-Streichan/The Stock Market. 54: Wolfgang Kaehler. 59: *t.* E. R. Degginger/Color-Pics, Inc.; *m.t.* E. R. Degginger/Color-Pics, Inc.; *m.b.* E. R. Degginger/Bruce Coleman; *b.* E. R. Degginger/Bruce Coleman.

Unit D Opener 1–3: *border* Robert Reiff/FPG International. 2: **Chapter 1** 4–5: *bkgd.* © Jim Zipp/Photo Researchers, Inc.; *l.* Kyle McLellan/© National Geographic Society; *r.* © Jeff Lepore/Photo Researchers, Inc. 10: NASA/Tom Stack & Associates. 11: *t.l.* Jeff Smith/The Image Bank; *t.r.* © 1996 Jim Richardson/Woodfin Camp & Associates; *b.l.* Comstock; *b.r.* Merritt Vincent/PhotoEdit. 24: *l.* Steve McCutcheon/Alaska Pictorial; *r.* Wolfgang Kaehler. 25: *t.* ©1996 Sylvia Johnson/Woodfin Camp & Associates; *m.* Wolfgang Kaehler; *b.* E. R. Degginger/Color-Pics, Inc. 26: Mark Segal/Tony Stone Images. 27: Sobel/Klonsky/The Image Bank. 28: Bob Daemmrich Photography. **Chapter 2** 30–34: *bkgd.* John David Fleck/Liaison International; *inset* © David M. Grossman/Photo Researchers, Inc. 32: Ken Karp for SBG. 35: *b.* Mitchell Funk/The Image Bank; *(t.)* Ken Karp for SBG; 36: The Image Bank. 40–42: Ken Karp for SBG. 44: Hans Reinhard/Bruce Coleman. 45: Keith Wood/Tony Stone Images. 46–48: Ken Karp for SBG. 49: *l.* Jerry Lessen/Bruce Coleman; *m.t.l.* E. R. Degginger/Color-Pics, Inc.; *m.b.l.* Brian Parker/Tom Stack & Associates; *m.r.* © London School of Hygiene and Tropical Medicine/Science Photo Library/Photo Researchers, Inc.; *t.r.* Moredon Animal Health Ltd./Science Photo Library/Photo Researchers, Inc.; *b.r.* © Moredon Animal Health Ltd./Science Photo Library/Photo Researchers, Inc. 52: David Madison/Bruce Coleman. **Chapter 3** 54–55: © Antonin Kratochvil/*Discover* Magazine. 56–57: Grant Huntington for SBG. 61: Kay Chernush/The Image Bank. 65–66: Grant Huntington for SBG. 69: *l.* © Andrew J. Martinez/Photo Researchers, Inc.; *r.* © J. Martinez/Photo Researchers, Inc. 71: Timothy A. Murphy/The Image Bank. 73: Grant Huntington for SBG. 74: Richard Hutchings for SBG.

Unit E Opener 1–3: *border* John Gerlach/Tom Stack & Associates. 2: *l.* Marty Snyderman. **Chapter 1** 4–5: *bkgd.* Tom Bean/Tony Stone Images; *inset* © Melinda M. Hutton. 6–7: Grant Huntington for SBG. 8: *l.* Donald Specker/Animals Animals; *r.* Grant Huntington for SBG. 9: Grant Huntington for SBG. 10: Doug Perrine/DRK Photo. 12: *t.* Michael Fogden/DRK Photo; *b.* Al Grotell. 13: *t.* Stephen J. Krasemann/Peter Arnold; *b.* © Dr. Jeremy Burgess/Science Photo Library/Photo Researchers, Inc. 14–15: Grant Huntington for SBG. 16: *l.* D. Cavagnaro-DRK Photo; *m.* © Farrell Grehan/Photo Researchers, Inc.; *r.* N. H. Cheatham/DRK Photo. 17: *t.* Hans Pfletschinger-/Peter Arnold; *b.* Jim Brandenburg/Minden Pictures. 18: *t.* © Tim Davis/Photo Researchers, Inc.; *b.* © Tom Bledsoe/Photo Researchers, Inc. 19: *t.* Breck P. Kent/Animals Animals; *b.* Scott Nielsen/Imagery. 22–25: Grant Huntington for SBG. 26: *l.* © James Steinberg/Photo Researchers, Inc.; *m.* © Gary Retherford/Photo Researchers, Inc.; *r.* Zig Leszczynski/Animals Animals. 27: *l.* Ted Levin/Animals Animals; *r.* Joe McDonald/Animals Animals. 28: *t.l.* Stephen J. Krasemann/DRK Photo; *t.r.* M. P. Kahl/DRK Photo; *b.l.* Stephen Dalton/Animals Animals; *b.r.* John